St. Louis Community College

Forest Park
Florissant Valley
Meramec

Instructional Resources
St. Louis, Missouri

THE MICROSOFT FILE

THE MICROSOFT FILE

The Secret Case Against Bill Gates

WENDY GOLDMAN ROHM

TIMES BUSINESS

RANDOM HOUSE

Some of this material appeared, in different form,
in *The Boston Globe*, the *Chicago Tribune*, the *Financial Times*,
Upside, and *Wired*.

Library of Congress Cataloging-in-Publication Data
Rohm, Wendy Goldman.
The Microsoft file : the secret case against Bill Gates / Wendy Goldman Rohm.
p.   cm.
ISBN 0-8129-2716-8
1. Microsoft Corporation.   2. Gates, Bill, 1955–   .   3. Computer software
industry—United States.   4. Competition—United States. I. Title.
HD9696.63.U64M537   1998
338.7'610053'0973—dc21   98-4450

Random House website address: www.randomhouse.com
Printed in the United States of America on acid-free paper

2   4   6   8   9   7   5   3

First Edition

For Madeline and Murphy,
with gratitude and love

CONTENTS

CONTENTS

INTRODUCTION

Is Microsoft's rise as the world's most powerful and successful company in the computer and information industries a classic example of the free market at work? Is Microsoft's success and the failure of other companies the result of the creative destruction that makes capitalism so strong and unique? Or was there another force at work?

This book will show that Microsoft, under the leadership of its founding genius, Bill Gates, has engaged in a pattern of predatory business practices over the past decade that have all but killed the market in operating systems and applications software, and now likewise threaten to stifle free competition in the Internet and electronic commerce arenas. What has happened to Netscape is just the most recent example of an alarming pattern that becomes evident from an analysis of the strategy and tactics of Bill Gates and Microsoft since the early days of the software industry.

The seeds of this book were planted back in 1989 in a Las Vegas parking lot, during an off-the-record interview with a senior vice president of a major U.S. computer manufacturer.

It was November, a huge high-tech conference was under way, and meeting rooms and restaurants were full to capacity. I'd set up office under the Vegas sun with a couple of folding chairs in a back lot, out of range of the crowds and chaos.

A number of CEOs and senior executives would meet with me that day for a series of articles I was planning.

I had not expected what I was about to hear, however. What the executive, and many others, told me almost ten years ago was the beginning of the story of the efforts of one man and one company to create and maintain monopoly power in what should be the world's most dynamic, imaginative, and competitive industry.

What would follow, over the years of interviews and research, was their account not only of how Gates came to dominate markets in the United States but how his market power was leveraged worldwide.

What Microsoft and Bill Gates are doing today at the close of the twentieth century parallels what John D. Rockefeller and Standard Oil tried to do at its beginning. For Rockefeller, fuel—oil—drove the century. Out of it emerged an entire culture and lifestyle. World powers were built on it: the economy became virtually synonymous with it. Rockefeller changed the world, just like Gates has.

Gates, however, is succeeding far better than Rockefeller. For Gates, it's no longer oil flowing through pipes that makes the world run. It's information. Like Rockefeller, Gates has shrewdly identified the choke points and has managed them well. He knows the significance of infrastructure and market penetration. They're both more important than immediate profit—which comes in a payoff of unimaginable lasting power, once the monopolist has gained control.

Like Rockefeller, Gates at various points has expressed his opinion that since he created markets, he should rightly own them. To both men market share was everything. Never mind all the short-term freebies and price cuts they had to give. Both knew it would all pay off down the road, as competition was eliminated and they were increasingly free to operate as they pleased.

Gates, like Rockefeller, knew how to cut off his competitors at the pass. Rockefeller nabbed oil shipments by planting his agents all over the globe. His motto was, "The coal-oil business belongs to us." If dealers bought a mere barrel of oil a year, they had to buy it from him. Likewise, Gates has left no stone unturned. For some time—until the feds partially put a stop to the practice—he had computer makers pay a royalty to Microsoft on every machine they shipped, regardless of whether any Microsoft software was on it.

Gates tried to make sure that no alternative from any company, large or small, would ever gain any penetration in his market. Intelligence was important to Rockefeller, as it was to Gates, and both were quite good at it. The goal: to control the infrastructure and access to all routes to market.

Like Rockefeller's did, Gates' profits, relentlessness—and monopoly power—have pushed him on into new fronts. Rockefeller spread out to railroads, shipping, steel, gas, copper, not to mention banking and trusts. Gates leveraged himself from computer operating systems to applications software, into the Internet and, now, the travel business, financial services, the media, and beyond.

Gates historically has slashed prices or given products away and pushed computer makers into contracts that made it difficult for them to stray to another product, no matter how superior. But that's not all. Gates slashed the information pipeline for his competitors. That is, what has unfolded in recent years for those attempting to compete with Gates is the equivalent of what the teamsters did in Rockefeller's day: They sought to sabotage the pipeline by dragging it to the surface and cutting it so the oil would spill. The pipeline had to be guarded.

For his part, Gates slashed through his competitors' information channels, making it impossible for them to reach the market, to make products that would run on machines controlled by him.

With the proliferation of computer networks, the world is so much easier for Gates to navigate, digitally, than it was for Rockefeller, who was often hindered literally by the physical restraints of his markets.

The Microsoft File will show, from inside offices around the world, Gates' campaigns to stymie free competition. It will provide a peephole into how key business deals are kept off the books; how psychological warfare is waged between those vying for power within the hierarchy of the Gates empire; and how Gates used a smokescreen of technological complexity to control the market and the scrutiny of Microsoft's activities.

At the same time, the federal government will be exposed for its fumbling of an important case. The players and their personalities and motives will be seen in the context of a circuslike atmosphere in which warring armies of attorneys, politicians, and corporate officers played out their personal dramas behind the scenes.

There are many who would offer one piece of advice: Let Bill Gates alone. And why not? That would be easy enough. The man and his great corporation have created thousands of jobs worldwide and catalyzed the creation of hundreds of companies that make products to run off the personal computers he has enabled with his operating system since the early days of the market. Why mess with Bill? His dominance has created standards in a marketplace that would otherwise have been chaotic, runs the argument.

Gates' contributions to a new industry, like Rockefeller's, are unquestionable. But less obvious is the hidden record—that shows how Gates restrained trade and inhibited the innovation of others who got in his way. Microsoft's activities behind the scenes and intentions in the marketplace are spelled out in the secret communications within his inner sanctum. The feds have collected a partial picture of what was going on, under subpoena, through continuous investigations—still ongoing. The record shows a classic monopolist, uncannily similar in strategies and intentions and ethics (or lack thereof) to John D. Rockefeller.

What has been Gates' intent? To build great products, as he contends publicly, or to lock up the entire marketplace to increase his ever-swelling coffers?

Only Gates' own secret communications, and the tales of those who tangled with him tell the full story. A portrait of Microsoft's strategies for market domination—from the early days of the industry to the current competitive battles in the space—is also painted by an e-mail trail.

The resolution of Microsoft's dominance of the market will have enormous impact on the burgeoning world of electronic commerce. Will it unfold freely, making it possible for all would-be participants to play in the market?

This resolution will not only affect market dynamics but will have an enormous impact on how we run our lives; how and what type of information will be accessible to us via the Internet, what our options will be in the future in personal banking and purchasing goods over electronic networks and the Internet, and who will be in control of the most basic backbone of communications—broadcast, Internet, cable—in the future. Will this be in the hands of a range of innovative companies driven by the customer, or will it be controlled by Bill Gates?

What Gates is doing now, as you read this book—his attempt to control electronic commerce and the Internet—is only a continuation of the tactics he has practiced and perfected since the early days of the DOS market.

In the process of creating this book, I conducted hundreds of interviews—in person and by phone and e-mail—over the past five years both inside the federal government and within the major corporations that were involved. These ranged from talks with chairmen, CEOs, and chief counsels, to midlevel managers and administrative assistants, and allowed me in many cases to closely reconstruct events.

As in any investigative endeavor, because of the sensitive nature of the material being covered, some allowed me to use information they provided but did not want to reveal that they'd been interviewed, while others were willing to go on record. Several scenes in the book were written based on my direct observation of the events, while other scenes were constructed from the accounts of those who were present or were briefed in detail and closely tied to or were otherwise familiar with the events. Also backing up my presentation of events are hundreds of pages of documents I collected in the course of researching this book.

At one point during the creation of this book, Bill Gates engaged in an e-mail correspondence with me over the period of several weeks. I also had a number of face-to-face encounters with him, during one of which he told me that he was "not allowed" to talk to me. Other Microsoft executives, including senior vice president and corporate officer Mike Maples told me that, although they wanted to talk with me, they were "not allowed to." This, they said, was an edict from Microsoft's corporate communications and legal departments.

Before this book went to press, Microsoft was presented with the opportunity to respond to a wide range of the allegations presented in it. A top Microsoft official told Random House that the corporation chose not to respond and had "no comment" on the thorough list of questions that was submitted. Other than that, Microsoft declined to officially participate in the creation of this book, although I had a number of Microsoft sources and documents.

As author Ken Auletta aptly pointed out in his *Greed and Glory on Wall Street,* "no reporter can with 100 percent accuracy re-create events that occurred some time before . . . A reporter tries to guard against inaccuracies by checking with a variety of sources, but it is useful for a reader—and an author—to be humbled by this journalistic limitation." I have tried to present events as they unfolded, by necessity sometimes from one side, based on the accounts of those who were active in the emergence of the power plays that have shaped an entire economic and digital era.

Wendy Goldman Rohm

CAST of CHARACTERS*

INSIDE MICROSOFT

BILL GATES, CHAIRMAN AND CEO

WILLIAM NEUKOM, CHIEF COUNSEL

STEVE BALLMER, SENIOR VP AND HEAD OF SALES

MIKE MAPLES, EXECUTIVE VP, WORLDWIDE PRODUCTS

JOACHIM KEMPIN, SENIOR VP, OEM SALES

JIM ALLCHIN, SENIOR VP

BRAD SILVERBERG, SENIOR VP AND HEAD OF OPERATING SYSTEMS

PAUL MARITZ, SENIOR VP, TECHNOLOGY STRATEGY

BRAD CHASE, VP, PERSONAL SYSTEMS

DAVID COLE, VP, OPERATING SYSTEMS DEVELOPMENT

BERNARD VERGNES, PRESIDENT, MICROSOFT EUROPE

JEFF LUM, VP, EUROPE

JUERGEN HUELS, HEAD OF OEM SALES, MICROSOFT GERMANY

STEFANIE REICHEL, VOBIS ACCOUNT MANAGER

COMPETITORS

RAY NOORDA, CHAIRMAN AND CEO, NOVELL

JOHN AKERS, CHAIRMAN AND CEO IBM

* Over the years, many of the individuals listed had changes in title and responsibility. For purposes here, the title during the time frame of most of the action in the book was the one used.

CAST OF CHARACTERS

Lou Gerstner, chairman and CEO, IBM
Jim Cannavino, head of PC division and chief strategist, IBM
Jim Manzi, chairman and CEO, Lotus Development Corp.
Philippe Kahn, chairman and CEO, Borland International
Jim Barksdale, chairman and CEO, Netscape
Scott McNealy, chairman and CEO, Sun Microsystems
Jerry Kaplan, chairman and CEO, Go Corp.
Alan Ashton and Bruce Bastian, founders of WordPerfect
Gary Clow, president, Stac Electronics
Bryan Sparks, president, Caldera

THE LAWYERS

Steve Holley, Sullivan & Cromwell outside counsel
to Microsoft
Tom Lemberg, chief counsel, Lotus
Andrew Berg, D.C. outside counsel to Lotus
Bob Kohn, chief counsel, Borland International
David Bradford, chief counsel, Novell
Sturge Sobin, D.C. outside counsel to Novell
Mike Sohn, Arnold & Porter, Washington D.C., outside
counsel to Novell
Duff Thompson, chief counsel, WordPerfect
Roberta Katz, chief counsel, Netscape
Gary Reback, outside counsel to Netscape
Felix Rohatyn, advisor to Lotus
Mike Morris, chief counsel, Sun Microsystems
Morgan Chu, outside counsel to Stac
Steve Susman, Susman Godfrey, outside counsel to Caldera
Ralph Palumbo, The Summit Law Group, outside counsel
to Caldera

THE FEDS

At the FTC
Janet Steiger, chair
Deborah Owen, Commissioner

CAST OF CHARACTERS

DENNIS YAO, COMMISSIONER

MARY AZCUENAGA, COMMISSIONER

ROSCOE STAREK III, COMMISSIONER

KEVIN ARQUIT, HEAD OF THE BUREAU OF COMPETITION

MARY LOU STEPTOE, SUBSEQUENT HEAD OF THE BUREAU
OF COMPETITION

STEVE NEWBORN, TOP LITIGATOR

MARC SCHILDKRAUT, ASSISTANT DIRECTOR, BUREAU OF COMPETITION

NORRIS WASHINGTON, STAFF ATTORNEY

AT THE DOJ

ANNE K. BINGAMAN, ASSISTANT ATTORNEY GENERAL AND
HEAD OF ANTITRUST

ROBERT LITAN, DEPUTY ASSISTANT ATTORNEY GENERAL

RICH GILBERT, DEPUTY ASSISTANT ATTORNEY GENERAL

DIANNE WOOD, DEPUTY ASSISTANT ATTORNEY GENERAL

SAM MILLER, LITIGATOR

STEVE SUNSHINE, DEPUTY ASSISTANT ATTORNEY GENERAL

RICH ROSEN, SECTION CHIEF

JOEL KLEIN, ASSISTANT ATTORNEY GENERAL AND HEAD OF ANTITRUST

DAN RUBENFELD, DEPUTY ASSISTANT ATTORNEY GENERAL

DOUG MELAMED, DEPUTY ASSISTANT ATTORNEY GENERAL

JEFF BLATNER, SPECIAL COUNSEL, INFORMATION TECHNOLOGY

DAVID BOIES, SPECIAL TRIAL COUNSEL

STATE ANTITRUST ENFORCERS

DAN MORALES, ATTORNEY GENERAL, STATE OF TEXAS

MARK TOBEY, ASSISTANT ATTORNEY GENERAL, STATE OF TEXAS

SAM GOODHOPE, SPECIAL PROJECTS, STATE OF TEXAS

THE JUDGES
FEDERAL DISTRICT COURT

JUDGE STANLEY SPORKIN (WASHINGTON, D.C.)

JUDGE DEE BENSEN (SALT LAKE CITY, UTAH)

JUDGE THOMAS PENFIELD JACKSON (WASHINGTON, D.C.)

THE
MICROSOFT
FILE

1

DOUBLE BILL

In the wee hours of the morning on January 20, 1995, Microsoft Corp.'s chief counsel, Bill Neukom, was in Washington, D.C., on the eve of a critical federal hearing. A Pandora's box was about to be opened. Meanwhile, on the same day, halfway around the globe, Bill Gates was on his way to Sydney, Australia, eyeing new global markets and preparing for the worldwide launch of his next big product, Windows 95. Microsoft was at a turning point—market dynamics were shifting like continents. The behemoth's world monopoly power was about to be challenged.

The technological day had subsided, and darkness came down over the city like a hood. Washington, D.C., was slowly being covered by a rolling fog as the winter night went balmy, softening the ragged edges of the Potomac as it slid past the White House.

Fog everywhere, way past midnight. Fog creeping up the white stone pediments and porticoes of the building where the First Family slept; fog slithering through the guardhouse at the west gate; fog tumbling up the sidewalk a half block away, where the facade of the exclusive old Hay-Adams blinked on and off like a cursor on a dark screen.

Now, at 3:20 A.M., bursts of light from an odd electrical storm descended from the clouds. Illuminated in his elegant D.C. bunk, the

3

six-foot-four-inch frame of William Neukom, watchdog extraordi-
naire and chief counsel of that juggernaut of American business
known as Microsoft Corp., lay supine. Neukom had reason to be
restless despite the familiar old upholstered chairs, faded rugs,
chandeliers, and white terry-cloth towels laid four across with HAY-
ADAMS embroidered in blue. As always, there were the new blow-
dryers mounted on the bathroom walls at the aging hotel; phones in
bathrooms and on bedside tables—with data ports, speaker phones,
and voice mail; brass lamps; smoke detectors; Perrier and Famous
Amos in the minibar; remote control; cable.

Yes, everything was as it should be. An old Vietnamese man
served drinks in the lounge. All just the same as before on
Neukom's visits to the capital, which had become routine by now.

The Hay-Adams Hotel, which had replaced the historic Hay-
Adams House that stood on the same corner in 1927, was a favorite
haunt of diplomats, White House guests, members of Congress,
well-heeled lobbyists. Many guests registered under assumed
names, with the cooperation of hotel management. The concierge
would often know the real names of his pseudonymous guests but
would never miss a beat, calling people by their invented monikers
throughout their stay with a bit of a smirk on his face.

There were often men with young women on their arms. On this
evening, a caucus of two seventyish gentlemen and four young,
blond women left the hotel restaurant. It was a typical sight.

Neukom usually registered under his own name. He had little
chance of running into anyone he knew here. Indeed, he had his
cheapest suit laid out. It would not do to be seen in front of federal
attorneys, with their paltry salaries, in an Armani—or a Zegna from
San Francisco's Bullock & Jones, one of his favorite places to pick
up a suit.

On many occasions he'd joked to his pals before his trips to D.C.
about getting out his most dog-eared duds—he'd paraded for three
years before the Federal Trade Commission and for a year now before the Department of Justice. And playing the bum wasn't completely new to him. While usually dressed immaculately—his
height, lean figure, and thick gray hair gave him a regal air—

Neukom had a guilt complex about his wealth. He'd drive his old beater—a Ford Taurus—to social gatherings, leaving the Mercedes and the Porsches back in the garage.

Now the Adams' filmy white curtains and heavier drapes could not keep out the violent flashes that seemed to emanate from Pennsylvania Avenue. The rumbling entered one's dreams, sounding like a plane engine, or a metal sheet being rumpled backstage somewhere.

Neukom had become adept at his performances before the feds. But in a matter of hours he would be facing that loose cannon Judge Stanley Sporkin in perhaps the most outrageous federal hearing in the history of antitrust law.

Neukom had the tough job. The years had heaped up almost imperceptibly, to the point where he now found himself in the unlikely position of playing watchdog for the richest man in the world, the other Bill, Bill Gates. Keeping Gates legal was more than a full-time job, Neukom would complain to his friends.

The deal he'd had to cut with the feds in recent months was all because Gates had gone too far—Gates and Kempin. Neukom couldn't keep up with the deals they were cutting around the world. He liked to describe Joachim Kempin as "the elephant who shit all over the place," pointing out, "I have to go shovel it up."

Nevertheless, Neukom had had his victories, and he was intent on having them again. The antitrust hounds continued to hurl subpoenas at him and the Gates empire, and were now questioning the deal he'd cut months earlier—a sweet tidbit indeed, which had effectively put an end to more than four years' worth of prying by the feds while not affecting Gates' moneymaking machine one bit.

Neukom, Gates, and their legal team had poked fun at Janet Reno, the Justice giantess, who had stood up to announce the deal as a victory for her antitrust cops. Neukom knew the feds had caved in. He liked to brag about the parts that never made it into the newspapers. Among them: the motion to quash he quietly filed in federal court just before the feds talked turkey. But things were starting to come apart at the seams.

A dark fog had settled in. The machinations of the business day had subsided. Driving in from the airport this evening, the tip of the Washington Monument had been subsumed in the deep gray mist. Tomorrow would be unpredictable.

Bill Gates—rumpled and tired—was drifting halfway around the globe. Traveling electronic passageways was his paradigm, sea and air like blank space on a screen; destinations opened like menus—Africa and Australia, his favorites.

It had been a long flight, and he had risen from sleep as from black grass. Sea grass. Spans of it by the ocean. Flying in from over the harbor bridge, a cliff-lined coast: Sydney, Australia. Murdoch country.

The air was soft this time of year. Life was like one of those vast but eroding beaches. Over recent months marriage had replaced Mother. How quickly the year had passed. On New Year's Day a year earlier, on another coast, he had taken his nuptial vows. It was something his mother wanted to see him do before she died. Love, at first, was like a prize won in a competition. Soon it became something else. Most everything had that tendency. It was one of the reasons he could not stand still.

Through a day of air and water. A storm had taken its course just outside the window, where the long grass had blackened and was being beat by wind. From above, two electric bulbs on either side of his berth—a makeshift place of random cushions and weeks collected.

Sleeping, a low hum in the chest, skin reddened by sun, head tight, seams of the skull traced like an etching across the crown taut with the monotony of time. It seemed he'd traveled farther than his thirty-nine years. Feet crossed at the ankles, lower lip slack as if having given up: all having been spoken.

Echo in the sleeping brain. Traveling across water. Miles of it. Air like water filling his lungs, dreams billowing like balloons grasped in a fierce wind.

Now a series of roads had brought him to Sydney's Ramada Renaissance Hotel. Meandering through the lobby, Gates had an unusual tentativeness for a man whose twenty-year-old company had transformed the world. Indeed, some considered him the most powerful economic force in America in the second half of the twentieth century. Yet he slunk more than walked across a room, as if testing the floor for solidity, or hoping to avoid some invisible mine. Head thrust forward, sternum collapsed, hips tucked under.

Halfway around the world, his chief counsel was doing some hand holding with the feds. They could not be allowed to stand in the way of all the "cool" things he wanted to do. ("Cool" was one of Gates' favorite words, and he used it to describe everything that surprised or excited him.) He had to expand. Things were at a turning point, and new markets meant everything. It had been a long time, and billions of dollars had changed hands, since the years when a mere string of code had been a place for him to inhabit.

Once he'd made a fortress of it: string after string of computer code piling up on a screen. Now the world was a different place—Gates' scope was growing so rapidly it was as if a Big Bang had taken place. He'd never imagined that being successful could cause so much trouble.

But he'd never become gun-shy. The Department of Justice antitrust chief, Anne Bingaman, had wanted him to get "the fear of Sherman." Her attempt to bring him down had only made him more aggressive. In the face of federal scrutiny on other fronts, three months earlier Neukom's team and outside counsel had helped him orchestrate a $1.5 billion bid for rival Intuit Inc., the tiny company that had outclassed Microsoft with its personal finance software—one of the only areas of software where he did not have a controlling lead. All he and his army of lawyers could do now was wait to see if that strategic bid would fly with antitrust regulators.

In the meantime, Microsoft's prior antitrust ghosts were again alive and kicking. All those whining competitors had to be squelched. Gates thought all had been settled the previous July and he could rest easy. But hell was breaking loose because of the Tunney Act, which gave a federal judge like Sporkin a chance to blow apart antitrust settlements with big corporations. John V. Tunney had been the son of a boxer.

Gates was furious. He tended to yell and insult Neukom every time something unexpected happened with the antitrust hounds. The two Bills had an odd relationship. Gates had put Neukom in charge of guarding his growing 18,000-person empire. Yet he mistrusted him. After all, even Gates' mother, Mary, had warned him that Neukom was untrustworthy, Gates would tell people. Consequently, Neukom had been one of the few members of Gates' inner sanctum of corporate officers he had not invited to his wedding. Mary Gates disliked Neukom, who'd been plucked years earlier from her husband's law firm to work for Microsoft.

Neukom gave the impression of being utterly dignified and gentlemanly. That dignity thing was one thing he had going for him that Gates would never have. Neukom had impressive physical stature, like Gates' six-foot, four-inch father. Many of the women lawyers at the Justice Department and the Federal Trade Commission seemed to fall all over themselves in Neukom's presence. One had even sent a card asking him for a date.

But Gates didn't have to like Neukom. The two had a love-hate relationship, and in some ways were rivals. While both were wildly rich and successful, they had in common a deep insecurity, which also served as their bond. Most recently Gates had made Neukom beg for a promotion. Then he'd only given him a new title, no pay increase. The word was Neukom had sat up in bed writing his own press release, that promotion had been so long in coming.

Now the hotel was beginning to fill up with a mixture of business executives and the pious. The Pope had come to town the same day as Gates.

Perhaps even more worshiped in Australia than he was in America, Gates was to speak at the Darling Harbor Convention Center to promote his next major software release: Windows 95. This country represented one of the fastest growing markets for Microsoft.

He'd gotten used to hobnobbing with the richest and most powerful men in the world and looked forward to paying a visit to Prime Minister Paul Keating, who would also be hosting the Pope that day.

Gates' fame now nearly matched that of the Pope. Microsoft's growth and power had become so pervasive that a fake press release had been sent out over the Internet announcing a merger between Microsoft and the Catholic Church. It was ridiculous that his public relations department had to issue a statement denying it. As if Microsoft could really do that!

Gates just didn't picture himself as a monopolist. True, years earlier he had told a group of reporters that he had a "natural monopoly." Some had taken that to mean the man believed he was fated, or had some god-given right, to his market power. But Gates had merely meant that Microsoft had won the market by being the best.

Well, sort of. His almost obsessive awareness that others were doing things better kept him fiercely driving his minions to seal up any possible chinks in the market while forging aggressively into new ones. His programmers, down to the lowest levels of the company, were quietly proud when given a surreptitious "dotted-line project with Bill." Such projects were mythical. They'd been going on in one form or another since Gates had barely reached puberty. Secret tasks. Pacts that no one else should know about. Like children cracking each other's code at a spy club. *Get Smart*, James Bond, and all that.

Gates had created a way to live his life that would be just like playing. But the stakes were high now. Dominions and turfs. Fiefdoms within fiefdoms. Screens within screens. The industry was a place of almost medieval divisions—markets within markets. He'd grown them all, why couldn't he play in them all?

———————————

Murdoch. Now there was a monopolist.

It had been more than a year since that bizarre lunch at Microsoft's 265-acre Redmond, Washington, campus. Rupert Murdoch had lowered his eyes, not wanting to look directly across the table as Gates shoveled great gobs of food into his mouth.

Now it was Gates' turn to be on the turf of the media mogul, about whom he had developed a certain anxiety. After all, things were at a turning point. Murdoch and his empire represented a world Gates knew virtually nothing about, but he was trying to learn fast.

Having conquered the PC software market worldwide, Gates had just begun to cut deals in Hollywood and the mass media world. He was still like a fish out of water, but the sheer size of that market made his competitive juices flow. The PC market was nothing compared with the market Murdoch played in. What was more, the media world was about royalties, endless returns on a one-time investment. Gates had built his empire on a similar model: building something once and collecting royalties for years while making very little improvement on the original.

Gates seemed panicked when that meeting with Murdoch was upon him. He'd been overcome with an irrational impulse to cancel it. Through the doorway to the conference room, Gates' colleagues had observed their leader pacing and in a frenzy. He knew that, as he was eyeing the media mogul's world, Murdoch was hiring technologists to get him up to speed on the information superhighway. What would he say? He was loath to be in the company of anyone who might be shrewder than he, particularly a man whose business he did not yet understand.

When Murdoch finally arrived and lunch was served, Gates did what he apparently did only when feeling in an inferior position. He did his "fuck you" routine to free himself of the burden of being the best, leapt up, piling his plate high in an act of abandon and contempt for etiquette. He then plopped himself back down in the chair and shoveled large masses of food into his mouth as if the act of eating was merely some sort of repetitive tic.

Murdoch found Gates the most peculiar man he had ever met, and remarked so to his colleagues right after the meeting. Gates' voice was nasal and self-conscious, as if he were at all times watching himself, listening to himself, measuring himself. Murdoch had also been appalled by the man's lack of manners. But he could perhaps be forgiven manners, with his twenty-hour workdays and outrageous fortune, which had reached $9.3 billion by October 1994.

The two men came away with no deal. (Gates had considered buying out a division of Murdoch's News Corp. ETAK had some mapping software that made Gates drool. He envisioned that this software be built into every laptop computer, so that traveling executives could find their way around any city. Murdoch had already licensed it to car manufacturers for built-in mapping in luxury cars.) Gates nonetheless had a chance to glean insight into Murdoch as a strategist—despite that lieutenant of Murdoch's, who drove Gates up the wall by referring to the software emperor as Black Billy.

Gates had always confronted his challenges head-on and was in the midst of some deals that would represent a turning point. Where others would cling to their past fortunes, Gates had always been ready to shake up his view of the world if it meant conquering some larger terrain. His longtime friends knew him as the one most likely to embrace a cactus. In the early years, out in the desert of Nevada, he had done just that. Or almost. His pals had stopped him before he inadvertently impaled himself on the strange vegetation that had sent him into a gleeful revelry. It had been Gates' first time in the desert.

In Sydney, January is a time for the bombaras, the ocean swells that come suddenly to beaches where rock oysters cling even more tenaciously. Now Gates was like a rock oyster in a bombaras: Gale-like forces threatened to reshape his world.

While the future was exploding, the past was coming back to haunt him. The feds were on his tail, and he had developed a reputation around the world for being unscrupulous and even an intellectual thief. Nevertheless, it was hard to turn down an opportunity to do business with Gates and his hugely profitable corporation.

He had his mother to thank for that. She had given him the world. Back in 1980, almost by accident, she had linked her son up with IBM. Things would never again be as easy as they were then, when he was dealing in small potatoes, writing early programming languages for the primitive PC.

He missed his mother's charm and grace. He hadn't realized how much the loss of her would hurt. No amount of money in the world could bring her back.

Who knows what his life would have been like if Mary Gates, a Seattle socialite, hadn't served on the board of the United Way with IBM CEO John Opel? Or if Opel hadn't been obsessed by catching up with Apple Computer in microcomputers? Opel had the hardware but was shopping around for an operating system. Mary had utter faith in her son.

Gates, of course, knew nothing of operating system software, but he quickly convinced another company, Seattle Computer Products, to license him its Q-DOS operating system. He slyly didn't mention a deal with IBM. Gates turned around and resold Q-DOS to IBM, and through a series of blunders Opel allowed Gates to collect all royalties for what would become Microsoft DOS, even though it would be jointly developed by IBM and Microsoft. DOS would become an industry standard, largely because of the blessing it received from IBM. The rest was history. Gates had eventually managed to get IBM out of the picture altogether with Windows.

Slowly, virtually every personal computer manufacturer in the world came to rely on Microsoft as the supplier of their operating systems, the underlying software that issues commands for the basic functioning of computers. Gates had used his market power to gain a lead, likewise, in applications software—software that allows computer users to perform specific tasks like word processing and creating financial spreadsheets.

New operating systems, and new markets, were critical to keeping his hold. Now it was months before his company's most controversial product release, and the market—and his personal wealth—fluctuated almost daily based on rumors of delay. A flood of bad publicity had afflicted the company over the past year as the federal government pried into his empire and its alleged monopolistic practices. Yet company profits continued to rise, like an irrepressible tide.

His willingness to throw himself into the most unlikely embraces, coupled with his vast market power and wealth, was leveraging him right into the most glamorous worlds. Just before arriving in Sydney, he had hobnobbed at a Las Vegas electronics conference with a man whose name tag identified him as "Steve Esser." It was Steven Spielberg, in baseball cap and glasses, on hand to nail a deal with Gates.

His new partners were at first skeptical, but Gates was managing to cozy up to Hollywood and the big media world.

Besides, there was no sport anymore in the PC market. IBM's chief strategist, Jim Cannavino, and Borland International's honcho Philippe Kahn were kaput, and soon Lotus Development Corp.'s Jim Manzi—whom Gates despised—would also be a nonentity. His competitors continued to drop like flies. Murdoch had felt the same way when his archcompetitor Robert Maxwell fell off his boat.

Gates made his way across the lobby of the Ramada and disappeared through a doorway. In the coming months he would become more visible than he'd ever dreamed. A market worth billions had succumbed to him, and he was intent on leveraging his success and power into new markets, linked by a digital network controlled by him, that would connect all aspects of American life.

But a lot of his past was catching up with him. The feds' intense scrutiny of the man and his strategies had begun some six years earlier, out of the public eye.

It had all started in an obscure, dusty office in Washington, D.C.—across town from the hotel where Gates' chief counsel was steeling himself for the storm of the next day.

2

FEDS

Flashback. As Bill Gates was cementing his monopoly power at the end of the 1980s, ennui had settled in at the Federal Trade Commission after the Reagan administration, which had all but killed antitrust enforcement. In the fall of 1989, the regulatory environment in Washington looked more like a soap opera. But some stirrings were afoot. The foundation of the subsequent Department of Justice suit and ongoing probes of the software giant was laid by the FTC.

D'Artagnan had kissed her in the elevator, the story went. Or *she* had started it. It depended on who you asked. The thought made Norris Washington and his colleagues a bit queasy. D'Artagnan was no Don Juan.

Such tales got Washington through a long, drab day at the Federal Trade Commission. The place had some spice, some of the time. True, D'Artagnan, the Musketeer nickname of attorney Steve Newborn, had become the favorite in the Bureau of Competition. But he was smart and worked hard. Washington's colleagues would later gripe about D'Artagnan moving up too fast while they were overlooked. But the thirty-one-year-old Washington liked the man, some years his senior, and knew he was as smooth as could be when it came to getting a case to court. D'Artagnan was an ace litigator. He was the hit man when push came to shove and a monopolist refused to settle. Washington couldn't help but admire him.

It was one of those early fall days in 1989 when the weather was just about to turn. Back down at street level, an encampment of the homeless was beginning to gather in the shrubs next to the stone horses that reared up so heroically before the Commission's Pennsylvania Avenue facade. Just two blocks down the federal triangle was the Department of Justice, whose own antitrust troops seemed always to be in a spitting match with their FTC counterparts.

Washington looked up from his standard government-issue steel-and-Formica desk. There went her head, bobbing down the hall like a beacon. Platinum blond. It glowed in the dusty, dusky hallways. She could be relied on to hold things up, throw a monkey wrench into any case begun by Washington and his attorney colleagues. Bizarre that these characters could rise to their posts as commissioners via political appointments.

The way she stepped off the elevator in that "Twister" dress. Big black polka dots, supershort—like she'd stepped out of the sixties. Great legs. The entire staff waited in anticipation for her to wear that dress.

That elevator had always been a chamber of intrigue. Or at least hilarity. Indeed, the only case of monopolization the agency had bothered to notice in recent memory was the one related to that lift: FTC Chairman Dan Oliver had made it his personal property.

Oliver's monopolization of the elevator had become legendary. The man was known for his secrecy. It so repulsed him to come face to face with his staff that he had an elevator key made that would allow him to go straight from the ground floor to his fourth-floor office—with no stops. Oliver was a reactionary conservative who had been appointed by Ronald Reagan. Under his reign no one had dared touch a big antitrust case, it seemed. Washington and his manager, Marc Schildkraut, assistant director of the Bureau of Competition, were nevertheless looking for some inspiration, a big monopolist to go after. Things had been pretty boring at 601 Pennsylvania Ave. for some time.

Washington and Schildkraut were a complementary pair. Washington, who was bright and diligent, respected authority and Schildkraut's opinion. He was dark haired, steady on his feet, of medium height and build, and soft-spoken. He seemed to prefer remaining inconspicuous, putting himself into detail work, witness interviews, and research behind the scenes.

The tall and lanky Schildkraut, by contrast, could be aggressive, confrontational, and even surly. Slightly balding, his dark blond hair lay in fine wisps against his brow. He wore a mustache, and his blue eyes flashed when he spoke. Schildkraut was animated and expressive. He had a knack for keeping the most well-rehearsed CEO off guard. In investigational hearings, he sometimes enjoyed playing off Washington's seeming naïveté in a good-cop, bad-cop routine, asking the younger attorney questions that he well knew the answers to for the benefit of the corporate officers for whom he wished to make a point. Washington would play the part brilliantly, answering his colleague bluntly with the facts as he knew them.

In computer industry terms, Washington operated as the back end of their system—guardian of a vast database of case details, while Schildkraut was the system's front end, representing his section's work to the bureau director and to the commissioners themselves—which sometimes required him to get down on his knees.

When it came to monopolization cases, the Bureau of Competition was beginning to look like some Kafkaesque study in inert officialdom—but not because the staff wasn't chomping at the bit to take on some master manipulator of market power. Until they had the word go, the newest commissioner, the forty-two-year-old Deborah Owen, at least would keep them awake with her blond head and slinky skirts slit thigh high.

It was early in the fall of 1989, and Oliver was at his personal best. "I've tried to do everything President Reagan would want a chairman to do—and less," he had said, having held forth before a group of antitrust lawyers during one of his infamous jaw-flapping sessions.

When Kevin Arquit got wind of that, it didn't faze him one bit.

16

He'd continued his day, crossing and recrossing the polished stone floors of the fourth floor to the commission offices. Those floors—laid when the place was built in 1914—could be slippery. At times he imagined he could see in them the specters of the old robber barons, grinning up greedily at Oliver as he barricaded himself in his fourth-floor office.

Undercutting and high-browed. That was the kind way to describe the FTC chairman. He had come to Washington back in 1981, intent on carrying on the Reagan agenda, and served as general counsel in the Departments of Education and Agriculture before his appointment to the FTC, where his goal was to relieve business of government regulation wherever he could.

Arquit—tall, suave, and sharp as a pin—knew firsthand what it was like to be at the bottom end of Oliver's worldview. Nonetheless, he was intent on becoming the director of the FTC's Bureau of Competition. When it came down to it, it was impossible not to like Arquit, even for Oliver, who regarded the younger man with some disdain. Arquit was a liberal Republican, and that made Oliver's skin crawl.

Further offending Oliver's pristine sensibilities, Arquit, with light brown hair and blue-gray eyes, had fallen in love with the chairman's twenty-five-year-old niece and married her. Oliver had protested wildly. He thought Arquit not of adequate breeding for his family. (Still, far more outrageous instances of romantic intrigue had unfolded within the agency's walls. One illustrious FTC employee during Oliver's reign was discovered en flagrante in a conference room with a female employee who eventually became his wife.)

But Arquit had the patience of a saint and the humor of a well-seasoned diplomat, with an uncanny talent for bridging the gap between the warring factions in the agency—laissez-faire economists and enforcement-minded young attorneys, politically appointed commissioners whose qualifications could run from brilliant to embarrassing. He was greatly loved for his ability to coax agreement out of the most recalcitrant personalities.

Where Oliver was high-browed, Arquit was high-minded. It

wasn't that he didn't notice the man's holier than thou manner of speaking, with a voice that resonated of New England's finest prep schools. Everyone at the agency was accustomed to that by now. The fifty-year-old Oliver was the former executive editor of the *National Review* and a buddy of the ultraconservative William F. Buckley. Since his appointment at the FTC, Oliver had been on a speech-giving circuit espousing his views on everything from the Iran-contra affair to the dangers of Washington. His gab schedule left him little time to do his job, which was just as he wanted it.

In hours of disillusionment, Arquit would sometimes remind himself that it was all in keeping with the FTC's sometimes outrageous history as a political animal—never mind its founding as an "independent" agency. The personalities might change, but the problems of the commission since its beginnings in the early part of the century seemed always to be the same: needless delay, senseless bureaucracy, and inordinate secrecy. These criticisms included poor planning, mismanagement of resources, failure to set priorities, preoccupation with trivial matters.

Turfs were so well defined inside the agency, they almost had a smell. As attorneys and economists in the 601 building butted heads, across the way the commissioners did their own war dances. Meanwhile, at the circumference of the big circle in which they dwelled was the Department of Justice—which inevitably set the tone for antitrust policies. Still, the lines separating Justice's and the FTC's areas of authority had never been clear and were sometimes nonexistent. Justice and the FTC had traditionally operated completely independently, according to different rules and policies. Indeed, the Federal Trade Commission had had a long and checkered past. Many thought it should be abolished.

Criticism of the commission dated back to its founding, Arquit knew, when it was almost immediately accused of political cronyism. Over the past fifty years, the agency had consistently been found wanting in its responsibility to administer a wide variety of antitrust and trade regulation laws.

"Bitter public displays of dissension among Commissioners have confused and demoralized FTC staff," scolded a 1969 report commissioned by President Nixon. "The failure to provide leadership has left enforcement activity largely aimless."

A study led by Ralph Nader tore the agency to shreds, calling its performance "shockingly poor." The political nature of its appointments, often resulting in "deadwood" personnel as one early Hoover Commission report stated, and the lack of accountability for its actions had been chronic problems.

Teddy Roosevelt would be turning in his grave if he could see how things had turned out, Arquit thought. The United States had invented antitrust law back in the 1880s, as a result of public concern about unfair business practices. During the late nineteenth and early twentieth centuries, corporate mergers were all the rage, with the rise of industrial technology and improved transportation. By 1888 antitrust was added to the presidential campaigns of all the parties, and between 1889 and 1891, eighteen states enacted antitrust laws. John Sherman, a Republican senator from Ohio, after two earlier tries introduced an antitrust bill in 1890 that passed the Senate by 52 to 1 and easily passed in the House.

At the time enormous economic power was being consolidated in a few hands, and oligopolists and monopolists were in their heyday. The purpose of the federal and state antitrust laws was to protect consumers from monopolistic pricing and to permit new competitors to enter the market freely. Antitrust enforcement was most promoted by the activist Roosevelt, beginning in 1901. He created a separate antitrust enforcement division within the Justice Department. Enforcement of these laws was handed to the Justice Department and the FTC, as well as to private parties, who could bring suit and be awarded treble damages.

The Sherman Act is in two sections. Section 1 prohibits contracts, combinations, and conspiracies in restraint of trade. Section 2 prohibits attempts to monopolize "any part of the trade or commerce among the several states, or with foreign nations."

Yet monopolization in and of itself is not illegal. And that was where Oliver seemed to rest his case. What is illegal is if a company, having attained monopoly power, has maintained that power through predatory practices. Now that could be a very difficult thing to prove.

The law states it is not illegal for a company to have achieved market power by possessing "superior skill, foresight and industry" and to have maintained its power through "reasonable industrial practices." Monopolization is illegal if it can be proved that there is specific "intent" to monopolize, anticompetitive or predatory conduct directed at accomplishing this, and a "dangerous probability" of success. Violation of the Sherman Act is a felony, and corporations can be fined up to $1 million per offense.

In general, criminal enforcement is appropriate only for outrageous and blatantly illegal conduct, such as bid rigging and price fixing. A director or officer of a company who participates in such a violation may be fined up to $100,000 and sentenced to three years in prison.

Of course, the Reagan administration disagreed with the economic foundation of most of these laws and only selectively enforced them.

Even then, historically, enforcement of the laws has not been easy, and has wavered depending on forces working in the economy and politically.

The Clayton Act, passed in 1914, addressed anticompetitive problems in their incipiency. Section 2, the Robinson-Patman Act, prohibits price discrimination, and Section 3 concerns sales and distribution agreements, prohibiting "tying arrangements" and agreements not to use competitors' products.

The third major antitrust law was the Federal Trade Commission Act of 1914, which prohibits "unfair methods of competition." Courts have determined that this covers all activities prohibited by the Sherman and Clayton Acts as well as others that may be identified by the FTC. The antitrust remedies available to the Commission are limited to the issuance of "cease and desist" orders. Further penalties are permitted only in the event of noncompliance with those orders.

All very well and good, at least for those who were passionate about seeing that the law was enforced.

Arquit and D'Artagnan, who had become great pals, were endlessly comparing notes on the bizarre environment they had worked in for years. The Little Old Lady of Pennsylvania Ave., as the FTC had been dubbed by Washington insiders, had become comatose. Antitrust enforcement during the Reagan administration had been the most lax since the Sherman Act's first decade.

Schildkraut and Washington—and everyone else for that matter—admired Arquit for his ambassadorlike charm and intelligence, even though he was now a relative of Oliver's.

As for Oliver, he could be heard complaining about his difficult job. "What does a deregulator put on his resume—all the cases he didn't bring?" he asked his antitrust peers repeatedly.

Norris Washington, just down the hall from Kevin Arquit, could not ignore what he was now reading. The article lay open on Washington's desk. It said: Last week Microsoft chairman Bill Gates stood up with IBM Corp. senior vice president James Cannavino to announce that Microsoft will hold back certain features for its Windows operating system software in order to spur market acceptance of OS/2, the competing operating software that has been jointly developed by Microsoft.

Washington thought he smelled a rat.

3

BUGS

IBM Corp. had made the mistake of letting Bill Gates take control of the operating system in its original deal with him. In late 1989 Big Blue and Microsoft were warring over future control of this technology. Gates was pushing Windows, and IBM was promoting its new operating system, OS/2. After an odd press announcement made in an attempt to clear up market confusion, the feds thought the two companies were engaged in collusion to divide up the market between themselves. Of course, neither company ever made public what its corporate officers were doing and saying behind the scenes. It took a while for the feds to catch on.

In the scheme of things, the wars of childhood had become the wars of a marketplace.

The beatings Jim Cannavino had taken as a boy had led inevitably to his independence, a fierce drive for survival, and his meteoric rise through IBM. Now IBM's PC chief would not be licked by Bill Gates.

In Las Vegas for the biggest computer conference of the year, the forty-five-year-old executive, his dark hair cropped in a Napoleonic cut, had been waiting in his hotel suite for some time. His security man was to sweep the place for bugs.

Cannavino was not one to shy away from a good fight. He looked forward to the performance he would put on for the press the following day with Bill Gates; Gates' right-hand man, Steve Ballmer; and Gates' "special strategies" czar, Jon Lazarus. Of the latter two members of Gates' inner sanctum, Cannavino would tell his colleagues, "Standing amongst those two thorns, it's kind of hard not to look like some kind of a rose."

Gates was smart, Cannavino acknowledged, and his latest prank was the pièce de résistance. Gates had been fooling IBM, he believed, pretending to be fully devoted to codeveloping a new operating system—OS/2—with Big Blue while secretly putting all his effort into Windows. Would he even have the guts to show up, Cannavino wondered, now that the younger man knew Cannavino was on to him and he'd be publicly held to his commitment? Cannavino recognized that if Gates won control of the desktop with Windows, he would be in a position to call the shots with computer makers worldwide.

Cannavino vowed that he would not be beaten, although he had warned IBM's CEO, John Akers, months earlier that he felt that he was on a kamikaze mission.

Odd to think back. It had been three and half decades since that nun had beaten him. Cannavino had returned home to his mother, who punished him—it was his fault that his teacher had become angry. By age twelve he began earning a living on the streets, shining shoes at ten cents a shot. The boy was pleased with himself and his new profession.

These days his "employment" was no longer about earning a living. No, it was much more than that. The relationship with Bill Gates was nothing short of a disaster.

Akers had been warned. About Gates and many other things.

Just a year earlier Cannavino had been moved out of mainframe software to run Personal Systems. Akers' edict to him was, "Fix this. We're losing a billion a year." Cannavino, a software engineer, was brought in to replace the marketing executive who had been running the division. He had asked for three months to evaluate the situation. Akers gave him two.

In late 1988 Cannavino met again with Akers, President Jack Kuehler, and the rest of the IBM management committee. "Your technical plan is not executable," Cannavino concluded, knowing full well that his news would be hard for the group to swallow. Akers had that look he always had—a mixture of stoicism and suspicion. Cannavino forged ahead nonetheless.

"The products will not come out," he began, noticing Akers drop a fraction of an inch in his chair. "They're going to be way behind." Kuehler sniffed.

"And I see no redeemable engineering structure in the place," Cannavino concluded somewhat triumphantly.

The group looked stunned. Kuehler, in a huff, called for an audit.

Two weeks later, Cannavino was back in front of the committee. Akers glared at him.

Cannavino had a long aquiline nose and a head so Romanesque it might have been transposed from a Pompeii relief. Short and stocky, he looked like he could not be knocked off his feet. His arms, hanging by his sides, were slightly curled, like a prize-fighter's.

Akers was not about to speak. Kuehler made the first move. "Cannavino is right," he said. "We have to get rid of a lot of people."

Cannavino was known to stir up the soup. Before giving Akers the dire news about IBM's operating system strategy, he gave him a little lecture on distribution. He advised the committee that distribution systems would change rapidly—and that IBM was not prepared for this. "You need alternate forms of distribution," he said. "And some direct sales with your largest customers. Second, you need a direct-response marketing partner—like a Gateway or a Dell. Third, you need to be in retail."

Kuehler said, "We're not going direct to our largest customers. And direct-response marketing is out of the question. Go ahead and try retailing." It was the model for the future, and IBM was doing it halfheartedly, Cannavino knew.

He suggested that IBM buy Packard Bell. The company had a business model that was working and making money. "Why don't we just make that our retail deal?" Cannavino asked Kuehler. At the time, Packard Bell had perhaps 7 or 8 percent of the retail market. Soon that grew to 40 percent, then to more than 50 percent.

But IBM failed to really go after retail. "We didn't go after direct-response marketing, and we didn't go after direct account sales. So we're zero for three in distribution," Cannavino would say.

When it came to software for personal computers, Cannavino was perplexed about what his colleagues had in mind. "You guys tell me about the software. This is not going to work."

"It must work," Kuehler said. He then dismissed Cannavino from the room.

When he returned, Akers, Kuehler, senior vice president and head of U.S. operations Terry Lautenbach, and the rest glared at him. "We want to hear you out," Akers said.

Cannavino grinned. "OK. First off, you think your best buddy is Bill Gates. But he's got a different plan than you. He's doing a Windows strategy," he said.

In fact, many a CEO's office had been buzzing at the time about the deceptions of Bill Gates. The man was gaining a reputation for screwing his alleged business partners.

In April 1989, Akers again sat at the big polished wood table at IBM's Armonk headquarters with his top men. Again, in the center was Cannavino. They were grilling him.

Akers looked as if he thought Cannavino had been eating LSD. "No way," he said.

Cannavino persisted. "Gates has a small team of people tied up making OS/2 shit. His real strategy is to do Windows," he said. Microsoft had officially committed to codevelop OS/2 with IBM as the next-generation operating system that would replace DOS. By that time, Cannavino had met about four times with Gates and gone over the company's software plans.

"I've gone through the plans and added up the number of people they have working on our stuff and the number they had in the same operating system group doing something else," Cannavino said. "I don't think Gates has any overhead, so he must be doing something else."

He went on, "It's not worth their while to do weird shit, like Unix or something. But there is a group of guys working on something else."

To determine what was really going on, Cannavino had talked with the applications software developers—known as ISVs or independent software vendors. He talked to the large ones, like Word-Perfect, as well as the smallest companies.

"What is Microsoft telling you to develop software for?" Cannavino asked. The answer was Windows, Windows, Windows.

"Meanwhile, Gates is coming and telling us at IBM that DOS and Windows are dead," Cannavino told the committee.

Akers was silent for a while. "How come I hate your story and I like Gates'?" he finally asked.

"Because Bill's story is what you want to hear. Mine is the facts of where you are," Cannavino replied.

Dead silence fell over the room.

"What do you think we ought to do?" Akers asked.

"Well," Cannavino said, "my opinion is that we kill OS/2 and buy 40 percent of Microsoft."

When Akers had recovered from Cannavino's words, he began grilling him again. "Buy part of Microsoft? What would Lotus think of that? They'd be really pissed. And our shareholders would be furious," he said. "And, Jim, I thought you didn't like Gates."

"No, I like Gates," Cannavino replied. "I don't like the strategy he's got. It's disingenuous, but he's smart. He's been hanging around hardware and marketing guys."

"We're going to have to think about this," Akers said.

In the ensuing weeks, Cannavino started getting testimonials from customers about what Microsoft had said to them about IBM. "They're saying, 'Microsoft is telling us that IBM is fucked up,'" Cannavino related. "And they're saying that Akers doesn't know what he's talking about." He knew the personal reference would get Akers' goat.

In the next management meeting, Terry Lautenbach conceded to Cannavino, "You've got a point."

"Bill wouldn't do that to me. I know his mother," Akers jumped in.

"He doesn't have a mother. She's obviously rented," Cannavino shot back. Kuehler tittered.

Cannavino was serious now. "Let me give you a customer's point of view," he said. "Here's what Microsoft is saying to GE and Boeing. You don't have to take my word for this, John. Call Boeing."

But Akers had had enough. "Just fix OS/2," he commanded.

Cannavino was now acting like a stubborn ten-year-old. "It's not what I'd prefer," he persisted.

"Are you with us, Jim?" Akers asked.

"I'd prefer a 40 percent stake in Microsoft," Cannavino said.

"Can you make this OS/2 work?" Akers again asked.

"That's not the question, John," Cannavino said. "The question is 'What are the odds of this succeeding?' There's a single-digit chance of success. Are you prepared to make a $1 billion to $2 billion bet?"

Akers conferred with the other members of the management committee and all decided against taking a stake in Microsoft and instead investing in "fixing OS/2."

"You know, John, I might not be the right guy to lead this effort," Cannavino said. "But I'll work as hard as it takes. Why don't you try to get one of these guys to do it?" He motioned to the other suits around the table. Everyone went pale.

It was the first time Akers knew he wasn't fucking with him.

Yes, Akers had been warned.

The Nevada heat was beginning to invade the hotel room. Cannavino got up to let the detective in with all his gadgets.

The man had quite an assortment in his bag, which he unloaded as if preparing for an operation. Cannavino watched as the man's bald pate dipped under the bed.

The security man was now fiddling with his equipment while

Cannavino stood by the window. It was a balmy day in the Nevada desert and the midday glare turned the IBM executive to granite against the pastel decor of the room.

Although Cannavino had it tough in the past, he now lived in a 250-year-old estate that was his version of Paradise. In the face of adversity, he had a twinkle in his blue eyes that could not be extinguished. Mischievous. He rode on horseback after his hounds every chance he could get, chasing foxes and coyotes through the underbrush. Not one prone to artifice, he would point out to his curious colleagues, "We always use wild animals."

Cannavino, though quite wealthy in his own right by now, loved the working class and was known to pal around with busboys, mechanics, waitresses, and other members of that segment of society that represented his roots. He had an almost Chekhovian fondness for the "little man." He could often be overheard in hotel lobbies thanking desk clerks for their politeness by calling them "silvery tongued devils."

Gates had found him old-fashioned and sentimental, and had no time for his small talk.

The detective's bald pate was now almost at floor level as he scanned again beneath the bed frame.

Tomorrow it would be Cannavino and Gates. How ironic it was that years earlier, when things were friendlier between the two companies, IBM had given Gates some advice on security. John Akers, Jack Kuehler, and Gates had had a powwow. The older men had taken Gates under their wing to get him up to speed on security concerns. Now the man was becoming more powerful than them all. Gates' personal fortune had just passed $1 billion.

It had started with his control of DOS. How stupid IBM had been to let Gates gain control. But that was someone else's mistake. Cannavino had only a year earlier been brought in by Akers to try to turn the situation around.

In the DOS market, Gates had sailed with no challenge until that upstart DR-DOS appeared in 1988. That, Cannavino realized, in addition to IBM's plans to grab the market back from him with OS/2, spurred nothing less than Gates' silent declaration of war.

Cannavino followed the head of the detective as it bobbed around the room. Suddenly the device in his hand began beeping madly. The man now was moving in on three different spots in the room.

Akers should have listened when Cannavino advised him to drop OS/2 and buy that stake in Microsoft, he still thought. But Akers wanted OS/2 fixed, so it was his job to get Gates under control and OS/2 in shape as a product that would make DOS and Windows irrelevant.

The knobby hand of the detective was now in Cannavino's face. Cannavino tilted his large head to one side, as he was prone to do when he found something mildly amusing.

In the upturned palm were three bugs. The man took out a bottle with black powder and a little brush. He dusted the three devices carefully. No fingerprints showed up.

Mel Hallerman's eyes were wide with excitement when he burst back into the room. Cannavino and a group of top IBM executives looked up. "You're not going to believe this," Hallerman said.

Earlier that morning of November 11, 1989, Hallerman had been winding his way through the corridors of a hotel in Las Vegas. The hotel, like every other place in town that week, was deluged with computer industry conference goers. Hallerman was on his way to the much-anticipated joint announcement with Microsoft.

One of the designers of the original IBM PC, Hallerman was a member of Big Blue's elite Corporate Technology Team—the top IBM engineers who were responsible for strategic product planning five to ten years into the future. Cannavino was one of his bosses.

IBM and Microsoft had been squabbling just hours before the announcement and only the night before had come close to calling the whole thing off. In the meeting room the IBM executives waited anxiously. Jim Cannavino looked as though he might need a double dose of his blood pressure pills.

Finally, Bill Gates showed up with Steve Ballmer, an intense and temperamental Microsoft executive who was one of Gates' closest confidants. With much relief from the IBM contingent, the event came off as planned. It was an "I'll take the high road, you take the low road" type of agreement. The two companies told the world that OS/2 would be the business solution for more powerful computers and that Microsoft would offer applications for it first, before bringing Windows software to market. Windows would be relegated to less powerful computers. Cannavino and Gates had argued about these matters numerous times, and now an agreement was finally public.

On the way out, as Hallerman walked down the corridors, he bumped into Ballmer. They talked as they strolled through the hotel about the plans that had just been announced. Part of the deal had been the promise that IBM and Microsoft would both work to reduce the OS/2 program to a version that consumed much less computer memory.

Hallerman chatted happily, pleased that the market would now be certain that OS/2 was the best software for business environments. Other CEOs—like Lotus's Jim Manzi and Software Publishing Corporation's Fred Gibbons—had already invested millions in developing applications software for it, and they had been begging IBM to do something to jump-start the market. He thought about the development work that lay ahead. "Getting this thing down to two megabytes is sure going to be a challenge," he said.

"Oh. We're *never* going to do that," Ballmer replied.

Hallerman couldn't believe his ears. "But . . ." He found himself stammering. "What do you mean? That's what we just announced!"

Ballmer turned and grinned at Hallerman as if to say, That's what you think, buddy. He then turned his back and left the hotel.

Hallerman, went back to tell his colleagues about this strange conversation he had just had with IBM's supposed business partner.

Jim Cannavino just smiled.

The room was abuzz.

Dan Oliver was out and the cocktail-sipping crowd was now gleefully tipsy. It was December 1989. Norris Washington and Marc Schildkraut, in suits and ties, hovered to one side with big grins on their faces. Their colleagues had congregated for the annual Christmas party for that tongue-in-cheek organization known as the Casto

Geer Society. What seemed to be every member of the D.C. antitrust bar had gathered and were now chattering away like a bunch of squirrels in a tree.

Casto Geer was a legend of sorts. He was a short-lived FTC employee who, because of his friendship with a former commissioner, had been authorized to set up an FTC office in Oak Ridge, Tennessee—for no other reason than that was where he lived. When this scheme was found out by the White House, Geer was fired. A "society" of FTC alumni and current employees was playfully formed in his honor and established the tradition of meeting every Christmas. These soirees always turned out to be a Who's Who in antitrust. It seemed that every politician and attorney in town had at one time worked for the FTC.

The champagne was flowing, and for good reason. Oliver was indeed out; George Bush had just appointed Janet Steiger the new head of the agency. Commission attorneys, who had been horribly demoralized, were now showing some signs of life. It was known that Steiger believed in vigorous antitrust enforcement.

All eyes gravitated toward the tiny woman who stood in one corner of the room at the D.C. firm of Baker & Hostedler, where the bash was being thrown. The crowd had surrounded her in admiration. Her eyes were bright as she talked, and her close-cropped brown hair set off a small, delicate face.

The fifty-year-old Steiger had been a surprise appointment by President Bush, who was a close friend of her husband, Wisconsin Congressman William Steiger. William had died suddenly at age forty of diabetes. He had been the founder of the volunteer army, and many thought he would eventually run for president. His tie with Bush went back to their both having been freshmen members of Congress in 1966. Both were from Houston, and they were part of a group of twelve newly elected Republicans who hung around together. William Steiger was the first to recommend that Bush be on the national ticket.

When William died, George and Barbara Bush, close to Janet, vowed always to take care of her. She was appointed chair of the Postal Rate Commission by President Reagan in 1982 and served there until 1989. Then Bush insisted upon her appointment as chair at the FTC.

It turned out that Steiger was greatly underestimated. A Fulbright scholar, she would become known by her colleagues at the FTC as a "preparation freak." No occasion was too small for her to request a briefing. Over the years Steiger had been called in the press "a Republican housewife" and "a Republican widow." Now that was upgraded to a "professional bureaucrat." The *National Journal* referred to her as the "iron pixie," the moniker that perhaps suited her best. She was known to be tough-minded and resilient.

Washington's eyes drifted back to Schildkraut's. Now was his chance. "I've been looking into something," he said.

Schildkraut's eyes lit up. "What are you up to now?" he asked.

"I'm on to something," Washington said. "But I don't know if that bunch is going to be pleased." He nodded in the direction of a group of commissioners.

There was Mary Azcuenaga. She was an independent and a Reagan appointee reappointed by Bush. On the positive side, she was known to pay painstaking attention to the details of a case. But on anything but merger cases—which, by law, had to be done quickly—her tendency to scrutinize minute details had been known to immobilize her. Azcuenaga had a reputation for sitting for years on consent decrees that had been signed by all the parties involved. But the commission had no system of accountability to do anything about it.

In 1973 Azcuenaga came to the FTC right out of law school. When the Republicans named her commissioner, they sought an appointee who was a woman and a minority. Many perceived her name as Spanish. She was in fact of Basque descent.

Azcuenaga's attention to detail could indeed drive her colleagues to distraction. Commission attorneys recalled that when the FTC press office routinely circulated weekly newspaper and magazine clippings on the agency no one thought twice about it. They were placed in a binder with a cover attached. For the fun of it, a cartoon was chosen and circulated each week that seemed apropos to current goings-on at the agency. Azcuenaga asked the press office if they were certain they weren't violating copyright laws by sending copies of the cartoon around to the staff.

A bright light seemed to be approaching Azcuenaga. There was Deborah Owen, the newest commissioner, also appointed by Bush. She had virtually no experience in antitrust law and would become infamous for her fits of temper in commission and staff meetings. Owen had a "closed door" style, which meant she rarely discussed her opinions with her staff or anyone else. Schildkraut and Washington exchanged glances. This evening Owen was wearing a very conservative looking gray suit—except that it was slit almost up to her crotch.

Before her arrival at the FTC, Owen had served three years as a managing partner at the McNair law firm, based in South Carolina with an office in Washington. She was also the former general counsel to Sen. Strom Thurmond. Owen was a conservative Republican who had attended Harvard Law School. She was also becoming known for her bawdy sense of humor.

Uncle Buck would join the group by the following Christmas. That was the nickname given Commissioner Roscoe Starek III by some of his colleagues—for his vague resemblance to John Candy. Starek had come to the commission from his post as the number-two person at the White House personnel office. Nasty and unconfirmed rumors circulated at the commission that he had recommended himself for the FTC job. He had not a shred of antitrust experience.

The group would later be joined in 1991 by Dennis Yao, the commissioner the staff had the most faith in. He was the most qualified of the bunch. He was the youngest of the commissioners, the only Democrat, and an economist with a Ph.D. from Stanford. Yao had recently been appointed by Bush. After receiving his MBA in civil engineering at Princeton, Yao had worked as a car product planner for the Ford Motor Company and developed the business plans for the 1983 Thunderbird.

Finally Schildkraut nudged Washington, who appeared to be gaping at Owen's legs. Washington in turn spilled a few drops of his drink on his trousers.

"Well, so what's the big story?" Schildkraut asked.

"The story?" Washington had forgotten what he was talking about. "Uh . . . well, I've been reading again," he said. Washington was a voracious reader and had taken to keeping up with the computer industry trade magazines. While some FTC probes started with industry complaints coming in over the transom, the best cases seemed to be self-generated, inspired by the curiosity of the commission staff. Schildkraut also had been reading the trades. Both men were becoming computer buffs, having had personal computers on their desks for a couple of years now—quite an accomplishment in a federal office.

Washington started to explain. "There was a press announcement in Vegas last month. IBM and Microsoft said some things and—"

"Not IBM!" interrupted Schildkraut. His voice always became squeaky when he got sarcastic—which was often. The twenty-year-long IBM case had been the Department of Justice's nightmare, and one reason both agencies were now so shy of monopolization probes.

"It sounds like a market division agreement to me," Washington continued.

"Really?"

"Yeah," Washington said. "A clear-cut case of collusion. It's complicated. I'll tell you about it."

Washington knew that at their heart all personal computers rely on operating system software, which issues the commands that make them work and interprets the commands of all other software a person might use. Without this software, a personal computer is a useless tangle of metal and circuitry.

Bill Gates, two years Washington's senior, had reaped a fortune with this software, Washington knew. Early on he had recognized the enormous revenue stream and market power that would befall any company controlling computer operating software. Gates knew in his bones that personal computers would soon run the world and be as pervasive as television sets.

Washington now suspected that something was up with Windows—Gates' add-on to his flagship DOS operating system. Windows lets computer users point and click on graphical icons instead of using the arcane, character-based commands of DOS. With Windows, Gates hoped finally to provide an Apple Macintosh–like interface—which he had envied for years. Although he'd been working on it since 1981, and announced the first incarnation of the product in 1983, Windows had still not caught on in the marketplace. Nevertheless, Gates was still trying to make a go of it.

From his reading Washington knew that, by late 1989, IBM executives had become suspicious of Microsoft, which had agreed to codevelop OS/2 with the company. But Gates appeared to be devoting more and more resources to fixing up Windows, as opposed to sticking to OS/2 and its own graphical interface, known as Presentation Manager.

Among other things, OS/2 was a way for IBM to wrest control of the operating system market from Microsoft, which had become rich collecting DOS royalties from virtually every computer maker in the world. "Now, if the two companies can't choose between Windows and OS/2, it looks like they're attempting to neatly carve up the big market pie for themselves," Washington mused.

Schildkraut smiled and nodded. He was certain that Kevin Arquit, director of the Bureau of Competition, would have no problem giving the nod to an initial phase investigation—which would not require approval at higher levels of the commission. Washington was ready to do a little fishing.

Some sort of ruckus was now stirring at the edge of the crowd. It was time for the favorite Christmas ritual of the Casto Geer Society. Tradition had it that the newest commissioner would give a speech. It was Deborah Owen.

Washington and Schildkraut watched as she strode up to the podium. D'Artagnan, across the way with his merger cronies and his assistant, Ginger, had moved in for a better view.

Owen stood before her compatriots and reached inside her brassiere. "I always keep my speeches in my bra," she said demurely. A mild titter erupted and gradually rolled into a wave of laughter that took over the room.

Owen then went on to give a detailed oration on the consumer-protection issues surrounding edible underwear.

By February 1990, when Schildkraut told Arquit that Washington was ready to start an initial phase investigation of Microsoft, Arquit gave the probe his blessing.

Staff attorneys at the FTC are pretty much left to their own devices in the first hundred hours of an investigation; if their hunches hold up, they seek clearance to formally begin an investigation from the bureau director and then from the commissioners themselves.

"Let me know how it goes," Arquit said. "In a few weeks we can try to get clearance. Justice isn't going to like this, after what they went through with IBM."

4

LABYRINTH

A year and a half after the FTC had begun its probe of Microsoft, the investigation had changed shape a number of times as federal attorneys began collecting internal Microsoft documents under subpoena. Gates was inadvertently leading them on a serpentine trail through his strategies in a number of markets. Gates himself, meantime, was conducting business as usual, letting off steam through liaisons arranged by his colleagues. He was intent on maintaining his DOS monopoly by shutting out all potential competitors—like Digital Research Inc.—while also leveraging his market power for an advantage in other unrelated software markets. This put him on a collision path with Ray Noorda, Philippe Kahn, and Jim Manzi.

She was beautiful. It hardly mattered that she was paid.

It was a gentle day. Twenty-four hours earlier, the sun had been harsh, marking off the hours with an unbearable stringency. Now soft gray clouds rolled in, and rounded out the edges of things, making all one.

Perhaps he was more at ease when his mind was able to mix things up into a rich soup. There were times when it seemed that pieces of himself had distilled and separated under the glare of the bare sun; the world had a sharp edge during such times, like glass.

Gates' confidant had done well—as he had done all over the globe. You can have anything you want, don't you realize? he had said to Gates, who was not yet married. At your level, all men need a little rest and relaxation.

Indeed, Gates had a need to let off steam. The events of the past year had been a bit much. The Federal Trade Commission had managed to home in on his core business. Meanwhile, Ray Noorda, chairman and CEO of arch-rival Novell Inc., had to be stopped. The OEMs—computer makers all over the world—were being courted with an alternative to his DOS software. Joachim Kempin, Gates' VP of OEM sales; his senior sales VP Steve Ballmer, and chief counsel Neukom—who had drawn up the contracts with his legal team—had made sure that everyone in the world came to depend on Microsoft. Indeed, from quarterly royalty reports of computer makers all over the planet, Gates had his finger on the pulse of the market. He had a global view no one else had, at any level within any corporation or federal office. He could spot glitches no one else could see till much later, slight fluctuations in demand around the world.

But he didn't have to worry about the feds. Neukom—with the help of Gates' father—had gotten him out of quite a bit of hot water over the years. They'd take care of him. Neukom and Ballmer, one of his closest friends, knew about his "thing" for women.

Gates had almost forgotten it all now sitting in a restaurant with the woman. (There would be other times—once in a hotel room with his other lover, a low-level staffer inside Microsoft. They had even kissed goodbye, in public, right in front of the Manhattan site of a Microsoft product announcement. That had been thrilling. No one had noticed.)

Now this one was like a friend—she was smart and very, very beautiful. What did it matter that it had all been arranged?

His confidant had done Gates a favor. Gates liked him most of the time—the two men shared an attitude of being above the pack; both liked playing word games and head games, and Gates got a kick out of that, but others recognized that the confidant was no gem. Still, this locker-room atmosphere was not uncommon at Microsoft. In one sex discrimination suit filed against the company, one executive had bragged to a woman who worked for him that he was "president of the amateur gynecology club." Then there was the e-mail, distributed to the entire staff, on "Mouse Balls," containing sexual innuendo about male genitalia, and his offer to pay $500 to a black woman employee to be able to call her "Sweet Georgia Brown."

Top executives had seen a lot of Gates' private side. A number of them knew too much, he told his closest friends. Neukom also knew too much, but Gates needed him.

Gates had been apoplectic when, the previous summer, Neukom had told him of the federal investigation. Indeed, his chief counsel's staff was ready to see Gates jumping up and down on Neukom's desk.

The letter from the FTC had arrived back in June 1990. It had stated that Microsoft was under investigation for supposed collusion with IBM. The agency was investigating the companies' joint announcement the previous November and demanded access to internal documents pertaining to the business strategies of Microsoft and IBM.

Neukom thought it was funny. Gates got mad anytime the company was accused of wrongdoing, but this was outrageous. Everyone knew that IBM and Microsoft had no agreement on anything. It had all unraveled. The press had even written about the "divorce."

Neukom had arranged a flight to Washington. There was no way he was going to start fishing into the company's documents without a subpoena. Later that June he had made a visit to the FTC's Bureau of Competition with his associate general counsel Bill Pope and Microsoft Vice President Paul Maritz. In a conference room they'd been greeted by the inseparable Washington and Schildkraut, along with two other FTC attorneys and an economist from the agency's Bureau of Economics.

For about two hours, Neukom and Maritz had tried to demonstrate where the company was going with Windows. There was no agreement with IBM, they said, and that already was more than clear to the industry. A lot had changed since the previous November.

Neukom had a tendency to be sarcastic, especially in the presence of those he felt to be less sophisticated than he. But he made it clear that Microsoft would not cooperate unless it was issued a subpoena—which he knew would take some time given the feds' bureaucracy. Until the subpoena was issued,* Microsoft would provide only press releases and publicly available marketing material. Pretty boring stuff. Neukom was a master at stalling.

By now, however, the documents were flowing. Thousands had already been turned over. Gates confided in his friends; he was nervous about what the feds were after. Neukom just laughed it off. "Nothing will ever come of this," he assured him.

A waitress greeted Gates and his new "girlfriend" next to him. Happily, no one ever recognized him outside the Northwest or Sili Valley. It was good to be out of all that. Noorda was driving him up the wall. He'd made the audacious move of buying Digital Research in October 1991 and was now attempting to eat into Gates' market share with Digital Research's DOS, known as DR-DOS, the only alternative to Microsoft DOS on the market.

Gates' pal Ballmer knew how paranoid Gates was about DR-DOS. Ballmer had read the e-mail Gates had shot off to him, railing about the competing product. Lazarus knew, Neukom knew, Kempin knew, Mike Maples knew. Retail sales of the product had started to outstrip those of Microsoft DOS. It was all but a companywide policy to kill DR-DOS using every possible means. Forget about the feds. Stay in control. Don't let them do to us what they did to IBM: turn the company into a bunch of wimps.

DR-DOS had been a thorn in Gates' side for some time. He was obsessed with it, despite his statements in the press that it was an insignificant product. It was when DR-DOS came along in 1988, as an alternative to MS-DOS, that he had been forced to lower prices to computer manufacturers. He'd been used to charging

---

* The Federal Trade Commission and the Department of Justice versions of a subpoena in civil cases is known as a C.I.D. or Civil Investigative Demand.

$30 to $60 per machine prior to that, and had been able to relax, assured that nothing could touch DOS and its monopoly on desktop computers. DR-DOS could take millions of dollars in royalties away from Microsoft if it were allowed to gain even a tiny portion of the market.

The history of the whole thing had always been problematic. Digital Research Inc. (DRI) was the original publisher of CP/M, from which Gates had originally copied MS-DOS. Seattle Computer's Q-DOS was a clone of CP/M; Microsoft DOS still contained lines of code written by DRI's founder, Gary Kildall. In fact, IBM had been so paranoid about that when they realized Gates had sold them a clone, they paid Kildall about $800,000—a pittance given the billions Microsoft had raked in from the product over the years—in exchange for his promise never to sue.

Although Gates had stolen his thunder, Kildall and DRI kept plugging away with their version of DOS. There hadn't been any improvements to DOS till DR-DOS 5 came along in 1990, adding features—built-in memory management, disk compression, a full-screen editor, security, and backup, among others—that infuriated Gates because his own operating system lacked them.

Digital Research had also put its product on the retail market as an upgrade, something Microsoft had never done. That enabled thousands of computer users who had already paid for a version of DOS, since it was running on their computers, to pay again for a better product.

It wasn't enough that by late 1989 Microsoft had a market share with MS-DOS of more than 90 percent. Holding on was the point.

By 1991 account managers could read the terms of the licensing policy in their OEM manuals in brief form. The new licensing terms had started in the Far East, when low-cost clone vendors were happy to increase their slim profit margins by using a cheaper but better version of DOS—from DRI. Microsoft had implemented what eventually became known as "per processor" licenses, which effectively locked computer makers into contracts that required them to pay for the Microsoft operating system on every computer sold.

Account managers knew they could entice computer makers into such arrangements by offering them discounts and other compensation. While the OEM manuals briefly defined per processor licensing, Microsoft account managers around the world were verbally told of the "strategic" significance of licensing Microsoft operating systems through this arrangement.

Gates typically made light of this arrangement to the press and publicly. "The approach we take to system software licensing is not unique at all," he would say. In a statement to a reporter, Neukom was likewise nonchalant about the impact of such licensing on competition. "Microsoft believes that its licensing practices are entirely legal and in no sense anticompetitive," he would say.

Still, Gates was nervous. It was his nature. Unwind, his confidant would say. You don't realize who you are and how rich you are, Ballmer would say. I'm taking care of everything, Neukom would say.

Now here he was with his "date." He didn't disapprove of the woman. Everything felt right. This wasn't quite as good as taking some beautiful woman to his gatekeeper's house back in Seattle, but it was fun. The woman now dining with Gates lived in one of those offbeat, seemingly vacant parts of the city, where warehouses doubled for artists' studios and living quarters. He'd only observed such worlds from afar. Mary Gates had liked to feel part of the bohemian world through the arts; she was a theater patron in Seattle. But he and his family were a bit too affluent and comfortable ever to really understand the bohemian life. The closest he'd come to that was during his younger days programming, when a string of code became a place to inhabit.

Gates was like them, just as bohemian in his way. He had a different "vision" than most, could see further—he liked to think. And he saw it appropriate that all the money in the world eventually gravitate toward him.

She was beautiful. Beautiful women had rarely turned their eyes on him in the old days, when he was a dropout. But now he could have any woman he wanted. Well, almost. Later, a young woman in Germany would catch his eye, a Microsoft account manager. He needed to travel there anyway, to take care of the DR-DOS situation, which was still out of control.

Back in Washington, D.C., Norris Washington and his colleagues sat at their desks fascinated by the e-mail that was flying among the intense band of men in Gates' inner circle.

It was the spring of 1991, and Bill Gates' presence leapt from the mountain of paper heaped on Washington's desk and down the corridor to his office in carton after carton. Washington and Schildkraut had quite a collection after more than a year of gathering information under subpoena—much of it marked "Microsoft secret."

Months earlier, when the FTC had issued its first access letter to the company, Microsoft had been informed that it was henceforth prohibited from destroying any records or documents, electronic or otherwise. In internal memos, electronic mail, and letters to and from high-level executives at other companies, here was a corporate diary that fairly breathed of Gates' leadership and management style. No newspaper reporter, no industry executive, no Wall Street analyst had ever gotten as intimate a look at the workings of the company.

It had taken a Herculean effort to get things to this point. Back in the winter of 1990, Arquit, Schildkraut, and Washington had scrambled for clearance to proceed with a full-blown investigation. They could only get it after liaison officer Carl Hevner submitted a request to the Department of Justice.

This process was the formal way that Justice and FTC conducted their ongoing scuffles over which agency would handle what case. Since both had jurisdiction over antitrust enforcement, this often was a matter not only of who brought up the antitrust concerns in the first place but also of which agency had the most expertise in the industry being explored.

At times like this, the Federal Triangle had the tendency to resemble the Bermuda Triangle, for all the federal investigations, consent decrees, and cases swallowed up by the DOJ and the FTC historically, never to emerge again.

In this case, however, Washington's request for clearance didn't permanently disappear, it simply languished for six months or so. As weeks passed, the silence was a mystery to him.

Higher up in the bureau, his colleagues knew that a battle was under way. The case might have stayed permanently in limbo if Schildkraut had not taken an activist role.

The FTC and Justice had butted heads over who would be the first to gain expertise in the red-hot personal computer industry. Whichever agency dug in first could pretty much count on getting all subsequent cases arising in that industry.

The FTC throughout the decade had been showing up the Justice Department, even though the political environment was intensely anti-regulatory. Historically, the two had been in a spitting match, measuring each other's victories while jealously defending their respective turfs. During the 1980s the FTC had handled some of the biggest mergers in history, many of them in the oil industry. Schildkraut's division had claimed victories in challenging mergers in that industry while Justice was losing every case it touched. Schildkraut had also handled the mammoth RJR Nabisco acquisition by KKR and had won numerous divestitures at a time when the Republican administration was in no mood to challenge business.

Justice had fought tooth and nail to prevent the upstarts at FTC from taking on what was originally thought of as an IBM/Microsoft case. The antitrust staff at the Justice Department was worried that the FTC would be in a position to make inroads on what it saw as Justice turf based on the expertise it had developed with the earlier IBM case.

Assistant Attorney General James Rill's deputies had argued that they'd spent decades on IBM. "But that case has nothing to do with the personal computer marketplace," Schildkraut had responded. "That was on IBM's mainframe business. The two markets are nothing alike."

Schildkraut had persisted, demanding that clearance be granted. Rill's deputies were also persistent, charging that the investigation was not a good one, and that there was nothing to investigate. They would also insist, "We'll investigate. We have the expertise in this." At stake was the potential to take control of antitrust regulation in the hottest area of the American economy: the personal computer industry. The DOJ and the FTC had always competed for the biggest and most visible cases.

Schildkraut had turned red in the face, biting his blond mustache in frustration. "You're telling me you don't think it's a good investigation, and at the same time saying you want to investigate," he had said.

The fact was neither agency had expertise in the personal computer industry, but at least the FTC attorneys—unlike the Justice Department staff—had personal computers on their desks, Schildkraut had pointed out before making his departure.

The bickering went on for the better part of six months. Eventually, Kevin Arquit, stepping in as master negotiator, took the matter all the way up to Jim Rill. Justice came around to agreeing that Schildkraut and Washington's principles were correct, and clearance for a full-blown investigation had been granted in June 1990.

Washington now realized how silly his first premise had been.

Paul Saunders, IBM's outside counsel from the New York law firm Cravath, Swaine & Moore, had spent years wrangling with the feds. He had been the one to review that first letter from the FTC with IBM's in-house attorney Tony Clapes. They had wisely decided to comply immediately with all requests for information.

In subsequent meetings with Washington and Schildkraut, they had pointed out that documentation made clear how frustrated IBM was with its partnership with Microsoft. Washington and his partner explained how they had come to the concern about a market-division agreement.

Klapse was a man of few words who preferred to listen. He was adept at gleaning the strategy of his interviewers. Washington had begun to waver. He had started to notice, in IBM documents and correspondence with Microsoft, that Bill Gates was afraid of IBM.

Microsoft's internal communications were confusing: records showed that some factions were pushing to accommodate IBM and others were saying forget about IBM. It also appeared that IBM was desperately trying to regain control of the relationship by threatening Microsoft that it would enter partnerships with other companies if Microsoft did not stick to its OS/2-centric strategy.

FTC attorneys were trying to determine whether Microsoft had changed its mind after the fact or had known all along that it would not honor the agreement. Was it just a "head fake," a deliberate attempt to fool the market?

Jim Manzi was beside himself. The Lotus Development Corp. CEO, and his chief counsel, Tom Lemberg, could not believe how much money he'd wasted in porting his market-leading spreadsheet software, Lotus 1-2-3, to OS/2. And he couldn't believe how far off the mark the feds had been.

It was April 1991. The two men sat at Lotus' headquarters in Cambridge, Massachusetts, overlooking the Charles River, which today was steel gray and unmoving. What could be done? At least the regulators seemed as if they were starting to understand. Lemberg believed it was a case of "head-fake," as he had explained to Norris Washington. The rest of the industry knew that. Jim Cannavino knew that. And now Washington was listening. The IBM-Microsoft pact was a sham, he was told. Microsoft and IBM had not managed to divide up the market at all.

While IBM had talked up OS/2 to applications software developers, Microsoft had done the same, telling IBM and the marketplace that it would be supporting OS/2 as the "platform of the future." Soon, however, IBM and the rest of the software industry would accuse Microsoft of falsely promising them that it would support OS/2 as the standard operating system for graphical programs. In 1989 Microsoft had been quietly telling some customers and computer hardware companies that Windows would be the future graphical operating system.

Indeed, within months of that November 1989 IBM-Microsoft announcement, Microsoft had put Windows on the front burner, slowly killing off all its development for OS/2. Microsoft executives, after denying the company's lack of commitment to OS/2 for months, would brazenly announce: "OS/2 is dead, and we killed it."

Competitors complained that they'd wasted huge sums of money in displaced development efforts while Microsoft had gained critical time to market for Windows applications software.

The operating system was like the oil that everyone needed to fuel their computers. And no one could get their jobs done without applications software that could operate with that new "fuel." By changing the standard, the monopolist had also made the world's existing business software obsolete.

It was as if Standard Oil had said, "Build all your furnaces to burn oil; oil is the fuel of the future," while it went off and secretly produced a new type of fuel—along with a new furnace to burn it. In such a scenario, the monopolist not only would have changed the industry standard but would have used its knowledge and control of the emerging standard to be first with the only device that could work with it.

Microsoft vigorously denied that it had done anything shady, claiming that it also had been surprised by Windows' sudden success in the marketplace after its earlier lackluster sales. Bill Gates and his marketers, however, had for some time been quietly pumping millions into the launch of a new version of the software—Windows 3.0. With Windows, unlike OS/2, Microsoft would not have to share a penny in royalties with IBM, and it would be free to call the shots in the future. It would be secure in the thought that its DOS monopoly, coupled with Windows, would continue to bring in high-margin revenues for the foreseeable future.

In May 1990, when Microsoft launched Windows 3.0 and the biggest marketing and advertising campaign in the company's history, the industry knew that Microsoft's strategy had changed. It just took a while for FTC attorneys to catch up.

Manzi and Lemberg, with the help of Andy Berg, Lotus' Washington, D.C.–based outside counsel—and every other company in the industry for that matter—were now hurling mountains of evidence at the FTC, evidence of alleged predatory conduct by Microsoft.

It was clear as day to Lotus: Microsoft's head-fake was all a ploy, part of a much bigger scheme to gain more power in the operating system market while leveraging that power to take over a new market, the applications software market, which was Manzi's bread and butter.

The roar of the engines had become a soothing ebb of white noise. At 25,000 feet, Novell's chief, Ray Noorda, flipped through his briefcase for a scrap of paper—the back of an envelope on which to record the outlandish thoughts now rising in his head.

At times like this, he would recall his English teacher in elementary school. Part of him yearned for the heroic life of literature. But this time around it had been all business, not without its own Odyssean sense of adventure.

It was July 1991, and Noorda had just left Bill Gates, and the fifth in a series of almost unfathomable meetings, in the San Francisco airport. The occasion deserved nothing less than verse.

As he searched for the stub of pencil in his jacket pocket, Noorda couldn't get the odd picture of the man out of his mind. Bill Gates, only a couple of hours before, had seemed to be davening before him, bowing and rocking, mouth moving, as if lost in the stream of some ancient liturgy.

"But I did want to merge! I did want to merge!" the Microsoft chief was saying over and over again, his head nodding up and down and nearly hitting the table on the downswing.

Noorda had never envisioned Gates as supplicant. Even though his behavior, as far as Noorda could tell, was far from manly, Gates was by far the more powerful man.

Gates' timing was interesting to say the least. He'd called to set up this meeting on July 18, 1991, within twenty-four hours after Novell had announced that it intended to acquire Digital Research Inc. Noorda had been preparing for a conference call with securities analysts to discuss the proposed acquisition when Gates' call came in.

There was little that could surprise Noorda these days. By now, he'd taken on the aspect of an old bloodhound. His gait had slowed. In the years before his retirement, the CEO of Novell Inc.—the sixty-seven-year-old senior statesman of the young PC software industry—had been raging against the slipping away of his empire. His memory was shot, and his lieutenants had begun to mock him.

It had been only two months since the world had been informed of the FTC's antitrust investigation of Microsoft.

Noorda supposed Gates had reason to whine, now that everyone knew the feds were breathing down his neck. But he couldn't fathom the caninelike whimpering that was being directed at him. It reminded Noorda of one of his sons at about the age of four.

That had been another era, as had been the days the Novell chief had rescued his company, based in Provo, Utah, and turned it into a networking software powerhouse.

This merger business with Gates had started in the fall of 1989. All this time Gates had been gathering intelligence, Noorda thought. But Gates had at first used his right-hand man, Steve Ballmer, to accomplish the task. Back then Noorda had agreed to do a favor for Rod Canion, the CEO of Compaq Computer. Canion's company was unveiling a new line of computers, called SystemPro, in Las Vegas. Noorda had agreed to appear at the event to announce Novell's software support for the machines.

Ballmer had also been on the panel. Noorda had just learned of Microsoft's plans to get into Novell's market—networking software that allowed groups of computers to communicate and process data together.

Ballmer invited him to breakfast.

Noorda bit his tongue; he was tempted to call the man by the nickname he had invented for him. Noorda liked to refer to the Microsoft chairman as Pearly Gates and Ballmer as Em-Ballmer. That was because "one promises you heaven, and the other prepares you for the grave."

"So what is it?" Noorda had grumbled. He had a tendency to grumble more than talk.

"Bill wants to know if you'd be interested in a merger," Ballmer said, suggesting that the leading supplier of computer operating systems and the leader in network software become one.

So Noorda, looking out for his shareholders' interest, participated in the talks that continued through mid-January, wondering whether Gates was serious. It wasn't lost on him that Gates had gotten lots of information out of him about his company's business.

Visits took place between Redmond, Washington, and Provo. At the time Novell's market value was about $1.2 billion, and its annual sales were $350 million. Microsoft was worth about $4.5 billion.

Things had gone silent by January 1991, and Noorda called Ballmer to find out whether Microsoft was still interested. Noorda had always been suspicious that the deal would not work, but nevertheless he continued to engage in the discussions, and provide information to Microsoft on parts of Novell's business.

"Bill can't make up his mind," Ballmer said. "And he doesn't like the idea of having to travel to Utah to stay up on development efforts, if the companies were to merge."

"Well, I'll make up his mind for him," Noorda replied. "We're not going to have any more discussions."

"Yeah, well, that's probably the right idea, because Bill isn't all that interested," Ballmer snapped back.

Talk had been getting around the company, and a buzz was beginning to spread around Microsoft. Gates and Ballmer had begun to discuss technical things that Noorda felt were inappropriate.

Ballmer followed up the conversation with Noorda with a letter in March of 1991, just four months before Gates' San Francisco overture. It said that one of the reasons Gates had called off the talks was "the risk of U.S. government disapproval of the transaction."

Shortly after the first merger overture, Noorda had gone to two major software allies of his, and competitors of Microsoft—Lotus Development Corp. and WordPerfect—to suggest that the three start an alliance to combat Gates' aggressive tactics.

Noorda proposed what he referred to as his "360" program—a joint sales and marketing effort to better compete with Microsoft, which was moving into the applications and networking markets with alarming speed. ("360" was a double entendre. It both referred to the "full 360 degrees of a circle," an all-encompassing alliance, and was meant to ensure that all three companies could retain their 60 percent market share positions.) The collaboration never materialized.

While the industry dallied, dawdled, and dozed, Microsoft was getting fatter and more powerful, Noorda thought. As computer and software makers continued to agree to terms spelled out by the software giant, they were increasingly turning over the reins to Microsoft chairman Bill Gates.

"We need to stand up to that little sissy," Noorda would say time and time again. That "little sissy" fluctuated between being the richest and the second richest man in America. There were reasons for his success. His was the face, the body, and the soul of Microsoft. Gates' closest friends noticed that there seemed to be no separation between his own ego and his company. He took everything that happened to his company personally. And Noorda noticed that Microsoft also took many of its attributes from the personal style of its leader.

Even now these issues could make Noorda's pacemaker skip a beat. This was a new world—and there weren't many "tough guys" left. Noorda liked to think he knew what "tough" was and thought back on his days as a bartender in college, and earlier, as a teenager in Ogden, Utah, hawking those "extra" editions when Hitler was invading Austria. To Noorda, being a CEO was about being a tough guy. In his mind, he'd compare members of the club. GE's Jack Welch: now there was a tough guy. Pearly wouldn't last a second in a room with him.

Like back in the World War II days, what was needed now was a sort of League of Nations, he'd tell David Bradford, his chief counsel, to stand up to the aggressor. For Noorda, the enemy had always been there—in one form or another. Back when he was at GE, it had been IBM; when he was at General Automation, the archfoe had been Digital Equipment Corp. These days, however, the enemy had swollen greatly in size, and it had the name Microsoft emblazoned on its flanks.

Noorda was raised as a Mormon but—unlike his brother—never went on a mission. Yet the man always seemed to have a personal crusade. His holy war was now being played out in the industry, and he loved poking fun at the drama of it. "Bombs flying, bursting all over me, around me, inside me!" he would exclaim.

In fact, he became known as the turnaround man, a type of corporate savior sent in on itinerant presidencies to save companies in trouble. "I never went on a mission," Noorda would say. "That's what made me such a rotten guy."

In 1939 Noorda's older brother Bert—named after his father, Bertus—had gone off to Holland on a mission. "They shipped him back when he finished, and put him in the army," Noorda said. That brother had a wife and two kids, and was killed in the infantry while in the South Sea Islands. "He had it tough, and I had it really easy," Noorda would say.

Noorda would go on at length with his top executives about the damaging impact Gates was having on the software industry. They didn't know the extent to which "that little squirt," as he liked to call Gates, was on a campaign that would soon put every company in the industry out of business. Or so Noorda thought.

To his chief counsel, Noorda sometimes resembled Shakespeare's Lear on a mountainside railing against the elements. Noorda would sometimes mock his own fervor about the subject. "This stuff drives me crazy," he would say, "or senile or puerile!"

Nevertheless, he was convinced it was his mission to stand up to "Gates' atrocities." He would often flash back to his World War II days—and could not get over the similarities between Gates' methods and the propaganda campaigns of the Third Reich.

Later Gates would pen a private letter to Noorda complaining about the comparison of his strategies to those of the Nazis. Gates wrote that Noorda had been "stating that at Microsoft there are people who are the equivalent of 'Hitler and Goebbels and Goering.' " He went on, "Your comparison is offensive. . . . It is troubling to me that you, as the CEO of a major American corporation, would use such language to describe a competitor." Gates had typed the letter himself and sent a copy to one of Noorda's lawyers, Larry Sonsini, as if to illustrate what a bad boy Noorda had been.

Gates' latest overture was a curiosity. Despite his mistrust of the man, Noorda was dying to find out what he was up to this time.

Noorda knew he had rubbed Gates the wrong way by announcing his intentions to acquire Digital Research, the only company to offer an alternative to Microsoft DOS, which was running on more than 90 percent of the world's computers, thanks to Gates' brand of deal making.

In his phone call of July 18, Gates suggested to Noorda, "Let's meet at the Admiral Club, at the San Francisco airport," complimented Noorda on his company's success in networking, and apologized for discontinuing the earlier merger discussions.

Sitting toe to toe in the airport, Gates had brought up the subject of a merger again. By now, Novell's market value was between $6 and $7 billion, and its revenues had increased to about $650 million annually. Its market share since the last time they had talked merger had increased from 40 to 60 percent. Noorda became increasingly annoyed as he watched Gates' eyes traveling every which way as he talked, everywhere but in the eyes of the person he was addressing.

Noorda could not believe that Gates would bring up the subject again, given his alleged concern about government intervention, and told him that he felt he'd been conned the first time around. It was then that Gates began his bowing and rocking, and his wails of "I did want to merge! I did want to merge!"

This time he insisted, "And I want to talk about a merger again. I'll personally take full responsibility for making it happen."

Noorda glared at him as Gates continued, pausing to give an awkward little wave of his hand. He had one condition for such a deal.

"Of course," Gates said, "that DRI thing will have to go." Noorda watched as the back of Gates' hand made a brushing motion through the air, as if clearing it of pests.

Noorda was at first incredulous. "I think you're going to have some problems with the U.S. government," he said. "And IBM will not be happy with this." Novell had a close relationship with Big Blue.

Gates, with his shoulders up about his ears and in his nasally drawl, replied, "I know how to handle the government. And IBM doesn't count."

Noorda laughed mildly. "Well, Bill," he said. "I will not be involved directly in this negotiation, because it would look like I have a personal interest in my wealthy retirement!" But he was only half-joking. He and his board had a fiduciary duty to evaluate Gates' proposal. Any buyout of Novell shares could involve a significant premium.

Now Noorda sat back in his seat. The seat-belt light had been turned out, and the plane had reached its cruising altitude. He folded the envelope, with his penciled scrawl on the back, in half and put it in his jacket pocket.

He'd written a poem. He couldn't wait to show it to Bradford.

———————

Philippe Kahn had been stalking Noorda. It was getting a bit outlandish.

The oversized Frenchman, CEO of Borland International, finally tracked the Novell chief down in Sydney, Australia, at a private board meeting. Noorda escorted him to the parking lot and told him to get lost.

"Come on. Why don't you like me?" Kahn implored. "You're just like my father!"

Kahn also had developed a habit of showing up unexpectedly at Novell staff meetings. He was intent on a partnership with Noorda. "What are you doing here?" Noorda would say, not unamused by Kahn's antics. "I don't want to talk to you. Now get out of here before I punch you!"

Oddly, Kahn also had an exaggerated disrespect for those he admired. Like a surly and envious son, he would tell tales of his encounters with Noorda. He liked to talk about the time he was at a computer show when Noorda was giving a speech. The two attended a reception together. Kahn was surprised to find the Mormon the ultimate party guy. "The guy loves to have a little drink," he noted to his colleagues. "Put Noorda in front of a tall blond, and he loses it."

Kahn also complained of Noorda's not showing up for his commitments. He had invited the man to give a speech at a Borland Developers' Conference. It was to be the opening speech before a crowd of 3,500. He didn't show up. "What the hell happened?"

Kahn asked him later. "I took a senior flight, and they bumped me off," he said.

Kahn watched Noorda at an industry cocktail party. He couldn't believe his eyes. There he was, placing hors d'oeuvres inside his jacket pocket. Noorda looked up and saw Kahn watching him. "It's great to be rich and live for free," he gleefully explained.

An off-site Borland meeting was taking place in a Utah suite, and Noorda decided to come talk to Kahn. He arrived in his son's beat-up pickup truck. This impressed Kahn again, because Noorda was a very wealthy man.

Kahn regaled his colleagues as he stared out the window, "All right, all right, he's driving a beat-up truck!"

When Noorda arrived at the meeting, planning to talk about a potential merger between Novell and Borland, a party was going on in the lobby of the cliff lodge. A ski magazine was hosting the event, and dozens of testers of skis were present. Noorda decided to crash the party and carried tasty morsels back to his truck for later enjoyment.

"Isn't this fun?" he asked Kahn.

Now Kahn wanted to talk to Noorda about how the two companies together could stand up to Bill Gates. Gates was slowly making inroads into Kahn's market. Borland's QuattroPro had been a hotselling spreadsheet software program, and Kahn had been putting Gates to shame with his company's programming tools. Now Gates was disparaging the Borland products, and getting computer makers to bundle Microsoft's products instead.

Moreover, Gates had stolen the limelight from him in other ways. Way back in 1983, Kahn was working and studying at a French university and was hired to do some programming for the unrecognized Vietnamese scientist Andy Truong, the real inventor of the first true personal computer. Kahn had actually written the software for Truong in 1974. By 1996 Kahn had some satisfaction that the Boston Computer Museum was at least acknowledging that Gates was not the father of personal computer software.

Gates had also snubbed him at a Las Vegas conference in 1983, when Kahn was still a student and tried to convince Gates to pick up his Turbo Pascal—a programming language—and resell it. Kahn did not perceive himself as a businessman and could not fathom starting a company. He thought it would be a good idea for Gates to sell it, though, and pay him royalties. Gates turned him down.

Now Kahn thought Novell should collaborate with Borland, and help him market QuattroPro and other products. But Noorda viewed Kahn as a buffoon and had no interest in the applications software market. It was not his core business.

Bob Kohn considered himself Philippe Kahn's right arm. When Kahn was outraged, which was often, Kohn was outraged. As chief counsel for Borland International, Kohn had a favorite saying concerning competing with Microsoft: "The Beatles were wrong. Money *can* buy love."

Kohn was bristling now with nervous energy. He'd sent an urgent e-mail missive to top executives at Borland. He had just gotten off the phone with Norris Washington.

A few hours later, Kohn's message was being read by the Borland senior vice president Gene Wang. Wang had been courted by Microsoft continually and now was being offered unbelievable sums of money to defect to Symantec, whose CEO Gordon Eubanks had been cozying up to Gates in recent months.

Wang read Kohn's e-mail message with great curiosity. Eubanks would be fascinated by this as well. It explained in detail what the feds were after, which Gates was dying to know.

Wang read Kohn's words over again:

ATTORNEY/CLIENT PRIVILEGED
CONFIDENTIAL COMMUNICATION
I just received an important call from Norris Washington at the FTC. He called to ask whether we had any information and opinions on several questions (set forth below) that would help the FTC formulate its theory. I did not give him any answers on the phonem [*sic*], but I told him I'd get back to him quickly.

1. Whether we have any information on a "per [processor] licensing arrangement for either DOS [or] Windows"—i.e., where hardware manufacturers will have to pay Microsoft a fee whether or not they ship with Windows or DOS.

Specifically, have any Borland sales people heard of this practice and do we have any opinion on the impact of such a practice on any potential operating system entry into the market?

From what I understand, Microsoft has actually told the hardware manufacturers this and the FTC is looking for an independent confirmation of the fact. Even if we can't provide independent confirmation, we would express the opinion that to the extent Microsoft is able to do this, then it would make it impossible for products like DR-DOS to be marketed. If the hardware [manufacturer] must pay Microsoft for DOS on all units, regardless of whether DOS was on them, then if they wanted to use DR-DOS, they would in effect be paying twice.

Do we have any further information or further thoughts on this?

2. Do we know whether Microsoft has engaged in any behavior that would make it more difficult to write tools or applications to any alternative operating systems?

I understand that Microsoft will not release sufficient information about Windows to Novell/DRI; the result is that Novell cannot announce it will be compatible with Windows. It would be helpful if we can provide some information on whether and how Microsoft has put things into the DOS or Windows, or will be putting into Windows NT, anything that can cause those systems to be incompatible with other operating systems (and cause applications manufacturers to do ports).

3. If Microsoft gains any type of command in the computer language market (as a result, for example, of their practice of leveraging their control over the operating system), would it

make it more difficult for other companies to make tools for other operating systems?

Do we have any technical information we can provide? Microsoft has been arguing to the FTC that if Microsoft was really doing all these nasty things, applications companies like us would stop writing to their operating systems and write to systems like Unix. Of course, this is unrealistic. The markets for tools for other operating systems are comparatively small markets. As evidence [sic] by our pull out of the Mac market years ago, there is not enough money to be made in other operating systems. If Microsoft drove other tools makers out of the business of writing tools for Microsoft's operating systems, we could not recoup enough money from writing tools for other platforms to stay in the business.

4. They are interested in the circumstances surrounding the debug [Kernel], but these issues will not come up in the "first round." However, to the extent these issues affects [sic] Microsoft's dominance in the operating system market or makes [sic] it difficult for companies to write tools for other operating systems, they would like to know.

5. They would like us to bring them up to date on recent activities of Microsoft relating to our business.

He said the FTC was moving forward with their investigation and they are "under pressure to do something as soon as possible."

We need to formulate answers quickly. I imagine that they might require us to sign affidavits they could use later on, so we need to be specific. I will start formulating answers from the previous information we've given the FTC and will give them a second update on them on the recent issues regarding trademarks, Windows end user registration, etc.

Meanwhile, please respond with any information or opinions you may have on the above questions. Thanks.

Wang apparently believed Eubanks would appreciate the extent to which he had the inside skinny on what the feds were up to.

Without a second thought, he clicked on the forward button, then typed at the top of the page: "fyi. gene."

Eugene Wang would soon be the subject of a criminal investigation and a police raid of his office and home. Gordon Eubanks, the head of Symantec, had already made Wang a job offer and was a friend of Gates' who would soon give positive testimonials about Microsoft to the FTC and later the Department Of Justice. Wang had leaked confidential Borland information to Eubanks at a time when Gates was trying to determine what his competitors were telling the feds.

David Bradford had an acerbic wit that could undercut even Ray Noorda's razor-sharp quips and gibes.

Bradford had been around the block in his years as Novell's chief counsel, yet he was endlessly flabbergasted by Microsoft's activities in the marketplace. It was now the winter of 1992, and Novell executives from around the world kept him busy indeed with reports of predation from the company's archcompetitor.

Meanwhile, about a month and half after the Microsoft merger talks had been reactivated, Noorda had called Gates and again said he didn't think the government would allow the deal. "But we might use the talks to make sure our products work together," he pointed out. He also told Gates that he was not going to get rid of DR-DOS, as Gates had requested, and that he was morally obligated to close that deal. He refused to discuss it further until the DRI acquisition was closed.

In October 1991, right after the deal was final, Gates had again called Noorda. "I'm ready," he said.

Soon after, Bradford and a raft of his lawyers flew to Palo Alto, California, where they met with Bill Neukom and a team of Microsoft's lawyers who'd flown in from Redmond. Much of the discussion focused on Novell's belief that the deal was not right for the industry, and that it would create a singular monopoly unacceptable to the FTC.

Microsoft's Neukom and Gates and others insisted that they could get the deal to play and estimated a 75 percent chance that the feds would approve such a transaction. Novell saw only a 10 to 15 percent chance that the merger would be approved. In the meantime, Novell had delayed its integration of DRI.

Finally, in February 1992, Novell asked Microsoft to send a letter stating its intentions. Microsoft's CFO, Frank Gaudette, did as Novell asked, stating in a letter dated February 13 that Microsoft wanted to buy Novell and was willing to pay a premium of about 20 percent. At the time the letter was sent, Novell's market value had shot up to about $9 billion. Microsoft was willing to pay $12 to $13 billion. Microsoft's own worth had risen to more than $22 billion since the first merger talks in 1989.

The Novell board was confused by this letter. If they signed the deal only to have the government knock it out, what would they have done to Novell? In the meantime, Microsoft kept asking if Novell wished to make an announcement and sign a letter of intent, and Novell requested more time.

Then, out of the blue, in late March, Microsoft announced that it was acquiring the database software maker Fox Software.

Bradford told his colleagues that the board "wouldn't have been more dumbfounded if you smacked us over the head with a two-by-four." He called Neukom to find out what was going on.

"Don't worry. We're still interested in Novell," Neukom told him.

Bradford remained perplexed. "What? You're kidding! Now you're trying to dominate databases as well as spreadsheets, and you still want to buy Novell?" Microsoft's strategy of buying a dominant position in every market was appalling to him.

Microsoft never retracted the letter, and Novell ended the discussions soon after. The board decided it had been perversely manipulated by Microsoft.

After Microsoft's surprise bid for Fox, Noorda was disgusted. "Oh, Jesus, let's forget this thing, it's a waste," he told his colleagues. Meanwhile, Microsoft was gearing up its attacks on DR-DOS.

Bradford was scratching his blond head and smirking. The Novell board had weighed the proposed merger with Microsoft for months.

Noorda gave some much needed comic relief when he danced into Bradford's office and pulled the fragment from his coat pocket.

Bradford read:

MEETING DATES—SAN FRANCISCO AIRPORT
A POEM BY RAYMOND J. NOORDA

We sat in a room together, you and I
Alone together for the fourth time
Perhaps for the last time
Perhaps not!
We had much to talk about—
About the other three meetings.
About the excuses and the regrets
Over you not doing what you said you would
*   and wanted to do*
About how I had won what you wanted to win
And about how much you had really
Wanted to come together as one
And I said you didn't.
And you said you did
It was a disgraceful game
SHAME!
SHAME! SHAME! I know your name
It is Pearly

In the meantime, Novell had gone out to solicit DR-DOS business from computer makers like Compaq and AST and discovered there was no chance of doing business at any price. Microsoft kept dropping its price to computer makers and bundling DOS with Windows, with promises that they would get for free its forthcoming Windows for Workgroups. It occurred to Bradford that this violated U.S. antitrust law, which forbids "product tying."

Noorda, when he'd finished railing about what Gates was up to, was encouraged by Bradford's legal analysis and the attention he was getting from the rest of Bradford's staff. He and Bradford had been reading about the antitrust investigation of their archfoe but had not spoken to the regulators about Novell's problems.

Bradford was in midsentence when Noorda's secretary burst in. "You have a phone call," she said. "It's the FTC."

Noorda cleared the room.

Norris Washington was on the line. He wanted Noorda and his chief counsel to help with his investigation.

5

MICROCOSM

Bill Gates' personal and business strategies all over the world were being played out in microcosm in Germany, where the largest computer manufacturer in Europe was still not under Gates' control. Gates was about to turn an entire country market around. He would stop at nothing, including paying "reverse bounties" to a company in exchange for an agreement that it would never sell another copy of a rival's product.

The old castle had belonged to royalty and was a favorite haunt of members of Parliament. Stefanie Reichel could not believe that she was here, at the Hotel Cliveden, just outside London, with Bill Gates.

Cliveden, which had been Lord Astor's estate, had become known as a place of intrigue in the 1960s, when a young woman named Christine Keeler inadvertently brought down Britain's conservative government. Members of Parliament and British aristocrats had used the place for orgies until Keeler squealed after a love affair with a defense minister and a military attaché from the Soviet embassy. (It had become known as the Profumo affair.)

The place was still breathtakingly beautiful, with its hunting grounds and gardens. The dining rooms and meeting rooms were palatial. Microsoft had rented it for its annual board meeting in August 1992. There had been traditions for this summer board meeting; it was always held in an exotic place, and Gates' mother and father usually attended.

Gates had first spotted Stefanie Reichel, wearing a striking red suit, in April 1992 during a business meeting with computer makers in Monte Carlo; he couldn't take his eyes off her. He canceled his flight back to the States for a chance to get to know this beautiful young woman, who spoke three languages and was an employee of Microsoft Germany.

Just the previous day Gates and Reichel had arrived at Heathrow and had a rendezvous at the Sheraton Heathrow hotel. From there they continued to London's Park Hyatt. That night they had tickets to see *Miss Saigon* and dined at the British actor Michael Caine's Indian restaurant.

Now Gates stepped into the Cliveden's richly appointed library, where a predinner cocktail hour was unfolding, with Reichel on his arm.

All found it unusual that Gates had not taken a room at the Cliveden like the rest of the Microsoft entourage, who had flown in from Seattle. But Mary Gates was happy to notice that her son had a pretty young blond with him. "Ohhh, hi! Who are you?" she asked Reichel.

The two spoke at some length, and Mary, who was known to light up a room, made every effort to include the young woman. "Oh, we should invite you more often to these things, Stefanie," she said.

Gates was slightly embarrassed by his mother's attentiveness to his new girlfriend.

The board members were filtering in, and many of the men were lighting up cigars. There was CFO Frank Gaudette and President John Shirley and his wife. Microsoft's cofounder, Paul Allen, was not present. Bill Neukom meandered into the room. Reichel's presence startled him. He had heard that Gates was intrigued by a woman in Europe, but later Neukom told Reichel that his heart sank when he realized it was she. He had met her months earlier at headquarters and been taken with her himself.

Earlier this day Gates and Reichel had had a lunch meeting with Theo Lieven, the chief of Europe's largest computer maker, Vobis Microcomputer. In a "Microsoft secret" report, one executive had months earlier provided a snapshot of what was going on at the Vobis account. "It looks like DRI is urging them to focus on DR-DOS," it stated, adding that "Lieven is complaining about the per processor license—he does not want to pay $9 with every computer system and thinks about shipping both DR-DOS and MS-DOS."

Before the Vobis lunch meeting at one of London's best restaurants, Nico at Ninety, Reichel and Gates had sat in a limo together. She had prepared a detailed briefing on the Vobis account for the big boss and handed it to him in a neat binder. Gates was impatient. "Just tell me what it says," he told her. Reichel laughed, a bit flustered. Gates had been sending her e-mail and love letters since he met her the previous April.

"Du." From the beginning, Stefanie Reichel was struck that she was being addressed as *du*.

German citizens knew there was something different about the American company from their first day on the job. Microsoft Germany was operating much as the company operated in the United States. That is, the sensibility of Bill Gates had filtered across the ocean with great intent.

Despite the influence of Western culture around the globe, inside most German companies, employees addressed each other using formal names. *Sie,* the formal version of "you," was the correct usage. The informal *Du* was reserved for after-hours socializing and personal relationships. An internal directive instructed Microsoft Germany employees, however, that "we do not address each other formally." It was one of the first things Reichel was told when she joined Microsoft in 1991.

Now she was helping to orchestrate in Germany a microcosm of how Microsoft operated and took over markets worldwide.

Reichel, though raised in Germany, had lived for many years in the United States, where she attended an Ivy League university and worked in Silicon Valley for several years. One of the first things she noticed as an employee of Microsoft Germany was how most new employees found the company's informality uncomfortable.

Reichel and her colleagues worshiped Gates. Germany was very structured. People did not drop out of college and become billionaires every day; there was a clear path for every accomplishment. In that respect, to the German culture Gates was even more of a phenomenon. Also, it was still pretty much a chauvinistic society. There were no other women salespeople or managers in the OEM group in Europe. And all the customers Reichel worked with were male.

Her hiring was a leap for the division and Microsoft Germany. Reichel soon found it easy to charm the men she met in business—not by being flirtatious or sexual but merely by being a woman. It didn't hurt that she was strikingly attractive, along with being intelligent and knowledgeable about both German culture and the computer industry.

In fact, Juergen Huels, her boss, considered Stefanie Reichel his secret weapon. He would send her into the marketplace to find out certain things. She was simply doing what men had done for a long time.

The two had met at another software company. At Microsoft, Huels, his boss, and his boss's boss had interviewed her. They were skeptical because she was female. But he was intent on hiring a woman to handle the most difficult, and strategic, account.

From day one Reichel was told that it would be like "mission impossible" to turn around the Vobis account. Vobis was the largest computer manufacturer in Germany—all of Europe for that matter—and at the beginning of 1991 , 100 percent of the computers it sold were being shipped with DR-DOS.

The edict had been handed down from Gates through the ranks: We want DR-DOS not to exist in this account. They had even set a date for her to meet the goal that the company be selling "no DR-DOS" but all Microsoft DOS and at least 50 percent Windows. "You make this happen, and you make us both stars," Huels told her. That meant more stock options for one thing.

Months earlier Gates had walked into a Vobis store to see only DR-DOS posters. He was enraged.

———————————

Gates and his top executives knew full well the strategic importance of signing up computer makers for "per processor" licenses, which would essentially require them to pay royalties to Microsoft for every computer shipped—of a particular processor type—regardless of whether the machine was running Microsoft software. In e-mail messages to a reporter, he would refute the impact of this type of licensing. "Whenever someone ships other software, that would be a system that they don't pay us for," he said. "People get to choose which is the most effective license type for them."

In the meantime, Theo Lieven had earlier been outraged at the per processor scheme but wanted to get the best prices he could. Margins were paper thin in the PC business. He recognized DR-DOS as the superior product but realized that he would end up paying twice for using an alternative to Microsoft's software. Gates would deny this as well, in e-mail to a reporter. He wrote, "I don't understand your argument that people can't afford to offer another operating system. They are NOT paying twice—who gave you that impression? It's silly. People license the way they choose based on the demand they see."

As to "who" gave that impression, in country reports circulated to Gates, his own senior executives noted that they had been pressuring computer makers to stop shipping DR-DOS, especially because they were bound by per processor licenses to pay Microsoft regardless. One report, circulated throughout the executive offices at Microsoft, stated about one computer maker, "He was advertising a system bundled with DR-DOS. This was quite an embarrassing situation, because we did not know this at that time. Novell was offering him a good deal. . . . We hear this from different customers right now. . . . We mentioned to [the CEO of the company] that this system is a system he is paying Microsoft royalties for."

Indeed, DR-DOS was such an attractive product that some computer makers were willing to pay twice in order to offer it to customers, despite the fact that Microsoft was reminding them that they were locked into paying royalties to Microsoft, and so offering other products did not make sense.

But Lieven, who had in October 1991 begun some shipments of MS-DOS 5.0, was still selling DR-DOS. Gates was about to help Stefanie Reichel turn him around.

The e-mail message that appeared on Reichel's computer screen in April 1992 was from Bill Gates. She had never before received a personal e-mail from him.

Gates explained that he had come to Monte Carlo with a lot on his mind, including talking to lawyers in the United States about lawsuits and helping Microsoft Europe president Bernard Vergnes make lots of decisions. (He did not specify what those decisions were about.) Meeting Reichel had "energized" him, he said, adding, "I hope I didn't stare or anything . . ."

The Microsoft chairman had no idea whether Reichel spoke English or whether she was married or "interesting," he said, noting that he is "somewhat shy," and so he didn't approach her and introduce himself.

Jeff Lum had nevertheless introduced Gates and Reichel, and Gates now noted that "it was great there was a topic of significance to discuss—our friends at Vobis."

As Gates was leaving the hotel to catch a plane with Vergnes, he told Vergnes that he wished to stay another night on the off chance he could talk with Reichel some more. Gates indeed did not take his scheduled flight for this reason, even though he had not booked any alternate hotel or made plane reservations to ensure that he could return to London for his meeting the next day. "I didn't worry about it," Gates wrote. "Believe me, this is not normal behavior."

Gates wrote at some length. "If you are coming to the US let me know," he wrote. "I mean a chance when no one from Microsoft is around at all," and went on to suggest dinner and to note that it had taken him a few days to figure out Reichel's e-mail address.

Gates had asked Reichel out on a date. She couldn't believe the correspondence Gates was having with her, and confided in Huels, who read the e-mail with relish.

In early summer another e-mail message from Gates appeared on Reichel's computer screen. A number of weeks earlier he had met her during a business trip to San Francisco.

He recounted their visit together in a litany of the passing sights of the night he had spent with her and their first kiss.

He was waxing poetic, nothing like his business e-mail, Reichel thought.

Gates apologized for not e-mailing Reichel sooner, noting that he'd been busy, with a trip to Washington to see President Bush. He went on, "We had an OEM review yesterday and of course Vobis came up. Steve [Ballmer] asked if the account manager was a German or an American, and I said nothing since I'm not even supposed to know how to spell [your name]. It was very hard not to smile."

Gates concluded, assuring Reichel that they would find a way to spend more time together.

There was a part of Gates that was quite romantic, Reichel was surprised to learn. Huels, who'd read everything along with her, loved it.

Now Gates was really going to help her get the biggest deal of all. She still could not believe how interested he was in her. It also frightened her; she was drawn to Gates' intelligence but wasn't sure she wanted anything romantic. From the beginning, courting the largest computer manufacturer in Europe had been a challenge.

She remembered the day Heinz Willi Dahmen, a Vobis manager, had greeted her on one of her first visits to the company. His massive physical presence (he must have been approaching three hundred pounds), combined with the light that tended to reflect off his shiny head, gave him the aspect of an aurora borealis.

At first, CEO Lieven refused to meet with her or anyone else from Microsoft. After doing some research, Reichel discovered Lieven was a wine connoisseur, and sent him a bottle of a California cabernet. Soon she was in his office face to face. He complained that Microsoft had threatened to cut off technical support and access to information if Vobis continued to sell DR-DOS.

———————————

John Teagle of Cleveland, Ohio, was not one to make a fuss or stick his neck out. The last thing he wanted was to find himself embroiled in a controversy.

George Rice had stood up before a congressional committee a year earlier. Rice had said a particular agent of one mammoth corporation had been "threatening the trade that if they bought of me they would sell them any more."

Now it was Teagle's turn to speak up. "They would have their local man, or some other man, call upon the trade and use their influence and talk lower prices, or make a lower retail price, or something to convince them that they'd better not take our oil, and, I suppose, to buy theirs."

The year was 1898, and John D. Rockefeller had ushered in a new age; he believed that all the oil business was rightly his. Gates had ushered in the information age and believed that all of it should continue to belong to him.

It had been said of Rockefeller that he was "the victim of money-passion which blinds him to every other consideration in life." For Gates, making money and getting 100 percent of all markets that he targeted was about winning, and there were no black or white areas in winning. It was an all or nothing deal. "Your mission is to get Microsoft system software on every personal computer," stated the secret "OEM Business Manual" distributed to account managers.

Rockefeller stopped oil shipments by sending telegrams to agents who had already made deals with independent suppliers and offering them further discounts. One such telegram read, "If you can stop car going to X, authorize rebate to Z [name of dealer] of three-quarters cent per gallon."

In Microsoft's case, a dollar here and a dollar there, even when computer makers had already spent cash buying competing products, meant a lot to their razor-thin margins, especially when tens of thousands of computer shipments were involved.

Earlier on August 19, that day of the board meeting, the Vobis chief, Theo Lieven, had flown in on his personal plane from Belgium, tickled that the Microsoft chairman would be meeting with him. Reichel explained that Lieven wanted to meet Gates before finalizing a deal that had been discussed weeks earlier.

Gates, Lieven, Reichel, and Huels dined for about four hours at London's Nico at Ninety.

The German OEM group would become one of the most profitable in the world. Huels and Reichel had turned it around, creating a cash cow that strategically influenced what was happening throughout the European PC market. The German market was a bellwether for the continent and was six to eight months behind the U.S. market.

Reichel noticed almost immediately that things happened at a much faster pace at Microsoft than at other software companies. After all, it was addressing a low-end consumer market, versus the high-end market at her previous job. The sales cycles were completely different. Reichel had always been a Mac enthusiast and used the PC for the first time at Microsoft. Huels had coached her closely on the strategic importance of OEM licensing, which Gates and Kempin understood well.

Between bottles of wine, Gates, Lieven, Huels, and Reichel now discussed, among other things, an agreement to "get DRI/Novell out of Vobis," a strategic partnership between the two companies, and a commitment that Vobis would agree to sell "no Novell Net-Ware Lite" but instead would contract for 25,000 copies of Windows for Workgroups—a new product for Microsoft in the market for computer networks in which it had no presence.

These agreements to cease selling competing products would be finalized weeks later when Lieven flew to Seattle.

Reichel was thrilled at how well the meeting had gone. Now the Microsoft board members were led into an enormous dining room of the Cliveden with a spectacular chandelier. A five-course dinner was served. Gates was seated with Reichel at his side. Across the table from her was Neukom. At her other side sat CFO Gaudette, who, along with Mary Gates, grilled Reichel on where she was from and how she had come to know the Microsoft chairman.

Mary Gates kept leaning across the table to compliment her new friend. She said to Reichel, "Why, you remind me so much of Bill's old friend Ann Winblad. So smart and cute!"

Reichel was doing just fine fitting in with Bill Gates' clan. She would soon head back to Germany. Gates would stay on for additional meetings with the board.

Reichel noticed that across the table from her, Bill Neukom was being particularly attentive. Toward the end of the dinner, he grinned incessantly at her, a cigar dangling from his mouth.

"At my sailing club, men and women alike smoke cigars," Reichel said, keeping up a sociable banter. "I like them myself."

Neukom grinned some more. "I *bet* you like cigars," he said.

Days later, at her office in Munich, Reichel received an e-mail message from Neukom. He was coming to Munich the next week and invited her to dinner.

In the ensuing weeks the e-mail was flying among Microsoft vice president Kempin, Reichel, Vergnes, and Gates, going over the details of the Vobis deal that Reichel and Gates had made with Lieven. It was standard for Joachim Kempin to come to Germany every quarter to make sure things were on track. He had been the star general manager of the country. Huels knew that Neukom and his legal team were reviewing every deal Kempin made. On the other hand, inside the company the joke was that Neukom's philosophy had become that of Gates: if a law is not clearly defined, you can write it yourself. A sterling bit of Neukom's wisdom remembered by his colleagues was "It is better to ask for forgiveness than to ask for permission."

Kempin, Lum, and Huels would talk informally about their concerns that the feds might find some "funny" stuff in their computers about the dealmaking that had gone on.

Kempin knew of the concern about DR-DOS at the highest levels of the corporation. Back in March 1991, it had been his goal to get a per processor contract with Vobis before MS-DOS 5.0 shipped. (By October 1991, Vobis would indeed be locked into a per processor license for the product.)

He, like Gates and other top executives, knew the impact on the market of per processor licensing. In fact, in an October 1990 memo, Kempin was shown to be pushing computer makers like Hyundai to sign such agreements. "This will block out DR once signed," the memo said.

In December 1990, Microsoft vice president Brad Chase sent an e-mail to Jeff Lum that emphasized Steve Ballmer's concerns about turning Vobis around. "Steve told me to eat, sleep and drink Vobis, so I will be on everyone to let me know what's going on with this account," Chase wrote. Other Microsoft memos acknowledged that winning Vobis over to MS-DOS would "lead other OEMs" in product endorsements. Vobis had enormous influence in Europe, like IBM did in the U.S.

In a January 1991 memo, Lum instructed Kempin of the need to "kick DRI out" of Vobis. The only obstacle, he said, was "Lieven's personal commitment to DRI." Lieven had been selling about 15,000 copies of DR-DOS a month, at the price to Vobis of $13 a copy.

Microsoft had been insistent on Lieven signing a per processor license, despite the fact that he said he would sell it on only half of his systems, as he was determined to give customers a choice.

Kempin offered to undercut DRI's price with a per processor price of $9 a machine. His price for Vobis selling half of its shipments with MS-DOS would be $18, twice as much.

When Lieven protested that he wanted to keep selling DR-DOS in addition to Windows, Kempin told him that he would have to pay a higher price for just DOS than for a DOS/Windows combination. He threatened that if Lieven did not take a per processor license, with DOS at $9 a copy and Windows at $15 a copy, then his price for Windows alone would be $35. (Under oath, Lieven would later say that that threat was the reason he agreed to the deal.) Microsoft would also give him the stated per processor prices if he agreed to a minimum commitment of 200,000 copies. That is, regardless of whether he sold that many computers, he would owe Microsoft for selling a minimum of 200,000 units.

In October 1991, Brad Chase sent an e-mail to other Microsoft executives that discussed Microsoft's strategy of putting competitors "on a treadmill." Such deals as the one now unfolding at Vobis would do just that, in the case of DRI.

By now, the feds were more than a year and a half into their investigation, which seemed to keep changing shape and focus. The European Commission had informally started its own scrutiny of the software giant's business practices.

Within Microsoft's domestic and country offices, senior executives were clearly worried. Informal discussions between Microsoft Germany's top brass took place in German beer gardens. They were convinced that while Microsoft could easily be viewed as having achieved a monopoly position in operating systems through legitimate means, it clearly had a cloudy conscience about how it had maintained that position, and about what was now going on in the applications market. "We were leveraging control of the operating systems market to get ahead of Lotus and Borland in the applications market," one executive mused. The e-mail between senior VPs could not have been clearer on this count. Bernard Vergnes, who had regular briefing sessions with Gates, said in an e-mail message, "It is key to keep Lotus out of that customer [Vobis] but still maintain reasonable profitability."

There had been some discussion about this among U.S. and German Microsoft executives, but most were heartened by the fact that the feds seemed to be totally on the wrong track.

The word was that the feds had been too stupid to make sure they'd received backup tapes, and they seemed to be ignoring evidence at Microsoft branch offices altogether. Indeed, in Germany it was normal procedure to purge data when individual computers became full. It was the Ollie North scenario. The truth about North's activities had been found in the backup files in a basement computer at the Old Executive Office Building—originally no one had thought of looking there for evidence. Likewise, the full document record resided on the archived backups of Microsoft's servers, through which all company e-mail passed.

Indeed, the feds were a bit slow in understanding the impact of personal computers on the way people communicated within corporations. As a result, not all the evidence seems to have been produced.

On September 24, 1992, Theo Lieven met at Banner's Restaurant, in Seattle's Sheraton, with Steve Ballmer; Bengt Akerlind, director of European OEM sales; and Stefanie Reichel. The meetings that had begun in London were nailed in a dinner meeting that night at the Seattle Hunt Club, in the Sorrento Hotel. In attendance were Lieven, Kempin, Akerlind, Huels, and Reichel.

Lieven was made a modest proposal. Kempin promised that if he agreed to stop shipping DR-DOS, even though he had earlier ordered and paid for 250,000 copies of it, Microsoft would issue him a credit of $50,000. (Lieven had $50,000 worth of the product left to sell.) Of course the company would not pay him cash, and the whole deal would be off the books; Microsoft knew how far it could go with the law. But they could easily say the $50,000 was for returned goods. (By 1998, catching Microsoft in similar instances of paying companies to stop doing business with competitors, the Justice Department defined such payments as "reverse bounties" used to induce companies to refrain from doing business with others.)

The Microsoft OEM master negotiator Kempin, former head of Microsoft Germany, was present and greeted Reichel warmly. There was Reichel's boss, Huels, and Bengt Akerlind, a tall Swede who was very ambitious.

The chemistry among the men was fascinating. Huels was ambitious and independent. Kempin easily controlled him. Huels coveted Akerlind's job, and Akerlind was his boss. But up until recently they had been peers. Huels and Kempin on the other hand got on splendidly.

Kempin said the deal would be agreed to verbally but would not be put in writing. He knew—as he and Gates had been advised by Neukom on many occasions—that such deals tread at the edge of the law. "We're not stupid. We know how to walk a fine line," one executive told another when the issue of legality came up.

It was standard practice for OEM contracts not to line up with Microsoft's own guidelines for pricing. "Deals would always be made if people agreed to also take the applications software," said one Microsoft manager involved.

In addition to an unheard of distributor agreement, the Microsoft executives offered a special "white box bundle" that would kill many birds with one stone. (A combination of Microsoft products would be put in a plain white package.) Not only would it keep DR-DOS out of the market but it would deal a blow to Lotus and Borland, as well as Novell, in that the largest computer manufacturer in Germany would now be bundling applications software for free. Vobis was promised it would get the applications software for virtually nothing if it would restrict both DR-DOS and Novell's NetWare Lite from the market. The German company was given the price of $9 per machine for DOS and $12 for Windows. "If you don't sell NetWare Lite, your pricing will be far below the pricing in our own internal guidelines," Lieven was told.

Microsoft would also be killing two birds with one stone in that it would also be getting a leg up on Lotus and other applications software makers. For Vobis, naturally, it would be more advantageous to sell Microsoft applications than to sell Lotus because doing so would mean a discount on DOS and Windows. It would also work handily just in time for the competitive Christmas season.

It had been customary for Borland and Lotus to cut deals with computer makers on applications to be shipped with their hardware, but Microsoft would then waltz in and undercut their deals, using the operating system prices for leverage. "Don't think we didn't talk about it," Microsoft sales vice presidents from around the world would joke with their account executives. But this was one area Huels and others were a bit squeamish about. While they felt Microsoft had legitimately won the operating system market, even given its lock-in licensing practices, using the OS dominance to take over the applications market was something the regulators had reason to yell about.

Essentially, Gates gave Vobis what no one else in Europe had—

a bundle of Microsoft Word and Excel, along with Windows. But Lieven had to promise that, even if customers asked for it, he would not ship a single machine with DR-DOS. Microsoft senior vice president Steve Ballmer's involvement also had great impact on inducing Vobis to cease shipping the competing product in the early stages of its contracts with Microsoft. It set the stage for the deals Gates would finally help close. In April 1991, Ballmer and Lieven had met in Nice. Ballmer had discussed other "inducements," as Lieven would testify, involving bundling Microsoft applications software with an operating system deal. A Microsoft Word/Excel combination was suggested as part of the DOS/Windows deal.

As the icing on the cake, Kempin offered to buy all Vobis' DR-DOS holograms, which were like currency as they were used for authentication when Vobis or other OEMs shipped a copy of DR-DOS. He added, "I'll wallpaper my wall with them!" and laughed a great laugh. "Even if you have per processor licenses, and even if you've already paid for DR-DOS, we don't want you selling it," Lieven was told. In sworn testimony, Lieven would later say that he did not ship any more DR-DOS because Kempin had "purchased" the rest of his holograms. Plus, he noted, he had promised Bill Gates that he'd never ship any more DR-DOS.

The "white box" deal—along with a "finished goods" distributor contract, marketing funds, and special in-store Christmas promotions funded by Microsoft—had been arranged to make Lieven happy. Gates was willing to offer almost anything as long as DR-DOS was dead. Kempin would always say he refused to lose any deal on price.

Among the e-mail messages not produced to the feds from the computers of Microsoft Germany was one that Bernard Vergnes sent to a number of other Microsoft executives on September 7, 1992. Along with documenting the Vobis deal, it showed Microsoft's intent to use its DOS contracts to leverage computer makers into buying Microsoft applications software in place of that from Lotus and others. It said, "Congratulations. Germany is also negotiating a deal with Vobis. It is key to keep Lotus out of that customer but still maintain reasonable profitability." He attached to his message an e-mail message from Reichel and Haink, summarizing the deal. After noting the success of Gates' meeting with Lieven, and the strong market presence of Vobis—number one in market share, over IBM—the memo said: "Lieven . . . is willing to no longer offer DR-DOS or Network Lied [*sic*]. . . . As you know, Lotus and Borland have been aggressively approaching our OEMs, and Vobis is no exception."

An exclusive applications software bundle would be offered, it went on, and based on this Lieven "is ready to commit to us exclusively and to throw DR-DOS and Novell out and also commit to 25K WFW [Windows for Workgroups]."

Under oath, Lieven would later say that Microsoft's "inducements" had nailed the deal. "After all, DRI has no Word, no Excel, and no Bill Gates," he said.

Later in 1992 Microsoft was readying itself for a visit from EC investigators, who were collaborating with the feds. It had arranged for an internal audit to check out what it had in its files.

Soon thereafter, Reichel and her colleagues were given new computers and their old computers and files were taken away. They were told they were being upgraded.

The tone of Microsoft's habitual way of doing business—passed on from the personal style of Bill Gates—was not unlike the "Viking" dinner held during one meeting of Microsoft executives around the time of the Vobis negotiations, in which those present dressed as Vikings with horns on their heads and gloried in the roles of legendary aggressors who pillaged and conquered their foes.

That such an attitude was business as usual at Microsoft could also be seen in one broadly distributed Microsoft memo describing a bizarre joke played after a car accident. It described the circumstances under which a Microsoft account manager had sped off down the German autobahn after an incident in computer maker Amstrad's parking lot.

Amstrad, like Vobis, was another European computer maker that was selling DR-DOS. The memo explained that the Microsoft executive had backed into the Mercedes of Alan Shivvers, an executive at Amstrad. After bashing the vehicle, the Microsoft executive had left a note on the damaged car with DRI's address on it.

Over the months, Reichel, Huels, and other account managers were present in meetings in which Neukom briefed Kempin and others on how they should conduct themselves given the federal investigation. This included the need to retain documents. He'd asked Kempin to get OEMs to testify that Microsoft did not strongarm them. Kempin had reassured him: "Don't worry. We have them in control."

———————————

In little more than a year, Vobis had been turned around from selling no MS-DOS and 100 percent DR-DOS, to selling no DR-DOS and more than 90 percent of its computers with MS-DOS.

Microsoft had won a new per processor agreement, with an eighteen-month commitment for $18 million worth of MS-DOS and Windows preloaded on 400,000 Vobis computers. It had also nailed the biggest commitment by a computer maker for Microsoft applications. It was the largest single contract from a computer maker in all of Germany, and Europe, at the time. Vobis had further agreed to bundle 25,000 copies of Windows for Workgroups long before the product was launched.

It had all been spelled out in Reichel's performance goals, an official Microsoft document. In a November 1992 review, she would be commended for increasing Vobis' "MS-DOS penetration to over 90 percent of their processors along with committing to a per processor contract for 400K units annually," and getting Vobis to "no longer offer DR-DOS." She was rewarded as well for gaining "Windows penetration of 90 percent" of Vobis processors and for the "exclusive bundling deal with Vobis on a European worldwide basis for White Boxes of Excel and Word . . ." products that were posing fierce competition to Lotus and Borland and other application software makers, given that Microsoft was making deals and leveraging its operating system to get computer makers to also preload its applications software.

While Lieven thought he'd made out like a bandit, the document bragged that "the price negotiated was the highest price attained in Europe for such a deal and will bring a revenue of more than USD $6 million of unforecasted money and higher market penetration for [Germany] alone."

With Gates on her side, Reichel had accomplished quite a feat in a short time.

By 1994, after DR-DOS was pretty much dead, Microsoft had doubled the price for DOS. There was no alternative on the market. Like a classic monopolist, once it had eliminated competition, prices soared.

6

THE TRIGGER

Recognizing that Gates had irrevocably tied up the operating system market, his competitors began lobbying the feds to restore competition in the applications software market before it was too late. The antitrust theory of essential facility, as well as a broad case focused on monopoly leveraging, had been upheld in courts but they had not been used to address commerce in the digital world. Meanwhile, the feds were busy gathering evidence for the far simpler case: Gates' stranglehold in the operating system market through illegal contracts and sabotaging of competitors' products. There was no lack of evidence.

Andy Berg, Lotus' counsel and antitrust expert at the D.C. law firm of Akin, Gump, had his hands full. Jim Manzi had hired him. Ironically, he had been a classmate of Gates' and Ballmer's back at Harvard. He got a huge kick out of this.

There was something much bigger that needed to be addressed, but it was going to be hell to educate the gang at the FTC.

In the history of antitrust law, Berg had his favorite cases. The one that intrigued him the most involved a group of railroads known as Terminal Railways, which controlled the only bridge leading to a valley crossing the Mississippi that broke through into the West. It was basically a bottleneck monopoly.

The twenty-first-century version of Terminal Railways' "bridge to the West," of course, was software. Things were beginning to look very much like the digitized version of the Ho Chi Minh Trail. It was an issue of who controlled the roads, who was granted access, and who would be able to make the perilous journey and get successfully to market.

Antitrust attorneys were preparing to argue that Microsoft controlled what computer markets paid for operating system software and who in the development community was allowed access to the technology. No one could build products compatible with Microsoft's operating software unless Microsoft gave them that access, they would argue.

Berg turned the pages; it all was coming back to him now. In the Terminal Railways case, the company was not broken up but was ordered to offer all those wanting access to the bridge and the switching yards on the other side of the bridge fair and nondiscriminatory terms. Justice!

But there was even more reason to believe that the government would have a lot to go on. In yet another case involving nontangible assets, Associated Press was judged an essential facility that couldn't blackball potential members for competitive reasons. Even direct competitors had to be given access to the facility.

And, of course, there was the landmark case of MCI and AT&T, brought because AT&T had restricted MCI's use of its local circuits to exclude MCI from the long-distance market. In that ruling the court stated: "The antitrust laws have imposed on firms controlling an essential facility obligation to make the facility available on nondiscriminatory terms."

Microsoft's activities could only be described as a "monopoly brew." Sturge Sobin had come up with that one. He was the D.C. arm of the legal army that belonged to Ray Noorda. But Sobin was against going after the huge case that monopoly brew would present.

Lotus and Novell soon found themselves in an unlikely brawl, despite the fact that they were fighting the same enemy. Novell, through the efforts of its counsel, David Bradford, and Sobin was pushing for a case focusing on the operating system market. Lotus was going for the whole kitchen sink. That involved Microsoft's leveraging its power in the operating system market to take over other unrelated markets, like applications software.

But now, as well as worrying about Microsoft, Lotus had to battle how Novell was persuading the FTC to bring a case that failed to address the concerns of most of the companies attempting to compete with Gates. The operating system market was by now dead and gone. Gates had eliminated all competition there. In applications software some hope still lingered, although there were signs that Gates was using his market power to kill off competition in that arena too.

If Noorda and Bradford got their way, Lotus' concerns would never get addressed.

Berg shot off sheaves of documents and legal analyses to Norris Washington, who was fascinated by the whole situation. That didn't mean, however, that Washington and his colleagues could find one neat theory of antitrust law to address all these instances of anti-competitive conduct.

It was truly amazing. Washington and Schildkraut read the secret memorandum that had been circulated inside Microsoft's sales and OEM offices. It was now late 1992, and the federal attorneys were still poring over e-mail and documents being passed between Gates and his deal-making wizards, Steve Ballmer and Joachim Kempin, as early as the fall of 1990. In that year they had locked up computer makers worldwide in "per processor" contracts for a product that didn't even exist, MS-DOS 5.

In a confidential memo, dated October 10, 1990, addressed to VP Richard Fade and distributed to senior executives in Microsoft's sales and OEM organizations, the extent to which the company had its thumb on the industry as well as its future was dazzlingly clear.

Jeff Lum, writing under Ballmer's and Kempin's guidance, analyzed the company's performance in the first quarter of fiscal year 1991—which was the fall of 1990—and presented the objectives for the upcoming second quarter. He was about to move from his position as group manager in the United States to director of European OEM sales.

Lum's team alone was 120 percent ahead of its budget, bringing in $9,085,218 for the first quarter. "DOS, the always-dominant product, contributed 66 percent towards product revenue (70 percent if you include the Shell). UPB [unpaid balances] write-down accounted for 9 percent of revenue with Compaq leading the way with $1.3 million write off. NCR was the only other account to dip into prepaids, all others exceeded minimum commitment payments."

Windows and mouse sales were strong, accounting for 13 percent of revenue. In a pie chart, Lum showed 8 percent of revenues, at this early date, to have come from Windows licenses, versus 4 percent for OS/2. Windows would not become as big a hit as DOS until 1992, when it was selling a million copies a month, in large part because Microsoft had coerced computer makers with freebies and price cuts they could not pass up to license it as a condition of licensing DOS.

Lum's report tracked major U.S. computer manufacturers' processor shipments for the fourth quarter of 1990. Reflecting Microsoft's practice of charging royalties for every computer shipped, Lum stated, "These shipments map directly to the revenue as reported earlier for FYQ1 '91."

Lum also discussed "heavy negotiations" with Hewlett-Packard and said that Microsoft was intent "to raise HP's DOS royalty significantly (have to start high with them!)."

He stated among his group's objectives to "close all remaining DOS 5.0 licenses by 12/30/[90]."

Federal attorneys noticed that in a later confidential communication Microsoft had blatantly told some computer makers they could not buy Windows at all unless they also licensed DOS. Mike Davis, an executive of Diamond Trading in the Far East, received this letter:

Dear Mike,
Further to our conversation yesterday, I am writing to con-

firm that Microsoft is unable to supply you Windows as a single product.

Microsoft will only sell you Windows as a combined [*sic*] packaged with MS-DOS version 5.

Yours sincerely,

OEM Sales

Microsoft Ltd.

Behind this strategy was Gates' paranoia about DR-DOS 5.0; he did not want anyone—particularly in the Far East, where small clone manufacturers were interested in a lower-cost alternative to MS-DOS—to run Windows on the competing operating system.

Washington and his colleagues also noted in memo after memo the traditional goal of the monopolist: to increase market share, take over markets by undercutting competitors, and then raise prices. Microsoft had argued repeatedly that it could not have done anything wrong because prices for consumers had continually dropped. But Washington knew current consumer prices were not the only measure of predatory conduct. Prices within the feeding chain—for computer makers—had increased once Microsoft had succeeded in locking competitors out.

DR-DOS had Gates going ballistic when it came out with DR-DOS 5.0 in April 1990, and now only months later his sales team was locking computer makers into contracts for Microsoft's version of the product, which it had publicly stated would appear also in 1990. (It would not appear until June 1991.)

Washington and his colleagues noted that over the months since its acquisition of DRI, Novell had tried to solicit DR-DOS business from computer makers such as Compaq and IBM and discovered there was no chance of doing business at any price. Meanwhile, in e-mail after e-mail, Gates had complained to Ballmer that DR-DOS had made it impossible for him to keep prices high. How could he continue to be profitable with DR-DOS around?

Novell's Bradford, and his hired gun Sobin, kept the data flowing; the hallways of the Bureau of Competition were knee deep in evidence. Microsoft kept dropping its price to computer makers and bundling DOS with Windows, with promises that they would get its forthcoming product Windows for Workgroups for free.

Over the transom, still more was coming in.

Lotus' Berg sent a letter to the investigators urging the FTC to take action against Microsoft for anticompetitive practices. Lotus was cooperating fully to show how Microsoft had violated U.S. antitrust laws, "in particular Section 2 of the Sherman Act."

Berg was worried that the FTC's case would ignore the predation going on in the applications software market, where Gates was increasingly leveraging his power to slowly eat into the market shares of even the top selling products of competitors.

He wrote, "We believe any enforcement action . . . should focus on the broad range of Microsoft's anticompetitive practices in the applications software and related markets (e.g. spreadsheets, word processing and e-mail), not simply certain narrow practices in the operating system market (e.g. DOS). . . . These anticompetitive practices are widespread and they have extensively harmed both competition and competitors in these related markets. We also believe that the potential for consumer injury is substantially greater in these applications and related software markets than in the OS market."

Berg pointed out that the essential facility approach with the operating systems case would help the feds address Microsoft's predation in other markets. "It is essential that any enforcement action taken . . . focus on Microsoft's use of its control over its OS software, which we believe constitutes an 'essential facility,' to dominate the applications and other related software markets, not simply the OS market," he wrote.

Lotus provided briefing papers, legal memoranda analyzing Microsoft's conduct under the U.S. antitrust laws, and a policy paper demonstrating that an enforcement action against Microsoft would not damage the competitiveness of the U.S. computer software industry in global markets. Also provided was a report by Philip Nelson of Economists Inc. assessing the economic impact of Microsoft's anticompetitive acts and suggesting appropriate rules of law and remedies.

In keeping with the feds' desire to go after the least complicated case, Nelson proposed narrow remedies that addressed Microsoft's most egregious conduct while not being overly regulatory or creating disincentives for Microsoft's otherwise legitimate procompetitive conduct.

For Washington and Schildkraut, every day seemed to bring surprises. They'd learned, for instance, that one of Microsoft's top programmers had had some "pretty wild ideas" after a few beers. Indeed. The words were outrageous given the subject of the internal brainstorming session.

The FTC attorneys were getting a peek into the private side of one of the most profitable corporations in the world. "We should surely crash the system," the e-mail had said. You couldn't get more blatant than that.

Back at the turn of the century, Senator Sherman—creator of the Sherman Act—had been right on to make a distinction between "intent to monopolize" and holding a monopoly position because of "superior skill." Microsoft's communications did not portray a company intent on winning through skill.

An e-mail message from senior VP Jim Allchin to Gates and others discussed the importance of not allowing Novell to get a toehold in the operating system market. It read:

"So one slip up and we get set back quite a ways. This isn't really that hard. If you're going to kill someone, there isn't much reason to get all worked up about it and angry. You just pull the trigger. Angry discussions before hand are a waste of time. We need to smile with Novell while we pull the trigger."

Microsoft's intent was coming across loud and clear. Now the only problem would be to fit all the evidence into a litigation strategy that would fly, given the way the FTC operated.

The documents before Washington and his colleagues hinted of potentially illegal behavior in areas they hadn't dreamed of when they'd launched the investigation more than a year earlier. They were breaking their backs to get the case solid enough to present to the commission for a vote on whether to seek a federal injunction against Microsoft.

There had been many odd events up to this point. The antitrust probe of Microsoft did not become public until May 1991, when the Wall Street analyst Rick Sherlund was tipped off by a WordPerfect executive. Sherlund, after discussing the matter with Neukom, mentioned the inquiry in a Goldman, Sachs investment report, and by the middle of the month every newspaper in the country was running the story. Microsoft acknowledged it was being investigated but insisted that the probe focused purely on its fall 1989 announcement with IBM.

A month later a Bureau of Competition evaluation committee approved expansion of the case into a full-fledged monopolization probe. In April of 1990, Neukom had received a letter signed by Kevin Arquit stating that Microsoft alone was now the subject of a broad investigation of its monopoly position in the industry. Microsoft leaked the news that the case was not "narrow" a few days later.

That April 1990 morning a reporter phoned Marc Schildkraut, asking him to confirm that the investigation had been expanded to cover Microsoft's overall business practices. Schildkraut replied that he could not comment on FTC investigations. But, the reporter pointed out, Microsoft itself had faxed the FTC's letter to members of the press.

Later FTC attorneys confronted Neukom about why Microsoft had leaked the letter. After all, nonpublic investigations were not conclusive until completed. Many probes ended up being closed for lack of evidence. "That's none of your business," Neukom replied.

Now Washington and Schildkraut read again the e-mail that had been flying among Microsoft executives back in September 1991, just before the company released its "Christmas beta" preliminary version of Windows 3.1. Evidently the executives had been intensely discussing how to promote the appearance of incompatibilities in rival products attempting to operate with Windows 3.1.

They read a memo from Microsoft vice president David Cole, and noticed that it had been copied to the Microsoft senior vice president Brad Silverberg, a confidant of Gates, and Phil Baron, another engineer.

"It's pretty clear we need to make sure Windows 3.1 only runs on top of MS-DOS or an OEM version of it," Cole wrote. He then pointed out that he checked with the Microsoft legal department, which was working up text that they would display if someone tried to set up or run Windows on an "alien" operating system. Microsoft would then give the user the option of continuing after the warning, he noted. However "we should surely crash the system" at some point shortly later, Cole said.

Cole then asked how Microsoft should proceed on the issue of "making sure Win 3.1 requires MS-DOS." He pointed out that "some pretty fancy internal checks" were needed. "Maybe there are several very sophisticated checks so competitors get put on a tread-mill," Cole wrote.

"Aaron R had some pretty wild ideas after three or so beers," he continued, noting that "the less people know about exactly what gets done, the better."

Brad Silverberg had responded, quite to the point. He wrote:

> What the guy is supposed to do is feel uncomfortable and when he has bugs, suspect the problem is DR-DOS and then go out to buy MS-DOS or decide not to take the risk for the other machines he has to buy for in the office.

On February 10, Silverberg sent e-mail to Steve Ballmer, suggesting that if Microsoft received problem calls because of the error message, that Microsoft should tell customers using DR-DOS that "we only support MS-DOS" and that they could call the company that makes DR-DOS, or "put a kind gentle message in setup . . . but not every time the user starts Windows."

He explained that such a "kind" message would probably not offend anyone and wouldn't get the press up in arms. To address the anticipated barrage of support calls from DR-DOS users, Silverberg went on to suggest the creation of a message in Microsoft's phone system. It could say, for example, if you are not using MS-DOS or an

OEM version of MS-DOS, then press double pound, he stated. Then the user would be given the message.

The clincher came next. Getting to the heart of the matter—how to keep customers locked into using Microsoft's DOS—he wrote, "The most sensible thing from the development standpoint is to continue to build dependencies on MS-DOS into Windows."

To Washington and his colleagues, that last phrase was a killer: "continue to build dependencies on MS-DOS into Windows."

Maybe Andy Berg was right about pursuing the essential facilities theory. Microsoft was making sure that no other company could have access to the heart of the machine—the operating system— like it could. Microsoft controlled the industry standard—MS-DOS—and all other companies had to figure out how to make their products run with it. Meanwhile, Microsoft was doing secret things to make sure only its own products could perform well. And if a competitor managed to do a good job making competing software— like DR-DOS—Microsoft would fiddle with the underlying code to create the *appearance* that a competitor's problem was causing a malfunction.

Gates, Silverberg, and Ballmer were denying such allegations loudly in the press. But their internal records showed the bald truth.

Now, here was chronicled everything from Gates' intelligence-gathering campaigns to his top executives requesting that programmers find ways to sabotage competing products.

Months earlier, when the FTC had issued its first access letter to the company, Microsoft had been informed that it was henceforth prohibited from destroying any records or documents, electronic or otherwise. In internal memos, e-mail, and letters to and from high-level executives at other companies, here was a corporate diary that fairly breathed of Gates' leadership and management style. Every-thing—down to the most petty requests to lowly programmers—was being driven by Gates. It was clear that his personal strategies and win-at-all-costs ethical code had been fully absorbed by his all-male inner sanctum. Some federal attorneys noted, when face to face in depositions with corporate officers, that they even imitated their chief's habit of rocking back and forth.

Washington now considered a single page before him. A hand-written note in Bill Gates' childish scrawl that had fallen out of a batch of papers he'd been leafing through. He stared at it for a while, and turned it over and over.

"Purge email," it said.

Washington had been hearing unsubstantiated rumors that Microsoft was destroying documents, but he couldn't believe that a major corporation would actually do something like that, which could result in criminal charges if discovered. The pile of documents in which this note had been wedged spanned late 1989 through late 1992.

He picked up the phone and called Neukom's office. "What is this?" he asked. "Is Bill destroying e-mail?"

"I'll get right back to you," Neukom said, and hung up.

Days later he returned Washington's call. This was a matter of "attorney-client privilege," he told him, and offered nothing further.

In mid-December 1992, back in Germany, Juergen Huels penned an e-mail message that was circulated widely within Microsoft but never turned over to the feds. It was among the documents that had been copied to chief counsel Bill Neukom as well as at least eleven others.

By this time, Neukom had helped Stefanie Reichel disentangle herself from Gates' continued advances, and she was now moving to the United States, in part because of the courtship of Neukom.

Huels now congratulated Reichel, in an e-mail to her and her colleagues, on the job she had done—aided by Bill Gates—during her tenure at Microsoft Germany.

"Stefanie has worked in the German OEM group for 14 months and contributed a lot to our success. She took over Vobis when she started and turned this account totally around. This account ships now almost no competitive OS." He also stated that in fiscal year 1993 Microsoft expected $13 million in royalties from Vobis.

Neukom had responded to Reichel in an e-mail of his own.

He wrote, "As they say down under: good on ya."

7

DISCOVERY

What Bill Gates did to tiny Go Corp. is a blueprint of how the bil-lionaire preyed on numerous companies attempting to innovate and compete in the software market. In perusing Microsoft's secret com-munications, federal attorneys discovered Gates had broken legal contracts in numerous areas, including violating nondisclosure agreements with would-be partners. Overall, there were grounds for quite a few private lawsuits against Microsoft, but the feds could not share this information with the companies involved. Microsoft's indi-vidual acts of predation could not be addressed after the fact. The feds had to focus on patterns of behavior that would continue to af-fect an entire marketplace. This was why Gates' software licensing practices in the DOS and Windows arena became the focus.

In the meantime, Microsoft's internal brainstorming about how to sabotage DR-DOS could be seen in hidden code discovered by Novell programmers and a consultant to the FTC. Moreover, the market was moving full speed ahead, and Microsoft was wrangling with computer makers over their DOS 6 licenses. Like a classic monopolist, it had raised prices while ripping off yet another small company—Stac Elec-tronics—to gain the features that made DOS 6 different from DOS 5.

It was no wonder that CEOs were comparing doing business with Bill Gates to having a date with Mike Tyson: one could expect to be raped.

Now the case of Go Corp. was on the table, and the feds had called Go's CEO, Jerry Kaplan, in for an interview. There had been some speculation in the press that Gates had screwed Go, but Gates and his executives had vehemently denied the allegations when questioned by reporters. The facts, however, could be seen plainly through Microsoft's secret internal communications now in the hands of investigators.

Back on July 8, 1988, Bill Gates signed a nondisclosure agreement with Go Corp. "You [Microsoft] will hold in confidence and not use or disclose any information . . . You will . . . notify Go of any unauthorized release of information," the agreement read.

On February 13, 1989, Gates' vice president of software, Jeff Raikes, also signed a joint project agreement and nondisclosure statement. "No written copies are to be made without the express written consent of the other party," the agreement stated, in an attempt to keep confidential business information belonging to Go from being distributed freely throughout Microsoft.

Now Norris Washington was gritting his teeth.

He looked Jerry Kaplan in the eye as he spoke. The two had talked on the phone many times. Washington's eyes wandered from Kaplan's eyes to his mouth and rested momentarily on his jaw, which was jerking up and down as the man continued on with his emphatic speech. Washington looked back to Kaplan's eyes.

He couldn't tell him what he had discovered in Microsoft's secret records during his nonpublic probe of the company.

In 1988 Jerry Kaplan had engaged Bill Gates in talks about Microsoft's interest in developing software for a new operating system and hardware technology that Go had invented for a new breed of machines known as pen-based computers.

Gates had flown to Go's office to glimpse what Kaplan had to offer. Go entered into an agreement to have Microsoft do some preliminary applications work for a system. Gates sent a software engineer and others to Go to study the company's work in detail. About two years later Microsoft showed its own version of a pen operating system in the marketplace, having copied from Go everything it could.

Kaplan and Washington went over the long list of intellectual property that Kaplan was certain Gates had stolen from him. "There's not a question about it," he said.

By the time Washington had reviewed Microsoft's internal e-mail on the subject, he knew that what Kaplan had to say was an understatement. He watched as Kaplan talked on, barely able to contain himself. What he had learned poring over Microsoft's secret documents would have made Kaplan fall over.

But Kaplan didn't even know the full story.

Washington could follow Go's tale through Microsoft's paper and e-mail trail just as Kaplan told it. Bill Gates had arrived at the very first meeting with Go with his colleague Jeff Harbers. Go executives followed up with a visit to Microsoft's offices in Redmond, and the groups—including regular meetings with the Microsoft executives Jon Lazarus and Mike Maples—traveled back and forth over time.

Agreements were signed so that there was no ambiguity, and Gates had given Go the impression that he was clearly interesting in doing business with the company.

"Microsoft will assign a minimum of one half-time person to work with Go to identify projects of potential interest to Microsoft," said one section of the contract. It went on: "Microsoft is interested in exploring potential business opportunities relating to the Go notebook computer. Potential projects include native applications, adaptations of desktop-based Microsoft products, and insuring smooth exchange of data between notebook and desktop applications. Go is seeking strategic partners to develop applications for Go's notebook computer." It had been clear that Go had developed its own operating system for the computer and was interested in a collaboration with Microsoft only in the area of applications software.

The e-mail record however told a different story.

The feds had discovered that what Gates said in his e-mail was the opposite of what he'd agreed to with Go. Gates said that Microsoft was not interested in collaborating with Go at all. He simply told his software engineer: I want you to go and find out everything you can.

In addition, Go gave the engineer confidential information, trusting it would be protected under the agreement Gates and the engineer had signed. Once back at his company, however, the engineer freely distributed Go's confidential business information to Gates and numerous other Microsoft executives.

Months later the engineer sent e-mail to Microsoft executives demanding back all the copies of the Go material. He knew that Microsoft had violated the contract and appeared to want to limit the paper trail.

Go's case would have been best solved through private litigation. The government's limited resources and the amount of effort that it takes to come up with evidence showing multiple patterns of behavior made such cases too much for the feds to stomach.

Monopolists should not be allowed to use their dominant economic positions to exhaust other companies, Kaplan argued.

Washington, Schildkraut and their colleagues continued to bite their tongues as they interviewed industry executives. They were not allowed to disclose to outsiders what they had found in Microsoft's documents.

Kaplan was chagrined that not even the government had been able to do anything about Gates' predation. In addition to making off with Go's design plans, after sizing up Go's plans for a new type of operating system, Microsoft announced in private meetings with computer makers that it intended to offer a system known as Pen Windows.

Microsoft was going around to computer makers who were trying to license Go's system and strong-armed them into not licensing it by a variety of means. This made it impossible for Go to get into the market.

Kaplan told the feds that Go had made detailed presentations and market studies for months to Compaq, and the company's CEO was ready to commit to using its operating software and building a system around Go's technology. But Microsoft talked to Compaq and said: "If you want to get good pricing on the stuff you do with us, don't work with Go."

Go had even managed to get one company—NCR—to license its technology. But subsequently Kaplan was surprised to see on NCR's price list that it had priced the operating system separately, so buyers had a choice of Microsoft's or Go's. And Go's cost twice as much.

Kaplan was flabbergasted. "Why is that, what is this all about?" he asked NCR executives. It turned out that NCR, like other computer makers bound to Microsoft's per processor licenses, had to pay Microsoft even if it shipped Go's operating system.

Grid Systems, owned by Tandy Corp., was an early manufacturer of one of the few pen-based computers on the market—and had actually taken a license, but it never shipped anything. To Grid, Microsoft had said, "What a shame it would be if you disrupted your relationship with Microsoft."

Kaplan told Washington, "They had such a dominant position, they were not afraid to use whatever threats were necessary to get people not to use our stuff."

Federal attorneys were noticing some patterns. These were exactly the same methods Microsoft used to lock DR-DOS out of the market. The company had threatened Vobis that it would not continue to get technical support from Microsoft if it sold competitors' products. Gates knew that computer makers could not live without doing business with him: their computers were useless without his operating system. He would regularly make threats that their future operating system contracts with Microsoft were in jeopardy if they should stray from the Microsoft fold in other product areas. (Later, Gates would use these same tactics to prevent products from Netscape and Sun Microsystems, for example, from succeeding in the marketplace. And later, Compaq Computer and others had been threatened that their Windows 95 licenses would be revoked if computer makers refused to bundle Microsoft's Internet Explorer.)

What's more, Microsoft had gone after the tiniest details of its competitors' technological designs. Go had developed a notebook metaphor for its pen-based computer, with handwritten gestures that would be recognized by the system. Microsoft had gone so far as to apparently crib from those gestures as authored by Go. "They went right to the edge of what they thought they could do legally," Kaplan told Washington.

"Have you considered a lawsuit?" Washington asked.

"Yes, very seriously," Kaplan said. In fact, he had an offer from the well-known intellectual property firm Brown & Bain—which had represented Apple Computer in its litigation with Microsoft— to take the case on contingency.

Washington understood well why Go, like scores of other small companies, would never actually file suit. When push comes to shove, litigation is expensive and time-consuming. "We were more interested in investing our limited time and energy into putting out a product," Kaplan explained.

"You have a very good case," Washington told him, without offering further details of what was in the Microsoft documents he had collected. "But I'm not sure we can help you. It is very difficult to find other people who are willing to come forward. For us to bring a case, we would need to find a pattern of abuse." What was more, Go was in a unique position; for the most part, there were no other companies in the PC operating system business aside from Gates. He had driven everyone else out.

Regulators would not base an antitrust case on a single instance of predation that occurred in the past, as it would have no remedies to offer for that. The goal of the federal agencies was to stop an ongoing pattern of behavior.

Gates seemed to have done similar things to other companies, but in different ways and different markets. Like he had done with Go Corp., in 1988 Gates had violated a nondisclosure agreement with Micrografx, promising not to distribute information about its development tool know as Mirrors. There had been suggestions to the FTC that Microsoft should limit the extent to which information flowed between its applications and systems software groups, as that information sharing gave it an advantage over other software developers since it had sole control of the operating system.

The FTC had collected evidence of inappropriate use of information between Microsoft's divisions, and violation of the Micrografx contract, at a time when the small company was about to introduce its Mirrors development tool for porting Windows applications to OS/2. The company was approached by Microsoft's manager of developer relations, Cameron Myhrvold, at a Software Publishers Association meeting.

Micrografx president Paul Grayson thought Microsoft might be interested in licensing Mirrors but was cautious about showing it. Micrografx did not want Microsoft's systems software group to get a glimpse of Mirrors for fear that it would be copied. At the same time, it was interested in possibly licensing the product for use within Microsoft's applications division as a porting tool.

Mirrors was briefly described to Myhrvold, who expressed interest in further talks with Micrografx on the product. Microsoft's Myhrvold confirmed his company's interest in the product at that time. "Micrografx executives told him their concerns and said they weren't interested in licensing the product to Microsoft for its systems software group," said Grayson.

After assurances that Microsoft would agree to limit its interest to the applications division, Myhrvold and other Microsoft executives requested further meetings to negotiate a licensing deal. In an early meeting, Micrografx chief executive Paul Grayson and chief of operations George Grayson met with Bill Gates to demonstrate Mirrors and to answer questions about how it worked.

Gates was initially skeptical and had many questions. "He had a list of fairly detailed questions that he was given all the answers for. At the end of the meeting, Gates was convinced that it could in fact be done, now that he understood it," Grayson said.

Microsoft continued to maintain its stance that it was interested in the product only for use by its applications division. A nondisclosure agreement and letter of intent was signed, which limited access to the technology to Microsoft's applications group.

Shortly thereafter, Gates assigned responsibility for negotiating the licensing contract to Mike Maples, at the time vice president of Microsoft's Applications Software Division. When Scott Ludwig, a member of Microsoft's systems software team, was also assigned to evaluate the product with Maples, it threw up a red flag to Micrografx. Ludwig had just transferred to Maples' applications group to do the Mirrors product evaluation.

Microsoft confirmed that Ludwig was indeed transferred from the systems group to work on the Mirrors project. "Micrografx expressed concerns about that and received assurances. Microsoft insisted that Ludwig was going to be permanently transferred to the applications group and would be assisting Maples' group in porting its applications," said Grayson.

So Micrografx continued to cooperate with Microsoft, showed source code, and allowed Mirrors to be tested. According to a number of accounts, the negotiations seemed to be going smoothly for weeks when Ludwig surprised Micrografx with the announcement that Microsoft had decided to scrap Mirrors and instead develop a similar product on its own to be incorporated in systems software.

Grayson said his company had in its possession the letter of intent "which we were operating under and considered to be a rudimentary contract, which clearly stated that the product was to be used only for application purposes and not for systems purposes." He noted, "We basically felt we had a branch of contract that we could sue for."

Indeed, Micrografx threatened Microsoft with a lawsuit but received little response. Microsoft increased its staff to work with Ludwig on its own porting tool, which eventually became a part of Microsoft's Windows Library for OS/2.

Microsoft executives at the time confirmed that after two months of work in the applications division, Ludwig was transferred back to the systems software group, where he then served as a systems software engineer. Ludwig had participated in the review of Mirrors and the subsequent development of Microsoft's own product.

"Microsoft made it part of their systems strategy and decided to compete directly with us," said Grayson. "Basically, they said, 'Tough luck, guys, we can't use your product; it isn't any good.' "

In subsequent weeks, Microsoft agreed to settle the situation with Micrografx by offering a cross-licensing agreement, which allowed Micrografx access to certain Microsoft technology. "We asked for more stuff and did a technology exchange and got something we hoped would be valuable. But we were distinctly unhappy about it," said Grayson. "If circumstances had been different, we might have sued them. We were convinced from talking to our attorneys that we could have won. But we hadn't gone public yet and were considering going public, and were pretty dependent on their support."

Ironically, months later, Micrografx entered into a development partnership with IBM Corp., which was to use advanced versions of the Mirrors technology to make Windows applications run faster under OS/2 than they did under Windows.

Responding to those allegations in 1989, Microsoft's Myhrvold said, "I was not a party to the negotiations. However, I knew about the Mirrors technology, and it was actually my group that did the initial demos at Microsoft of Mirrors. We continue to maintain a close technical relationship with Micrografx."

Myhrvold confirmed, "Scott Ludwig was for a time with the applications group." He also acknowledged that the concept behind Mirrors was central to what Microsoft was doing with its WLO product. "I'm sorry if Micrografx is disappointed with the way things turned out," Myhrvold said. "WLO is not by any means a high-profit item for us. Micrografx perhaps would not have made very much money on it, either." That remained a moot point from Micrografx's perspective, however.

Bringing an antitrust case to address all the various instances of Gates' predation upon individual companies would be very complicated. Federal attorneys knew that private litigation would have been far more effective in stopping such behavior than any case they could bring. But that was impossible for most small companies.

———————————

By now Go was dead. Kaplan would always wonder if this would have been true if, early on, Microsoft hadn't inhibited Go's ability to do business with computer makers. Kaplan would tell his friends, "This is like people who were exposed to asbestos for years and then get lung cancer. How do you prove it came from that?"

There were lots of other business factors that over the years mitigated against the company's success. And pen-based computing never became the blockbuster that analysts had expected.

In an emerging market, however, Microsoft's predation was a major influence. "People were unwilling to commit, unwilling to work with us, would not take licenses, despite the fact that everyone in sight said we had the only pen operating system around and it was a fine piece of technology. Far better than any alternative that was on the drawing boards for Microsoft," Kaplan said.

Gates had made a strange phone call to him just before he'd been contacted by the FTC.

The two companies had exchanged lawyer's letters, and Gates was paranoid that Go might be considering legal action against Microsoft. "He gave me this palsy talk. It was pretty funny actually. About how much money was wasted on this silly lawsuit with Apple and how difficult it would be for a small company to pursue a lawsuit against Microsoft," Kaplan said. Microsoft had even asked Kaplan to sign a document saying Go would never sue Microsoft, in exchange for future technical support.

Kaplan had just listened, his mouth hanging open in wonder.

Then Washington had called, saying, "We'd like to talk to you. We hear there's something going on." Two weeks later Washington asked Kaplan to fly to Washington, D.C., to meet with FTC lawyers. But it all had resulted in nothing.

Tens of millions of dollars were spent on Go's attempts to start a new market, and many people had put their lives into creating a piece of technology that was now dead. Kaplan would commiserate with his colleagues, "So fifty years from now they'll make a set of laws like they did for the monopolists of the railroads, where they were exposed for what they were and then made illegal. But I think the government is falling down on the job. In not understanding or willing to pursue a lot of the issues."

In 1991 Go spun off EO, the software part of the venture, financed primarily by AT&T. Going into the fall of 1993, Kaplan sold Go to AT&T, to be merged back with EO, and left the company. By June 1994 what remained of Go was totally shut down. When Kaplan heard the news, he realized that six years of his life had gone up in smoke.

Forget about lunch.

Andrew Schulman sat glued to his computer screen. He could not believe his eyes. Through a programmer's eyes, the strange encrypted code he found in Build 61 of the pre-released version of Microsoft Windows 3.1 could only be described as "obscene." He was catching up to what, unbeknownst to him, was a much discussed disparagement campaign by Microsoft that would soon become part of Novell's nonpublic, sworn testimony against the software giant.

Schulman had only days before concluded a phone interview with an FTC investigator who had questioned him about Microsoft's possible sinister intentions relating to IBM's problems running certain software drivers under OS/2. He had been skeptical about the concerns; not all of Microsoft's competitors' problems could have resulted from its sinister intentions. He had defended Microsoft on many occasions. After all, wasn't Microsoft great? Weren't its products brilliant? Hadn't it—almost single-handedly—spawned an entire industry? In an otherwise lackluster economy, Microsoft was a star of global proportions! Microsoft was apple pie and America at its best.

But now he was witnessing a phenomenon that he previously would have found unthinkable. How could Microsoft stoop to something so low? Or was this the work of a maverick, a programmer-equivalent to Ollie North? A digital renegade in some sort of surreptitious act of heroism? Or was it just a screw-up?

The latter idea was unlikely, based on the evidence that now presented itself. It couldn't be true. But there it was: code that was attempting to hide itself and disable the debugger he was using to pry into the secrets at the heart of the operating system.

Some weeks ago he'd been tipped off by a reporter who suggested he dig into the code of a prerelease version of Windows 3.1. She had some information that Microsoft had, at the last possible moment, planted code in Windows 3.1 to cause the product to appear to malfunction with DR-DOS.

This afternoon, curiosity had gotten the better of him, and he'd begun digging up his old prerelease versions of Windows 3.1. He found nothing unusual until he got to the final beta release of the product, dated December 20, 1991. He saw the same phenomenon in the "prerelease build" dated January 21, 1992, just before the commercial version of the product was released.

Running these versions of Windows 3.1 with DR-DOS produced error messages in five components of Windows: WIN.COM, HIMEM.SYS, SMARTDRV.EXE, MSD.EXE, and SETUP.EXE. The messages, which basically told the user that a problem had been detected, advised, "Please contact Windows 3.1 beta support. Press ENTER to exit or C to continue." Oddly enough, the "error" did not stop the software from running.

What's more, Schulman noticed that the renegade code that produced the error messages in the beta versions of the software was also present in the final retail versions of Windows 3.1. But wait a minute! A single byte had been added to prevent the message from appearing on the screen of the final version shipped to customers.

This seemed to be a brilliant ploy to determine which of Microsoft's beta customers were using DR-DOS. Then again, it also would probably frighten Windows beta users (of which there were tens of thousands) out of using DR-DOS. If they wanted to stop worrying about possible errors, they had to use Microsoft DOS.

The fact that the error messages were nonfatal—that is, even though they stated an error, they did not prevent the software from running—proved to Schulman that the code was deliberately incompatible. If the software continued to run despite the "error," it seemed the only error was that the customer was running Windows on a competitor's version of DOS.

The fact that the code was present in five unrelated programs in Windows 3.1 pointed to a concerted effort. And the way the code was attempting to obfuscate itself was outrageous, although the methods were in the end ineffective and even naive. Schulman viewed this as a deliberate attempt to thwart discovery, the sort of thing one expects from a teenager writing a virus, not from a multi-billion-dollar corporation.

When Schulman returned to his computer screen, there was one more astonishing tidbit. He knew it was routine for programmers at Microsoft to sign their work. He stared at his screen. There they were: the initials AARD. Was this the work of Aaron Reynolds, one of the most highly skilled and respected programmers at Microsoft?

By March 1993, Jack Frank was in a funk about the DOS 6 situation.

Frank had just stepped outside Building 8 on Microsoft Corp.'s sprawling Redmond campus. The calmly shifting branches of the giant firs above gave little indication of the tempest from which Frank, a systems vice president for Zenith Data Systems, a major U.S. computer company, had emerged. Frank had just catapulted himself from one of many screaming matches that had broken out in the course of his company's five-month effort to license DOS 6, the latest in computer operating systems, from Microsoft.

Microsoft was to publicly launch DOS 6 in a matter of weeks, and Frank still didn't have a contract in hand. Actually, he thought to himself, it would have been literally impossible to have it "in hand," seeing that the document was about a foot thick at this point. His engineers back home were worried that they wouldn't get the product in time to ship the new software on computers by the launch date.

Frank paced for a few moments on the small patch of lawn as he smoked. It was an oddly sunny day for this time of year in the Northwest. The air was cool. Frank consoled himself with the thought that back east his plot for independence from Microsoft, formulated with his product strategy team several weeks earlier, was already being set in motion. A slight breeze tickled the back of his neck; he felt his blood calming and smiled as he turned to reenter the building.

As he walked down the corridors, he noted stickers emblazoned on the office windows of the systems software reps. He had asked his own rep what the stickers were for and was told that they kept a running score of how many DOS 6 licenses each representative had sold. Microsoft employees often had competitions going with one another.

Frank thought about the past several years. He felt Microsoft had been ruthless in its licensing contracts. When the industry was in a slump, Microsoft was soaring. It had been the only supplier to raise prices year after year, subjecting his company to impossible margin pressure.

Months ago Frank had flown to Washington, at the FTC's request, to give his point of view on life with the software bully. The commission up to this point had been weighing unfair trade practices based on showing economic harm to consumers. What it didn't seem to take into account was the manipulation of computer makers by a dominant player in an industry. Frank felt firms were being held hostage by Microsoft's fickle licensing policies for systems software.

It had become a bitter joke among Frank's compatriots. "What's the most embarrassing question you ask your Microsoft rep?" Answer: "Can I see your standard price list?"

Historically, and for the time being, Microsoft had them over a barrel. It was the sole supplier of the industry standard operating system used on millions of computers throughout the world. And Microsoft, to all appearances, controlled the future of computing. A computer was nothing more than a mass of metal and wiring without operating system software at its core.

Frank was determined to have a complete contract by the end of his visit, but he was secretly hoping that DOS 6 would be the last operating system he had to license from Microsoft. Many outside his corps of product strategists would have told him that was a pipe dream.

All looked up when Frank reentered the meeting room. He was dealing this time with a new licensing representative, who had only one sticker on his window. The newcomer's boss sat in on the meetings. And when things got hot, Microsoft's master contract negotiator, Joachim Kempin, would step in.

It had been a particularly drawn-out process. At least twenty meetings had been held all over the country in the past five months. All the while, Microsoft had been insisting, "This is our standard contract." The fact was, there was no such thing as a standard Microsoft operating system contract. That is, except for small Far Eastern manufacturers. They were known to sign anything Microsoft handed them and often paid royalties of $70 to $80 per copy—easily 10 percent of the cost of a low-priced clone.

This particular meeting was probably the longest in the history of the company's licensing meetings with Microsoft. Six or seven major issues remained unresolved. For one, Microsoft had instituted a new upgrade policy for DOS 6: its computer vendor partners would no longer be allowed to upgrade customers. This change represented a bold step in wresting account control from manufacturers. The reason given was that "OEMs were doing a lousy job of it"—that is, upgrading customers.

This meant that Microsoft would get all customer names for those who had previously registered only with the computer company they bought their system from. Frank often daydreamed about Kempin playing God in his office, as he pored over the quarterly royalty reports that gave Microsoft a bird's-eye view of every computer vendor's business. Indeed, Microsoft had its finger on the pulse of the industry through these reports. They itemized sales of virtually every computer company in the world by processor type and operating system—regardless of whether Microsoft software was bundled with the computer.

Somewhere in the middle of the meeting, as Frank looked over the foot-tall stack of documents, a new paragraph jumped out at him. There in bold letters, Microsoft had the audacity to state that all machines shipped with DOS would contain a Microsoft registration card. This was a first for Microsoft, and the policy was initiated with DOS 6.0. In addition, computer manufacturers were required to ship their machines with the Microsoft manual as printed by one of Microsoft's printers. To save money, Microsoft was putting the registration card in the manual.

Frank's firm slipped around this by stating that it did not intend to include any manual with most of its machines, since they featured on-line help. Tension was high and the threesome in the meeting decided to take a lunch break. They headed for Building 24, which featured a new "multi-ethnic" cafeteria.

When Frank had flown to Washington to be deposed by the FTC, he'd had his colleagues ship cartons full of subpoenaed documents to the agency. However, once at the FTC office, he felt that he couldn't make his points strongly enough. The investigators seemed fixated on certain irrelevant things—like Microsoft's statements about OS/2—and seemed to be dismissing what he felt to be the key problems. Frank began to think it was hopeless. Every vendor in the industry had gradually knuckled under to Microsoft's demands. They knew they couldn't beat the immense marketing machine of the Redmond giant.

DOS 6 represented one of Microsoft's most monumental coups in terms of the ingenious way that the firm managed to find new ways to squeeze new revenues of its licensees. Frank's firm, like most other computer companies, had a clause in its existing DOS licensing contract with Microsoft stating that royalty rates could not be increased from year to year by more than a certain percentage. With DOS 6 Microsoft had broken the licensing terms into two components. It put most of the enhancements to the operating system—like disk compression—into a module called "Microsoft Enhanced Tools." DOS 6 itself, as it was licensed to computer companies, was nothing more than a shell. In fact, it provided virtually no benefits over DOS 5. If computer companies wanted to run the full DOS 6—featuring all those great enhancements that Microsoft had been promoting for months—they would have to sign up for two licenses: one for DOS 6 and the other for Microsoft Enhanced Tools.

The interesting thing was that the DOS 6 package for customers buying the new operating system retail or directly from Microsoft was a single product. Only to OEMs was DOS 6 presented as two products that required separate licenses.

Frank was beside himself. Microsoft had blasted away his company's resolve that no more than a certain percentage of its systems cost would be paid to Microsoft for royalties. His only consolation was that in six months his firm would be well on its way with a secret project: a new line of products that would require not a single byte of Microsoft software. In a meeting in a forest preserve only a few weeks back, he had finally agreed with his colleagues to do something no major computer vendor seemed to be willing to do: forge a road toward independence from the software magnate.

This would require new relationships with tiny companies. But it would be well worth the effort and the investment. Frank was also determined that his firm's new computer products would neverthe-less be fully compatible with the existing installed base of DOS and Windows applications. He was confident they could do it.

By the fall of 1993, Zenith Data Systems was ready to launch its first computers—which it would call "Personal Servers"—that would not require a single byte of Microsoft software. While allow-ing computers on a local area network to run existing software, the server, which controlled the network, would be driven by Novell DOS, which it had acquired from DRI. PC users on the network had no need to know nor care which operating system was running on the server.

Zenith had licensed DR-DOS from Novell to get around its re-strictive DOS and Windows contracts with Microsoft. At the same time, computer users would be able to run any software they wanted to at their desktop computers. (Microsoft's per-processor contracts had stipulated that any Intel-processor-based computer sold by the computer maker would owe a royalty to Microsoft. This, however, did not apply to machines that were physically incapable of running MS-DOS. Zenith had found a loophole, having spent months searching for one.)

In response to Zenith's plans, Novell chief Ray Noorda told the *Financial Times*, "These manufacturers are in a low-margin busi-ness. They want to get computers out the door and make a penny on every one of them. They cannot fool around with large dollar issues on the costs of what they ship. Paying Microsoft a royalty is a sig-nificant part of the total cost," he said.

But when Microsoft got wind of Zenith plans, it threatened the company that its future Windows contracts with Microsoft were in peril because of its plans to use a non-Microsoft operating system. (It would later make similar threats to computer makers who re-fused to preload its Internet Explorer software with Windows.)

8

TURNSTILE

By February 1993 the FTC had taken its first vote on pursuing an antitrust case against Microsoft and reached a deadlock. Through the spring and summer, an effort was on to win over at least one more commissioner. Inside the agency, attorneys were scrambling to salvage the case. Microsoft was on an intense lobbying campaign of its own. Meanwhile, e-mail showed Gates' senior executives scheming to cover up the intent of their sneaky code, should it be discovered by outsiders.

At noon on May 27, 1993, a line was already forming at the maître d's desk at the 701, a polished Pennsylvania Avenue restaurant with a bent toward nouvelle cuisine. Set back from the traffic at Seventh Street, the place was a stone's throw from the Federal Trade Commission.

On this breezy spring morning, the elegant eatery seemed to have whipped up a veritable gazpacho of antitrust influence as seen by the personalities congregating for the lunch hour. Among the flock: FTC Commissioner Dennis Yao; Anne Bingaman, Bill Clinton's newly named assistant attorney general for antitrust at the Justice Department; the colorful FTC commissioner Deborah Owen; and former FTC Commissioner Pat Bailey, recently hired by Bill Gates and his crew as a consultant to help penetrate the mysteries of the agency.

It had been a little less than four months since the February 5 stalemate on pursuing a federal court case against Microsoft. And in a little more than seven weeks, the FTC's four active commissioners on the case would try for a new vote. For the time being they had agreed to hold the powwow the week of July 19.

The fall and winter had been full of intense and unpredictable activity. The week before the commission had taken its first vote on whether to bring a case against Microsoft, Bill Gates had been seen doing high-fives with Bill Neukom upon leaving the office of Commissioner Owen—who would vote against bringing an antitrust action. Mary Azcuenaga had also voted against an action, giving no reason for her position.

The deadlock had come about because "Uncle Buck" Starek had recused himself from the case. Publicly, the reason was a mystery. Privately, it was that the oversized commissioner owned about 100 shares of IBM stock in a trust fund he shared with his brother and could not liquidate. Staffers could not get over the absurdity and insignificance of the situation.

But now it was lunchtime.

Commissioner Yao, tall, youthful, and in a dark beige suit, stood off to one side of the group now rushing the reservation desk. He was a supporter of the revamped complaint against Microsoft that staff attorneys were just putting together. He had supported the earlier complaint as well, but it looked as if a different tack would have to be taken if the case was to emerge from its moribund state.

The FTC Bureau of Competition, which had taken the lead with the Microsoft investigation since the beginning, welcomed a recent development: the Bureau of Consumer Protection had been brought in to address new evidence that Microsoft had allegedly violated the Magnuson-Moss Act, which defines unlawful uses of product warranty disclaimers. This was the latest heartburn of Bill Neukom.

While the tenets of the case continued to swirl these past several weeks, Yao wondered what the antitrust environment would look like with Anne Bingaman setting the tone at Justice. He'd have an idea soon enough: He was about to have his first one-on-one encounter with her.

The maître d' looked over the horde now confronting him, and with the transcendent air of a prelate rising above the hubbub, waved his arm over their heads, gesturing to one of his minions to bring a particularly well-heeled clan to their dining place.

Suddenly, a hand shot out to greet Yao. That wayward extremity protruding from a plaid sleeve was attached to the wily Art Amolsch, publisher of *FTC Watch*, a biweekly newsletter that archly observed the activities of the agency. Amolsch shook hands vigorously with Yao and was abruptly swallowed by another group of lunchgoers heading for their table.

Yao was led off to his table. Moments later he would be joined by Bingaman, who would be confirmed in a matter of days as the Justice Department's head of antitrust under Janet Reno. While Bingaman would not have direct control over the FTC's activities, since the commission was an independent agency, she would play a major role in setting the tone for antitrust policy. It was rare for the FTC to go against the policies of the Justice antitrust chief. Many at the commission felt Bingaman's appointment would bring change—for the better.

Amolsch, standing out in his plaid jacket, still had not been seated. He always looked as if he'd just popped out of a detective episode. His whitening hair was a bit rumpled, and he had a perennially mischievous look on his face. He'd traveled for two hours from the Shenandoah Valley for this lunch invitation. After all, the salmon at the 701 was not to be resisted.

Now he glided happily to a table. The man had a refreshing working-class air, delighting over the fact that what all in the room considered themselves to be doing—over such indulgent repast as Caesar salad with goat cheese and softshell crabs—was *working!* "It sure beats a factory line, doesn't it!" he exclaimed between bites of salmon. Amolsch, a self-described populist, was a Republican who at one time had supported Reagan.

Amolsch sat momentarily agape. His companion nudged him as the platinum head of FTC Commissioner Deborah Owen went bobbing across the room to a table, where it promptly subsided, obscured by a well-placed post.

Owen was still as colorful as ever. In the fall of 1992, a going-away party was being held for Kevin Arquit, the bureau of competition director, who was leaving the agency. All gathered at the "top o' the trade"—the nickname for the FTC cafeteria. Arquit's colleagues gave laudatory speeches in his honor. When it came to Owen's turn, speaking in front of some 150 guests at the party, she confided that she had only one piece of advice about life in the private sector: "Lock your door when you're having sex on your desk."

The place was beginning to take on the aspect of an antitrust chessboard. And now the royal blue streak coming toward Amolsch and his friend was Pat Bailey—the attorney/consultant who had been helping Bill Gates in effect psychoanalyze the Commission. Bailey grinned cheerfully as she gave Amolsch a pat on the arm and nodded to his lunch companion. She moved on to a table across the way.

The configuration of the room now roughly comprised a schematic view of the polarized Microsoft case. On one side was Owen, obscure but determined to stand her ground as one of the last true-blue Reaganites left at the agency. Across the room from her was Yao, lifting a fork to his mouth as he chatted with Bingaman. The pair represented a view of antitrust policy that would have seen the Microsoft case brought swiftly before a federal judge. And at a point in the room that would have connected the three factions in a neat triangle sat Bailey, a firm believer in antitrust enforcement yet now, as a consultant to Microsoft, in the unlikely position of having to play both sides of the fence.

More than three months after the February deadlock, two-thirds of the Microsoft case had been shelved—at least temporarily.

The basic problem was that after almost three years of effort by staff attorneys and investigators—often working twelve or more hours a day—the case had become unwieldy and overly complex.

In addition, the foundation of the case as it was presented to the commissioners on February 5, would have pointed to "structural" remedies—a practical and political minefield. For years the agency had avoided structural cases—involving the physical breakup of monopolies—like the plague. Such cases were known to go on for in excess of a decade and used up substantial resources. A number of the original tenets of the Microsoft case were problematic because of this.

One of the original areas of the investigation focused on the IBM and Microsoft "head-fake" in which the two firms appeared to have been jointly persuading applications software developers and customers to switch their development efforts from DOS to OS/2. It turned out that Microsoft had orchestrated a much different head-fake on its own, putting its investment in Windows and thereby getting a head start on the rest of the industry. But even looking at that case as a conspiracy of Microsoft's alone was troublesome. There was evidence to suggest that some groups within Microsoft believed some of what the company originally said about OS/2, although Gates' inner sanctum seemed to have taken a sharp detour.

The basic charge of monopoly leveraging, in which Microsoft allegedly used its market power in operating systems to leverage itself in other markets, such as applications software, was also problematic. Both the "head fake" approach and the charge of monopoly leveraging pointed to a path that the Commission was simply not willing to go down.

The FTC is an ends-oriented body; it would only bring a case that would result in remedies it could easily enforce. The Microsoft case was leading down a road that pointed to remedies that would limit Microsoft's use of its operating systems power in unrelated markets. Most at the agency did not want to come near structural remedies—involving the physical breakup of monopolies—that would impose walls between the company's operating systems and applications divisions, or even divide up the company. Even if attorneys at the agency could see their way around legal proofs for such a case, the Commission simply did not want to end up there.

What instead became the heart of the case was how Microsoft allegedly excluded other vendors from the DOS marketplace. It didn't hurt that Ray Noorda had threatened to take DR-DOS off the market if the feds did not act fast. The case was based largely on sworn testimony given in investigational hearings and roomfuls of documents provided by Novell illustrating Microsoft's attempts to keep DR-DOS off the market. This evidence had been provided from before the Novell acquisition of DRI in 1991 to the present.

Just prior to the February 5 meeting, the commission informed Novell that it was focusing on the DOS case. Novell was told that the Commission had reason to believe there had been violations of antitrust law in that area. The original complaint about Microsoft's exclusionary practices in the DOS market included "exclusive dealing," in which Microsoft licensed DOS (and Windows) on an all-or-nothing basis, coercing computer companies to pay royalties on every computer they shipped. For many companies, Microsoft's offer to allow licensees to buy the operating system on a per copy basis was out of the question—the prices to do so were exorbitant. Licensees received a substantial discount only if they committed all their machines to shipping with DOS.

Next was "direct tying" of the licensing of Windows to the licensing of DOS. Microsoft allegedly used Windows to keep OEMs in line on their DOS contracts. Basically, computer vendors charged that Microsoft told them if they wanted Windows, they had to play ball on DOS.

The issue of "technological tying" was perhaps the most damaging to Novell and DR-DOS. This involved Microsoft manipulating code in a beta version of Windows 3.1 to create the appearance that DR-DOS was not compatible with it.

In addition was "information tying," an allegation that Microsoft removed companies from its technical support list unless they had per processor licenses for DOS and Windows.

"Fraudulent and misleading public preannouncements" was another complaint. For example, in sworn depositions Novell executives alleged that during the week the company shipped its DR-DOS 5 software to customers, Microsoft wrote and distributed a product-to-product comparison of that product with Microsoft DOS 5, which did not exist in any form at the time. When MS-DOS 5 arrived on the market a year later, it did not include some of the promised features that had caused customers to stall or cancel their purchases of DR-DOS.

In the weeks leading up to the February 5 meeting, the FTC staff received an enormous amount of help from Novell. A joint Novell-FTC team worked eighteen to twenty hours a day. They had to be prepared for the possibility that the case would go to trial quickly.

During the week before the vote, seven Novell representatives came to the commission to give presentations—often two hours in length—to FTC attorneys, economists, and the commissioners. Members of the Novell team were often bumping into Microsoft and Lotus representatives, who were also giving presentations. According to FTC insiders, Gates himself was virtually "sleeping in the hallways" that week. Representatives of Borland International had canvassed the agency the week before.

D'Artagnan's day had come.

By April 22, Mary Lou Steptoe, Kevin Arquit's replacement as head of the Bureau of Competition, had empowered him to recast the Microsoft complaint so it would have one last chance before the FTC commissioners.

Norris Washington had not yet given up. There were more depositions to be taken before the second vote. And D'Artagnan and Steptoe surely wouldn't let the commission pass up this big case.

Following the February 5 debacle, FTC attorneys felt—as they had on numerous other occasions—that they'd been spinning their wheels. Their work had been exhaustive and thorough. Perhaps too thorough. They had collected millions of pages of evidence industrywide and roomfuls of depositions. All the *i*'s had been dotted and all the *t*'s crossed, and still the case wouldn't fly. Nobody quite knew why, but nobody was surprised: they'd seen it all before at the commission.

D'Artagnan, an FTC veteran of nineteen years, was known for his simple expository style and his ability to boil down the most complex of cases for a judge or layperson to understand. According to his peers at Washington law firms, he had a track record of winning preliminary injunctions at a time when the federal government won almost no other cases. These included cases involving the defense and aircraft industries. During the Reagan years D'Artagnan was infamous at the FTC for halting dozens of mergers when almost no other mergers were opposed.

By mid-May final depositions were being taken, and the Microsoft investigation was drawing to a conclusion. Evidence on the AARD code, was being consolidated. Aaron Reynolds was deposed. Steve Ballmer was brought in to address the strange code Microsoft had created apparently to kill DR-DOS's chances in the marketplace.

Weeks earlier Washington and his colleagues had been intrigued by the internal e-mail that indicated that Microsoft senior executives had gone to the trouble to think about how to explain things to the press should the code be discovered. The internal e-mail spelled out the way Microsoft later would answer questions publicly.

A programmer had questioned his superior, Microsoft Vice President Brad Silverberg, about how they would explain themselves if discovered.

> From: darbyw to silverberg
> subject: dos practices
> Thanks Brad. I don't think this addresses the issue of our encrypting the code. How do I explain that?

The reply from Silverberg explained how they could whitewash the situation. The answer to any questions about the error message, according to him, should be that Microsoft had not ever made their product incompatible with another, and that Windows was "designed and developed for MS-DOS." Microsoft did not test on other systems nor could it verify the stability of Windows running on anything other than MS-DOS, he said. If DR-DOS was really compatible with MS-DOS as its manufacturer claimed, "it would just run Windows," he said.

Washington and Schildkraut now knew that the only apparent reason DR-DOS was incompatible with Windows is that Microsoft made certain that this would be true. It was due, it seemed, not to any imperfection in the DR-DOS product, but because of Microsoft's deliberate campaign to sabotage DR-DOS, as spelled out in its internal communications.

Indeed, in May, Silverberg made some enlightening statements in an interview. He said that MS-DOS's 90 percent market share was secure because before buying DR-DOS buyers should ask, "Why take the risk with all the compatibility problems that DR-DOS has had?" He pointed out that the Windows 3.1 that was bundled with a laptop he'd bought came with the ominous warning that running it on an operating system other than MS-DOS could cause unexpected results or poor performance.

In response to very specific questions about the error code planted by Microsoft in the beta version of Windows 3.1, Brad Silverberg around the same time told a reporter, "There is no such thing. You're talking nonsense. Do you know this for sure?"

He was told that the code existed in five different programs inside Windows 3.1, and again asked if he knew what the code was. "No. I don't," he said.

He was informed that Aaron Reynolds had written the code. "So what? What's your point?" he asked.

From denying the existence of the code, Silverberg finally admitted that there had been code in the beta version of Windows 3.1 that "checked for MS-DOS." He added, "Windows is designed for MS-DOS. If DR-DOS is 100 percent compatible with MS-DOS as they claim, then it would never show up."

As Silverberg's own e-mail with other Microsoft programmers and executives showed, the only reason the error message came up was that Microsoft planted it there. He was the same Microsoft executive who earlier had written privately to other Microsoft executives, while the error code was being created, "What the guy [using the computer] is supposed to do is feel uncomfortable and when he has bugs, suspect the problem is DR-DOS and then go out and buy MS-DOS or decide not to take the risk . . ."

By midsummer, Washington and Marc Schildkraut were grilling Reynolds, the author of the code, and noted that he seemed to be an honorable sort. Even under oath he felt squeamish about squealing

117

on his bosses. "You'll have to talk to my superiors," he told investigators.

It was only weeks before a revamped complaint would be presented to the commissioners, and a final vote scheduled. Some in the software industry who remained close to the case were chagrined. They feared that the agency had set aside what they felt to be some of the most important issues. The case was being narrowed to the smallest common denominator in an effort to get at least three of the four commissioners to agree on its basic assumption: that Microsoft had improperly used its monopoly position to exclude others from the marketplace.

The complaint would also state that Microsoft appeared to have violated the Magnuson-Moss Act in its use of warranty disclaimers. Specifically, this complaint was based on evidence that Microsoft threatened customers that their product warranties might become invalid if competing software was used with Microsoft products such as Windows. The complaint would include a "Notice of Contemplated Relief," made up of a "cease and desist" order and "fencing in" provisions that would restrict Microsoft from engaging in activities similar to those deemed improper. Ancillary relief would also be sought, such as requiring that Microsoft give companies uniform access to advance technical information that affected their product development. No fines were expected to be imposed.

The commission had pretty much decided that it would reconvene for a final vote on the Microsoft case on July 21. Commissioner Owen was said to be annoyed when she was presented with the July date and was pushing for a vote as soon as possible. Vacation schedules, however, made an earlier vote impossible.

Meanwhile, Owen was vying with Janet Steiger and Dennis Yao for Mary Azcuenaga's allegiance. Azcuenaga still represented a ray of hope to those frustrated with the deadlock. And Owen was afraid that Yao and Steiger could bring her around to agreeing that Microsoft seemed to have violated the antitrust laws in the most basic of ways.

9

AUNTIE MAME

In June 1993, Anne Bingaman was being confirmed as chief of the Department of Justice Antitrust Division under Janet Reno. In July, in e-mail to his top executives, Bill Gates spelled out how he sought revenge on Ray Noorda, whom he blamed for the feds' scrutiny of his company. It was a classic example of Gates' obsession with damaging his rivals—which drove him to illegal practices to gain advantages in new markets. What happened to the FTC's case following a second deadlock defied all expectations. Gates was up in arms: he thought he had become the target of a game of double jeopardy.

Aunty Em. Auntie Mame. Antitrust.

Antitrust! It was a wonder the world still knew the meaning of the word. Certain liberal members of Congress were now archly observing the Senate ritual surrounding the ushering in of the first Democratic antitrust chief in twelve years.

Almost three decades had passed since Anne Bingaman held her first job in Washington. On June 9, 1993, just down the corridor from the Dirksen Senate Office Building on Capitol Hill, where she started her career, Bingaman, age forty-nine, sat before the Senate Judiciary Committee. It was her nomination hearing as the Justice Department's assistant attorney general in charge of antitrust.

Now here were Senators Joseph Biden, Paul Simon, Pete Domenici, Dianne Feinstein, Carol Moseley-Braun, Orrin Hatch,

Alan Simpson, and Charles Grassley, with Sen. Howard Metzenbaum presiding.

"Ms. Bingaman, to be frank, antitrust enforcement has never been in worse shape," said Metzenbaum. He was holding forth before his colleagues and making sure to get in a few good jabs at those Republicans he held responsible for what he saw as the current mess.

Hearing attendees, including many Washington veterans accustomed to being buffeted by the shifting winds that came with each new administration, were about to witness yet another shift.

The charms of that institution known as Congress could be seen in microcosm at this gathering: the overlapping voices, the understatements, overstatements, backhanded compliments, underhanded insinuations, and a litany of ways to mumble, chuckle, cough, and elbow-nudge.

(At the federal agencies, commissioners and their staffs engaged in a similar ritual during their meetings—with individual personalities and their respective agendas eventually converging into a single body that somehow managed to slowly creep ahead. This was government, with its multitudinous thumping organs—in the end a somehow cohesive body, despite its many legs at any given moment threatening to scamper off in all directions.)

Now Sen. Pete Domenici (R, New Mexico) was speaking. "Let me first say it is pretty obvious that I don't agree with everything the Clinton administration proposes or does, but I am here today because I wholeheartedly agree that this is a good, solid, if not exceptional, nomination."

The senators continued their banter. After a short speech supporting the nominee, Domenici tossed in a little barb for his colleagues' pleasure: "Mr. Chairman, I don't agree with you on everything."

"That is a surprise. I thought you did," Metzenbaum shot back. Laughter filled the room. Soon it was the turn of Jeff Bingaman, Democratic senator from New Mexico, with twelve-year-old son in tow, to give a tribute to his wife.

Metzenbaum had contrasted this nominee's activism with the systematic dismantling of antitrust enforcement begun during the

Reagan years. "To put it charitably, antitrust enforcement has languished during the last twelve years of Republican administrations," he said, again causing some of his Republican colleagues to bristle. "Antitrust officials, particularly under the Reagan administration, openly challenged the core values of our fair competition laws and in most instances refused to enforce them." He liked rubbing it in, thought some of his colleagues.

Finally, it was the nominee's turn to speak. "It's really the antitrust laws that are at the bedrock of our economic system," she said. "They give us the robust competition that encourages innovation, that makes us uniquely American, that makes us really what we are."

Bingaman's confirmation came off without a hitch: none could contest her qualifications for the job. She had known Hillary Clinton when both worked on a fund-raising campaign for the Children's Defense Fund. Her marriage to Jeff Bingaman, along with her recent practice at the D.C. firm of Powell, Goldstein, Frazer & Murphy, had given her an education about the workings of Washington. The Clinton administration was homing in on the economy, health care, and the information superhighway, that fantasy pipeline for billions of dollars in commerce.

In July, while the FTC was gearing up for its final vote on bringing a case against Microsoft, Bill Gates was beside himself with fury. He'd been obsessing over Ray Noorda's role in the federal investigation of his company. He wrote to Senior VP Paul Maritz, confiding his paranoia about Novell. It clearly showed how Gates personally ordered exceptions to standard Microsoft practices, in order to damage his competitors.

Gates had been furious about Noorda's participating in the FTC investigation, and sought retribution.

Gates wrote to Maritz: "Who at Microsoft gets up in the morning thinking about how to compete with these guys [Novell] in the short term, specifically—cut their revenue. Perhaps we need more focus on this."

Gates went on, spelling out his paranoia and his desire to get revenge on Novell and Noorda. "After their [Novell's] behavior in this

FTC investigation, I am very keen on this [cutting their revenues]. He went on to explain four ways to accomplish this—by undercutting Novell's product line with low-end versions of his own, using both Microsoft and Novell technology.

Gates spelled out how Microsoft could leverage its DOS dominance into Novell's networking market by bundling cheap networking "client" software; his motivation to lower prices was to cut quickly into Novell's market. He also indicated that he wanted to emphasize to customers his belief that Novell had held back supporting Microsoft's NT, something corporate information systems managers would be pissed off about. He wrote, "These approaches might require marketing money. I would be glad to consider a special request for something strong."

About the same time, Gates and his executives were accusing Novell in the press of being a monopolist.

In mid-July, at the apex of the Federal Triangle, between Sixth and Seventh Streets, D'Artagnan approached the rounded corner of the FTC facade, with its Ionic colonnades. It had been home to him for some twenty years. He stopped for a moment and looked up at the titanic horse being held back by a muscle man. The sculpture was a heroic portrayal of man restraining unbridled trade. His eyes settled on the lunging horse. Its nostrils flared slightly.

D'Artagnan blinked.

There were spectacles on the horse, and a sandy mane. He set down his gym bag for a moment and began to chuckle. The beast was Gates, and the muscle man, of course, D'Artagnan.

He had an idea about how to salvage his antitrust case.

D'Artagnan was not going to just sit around and wait for the inevitable to happen. Back in his office, he began to draft a letter that he planned to deliver to Mindy Hattan, who worked in Howard Metzenbaum's office.

Surely Hattan would help him perfect it, and the senator would want to put his John Hancock to it. The failure of the FTC to take action was a travesty. D'Artagnan knew the agency had one hell of a monopolization case. Mary Lou Steptoe knew it. Janet Steiger knew it. He was sure he'd have their support on this; no matter how bad it might make the agency look, the internal record would show who had held up the case. He was not going to wait for another deadlock. The final vote was scheduled for later in the month.

The letter, dated July 13, was addressed to FTC Chair Janet Steiger, and it indicated that it had been copied to the other four commissioners. At the bottom of the list was a fifth name: Anne K. Bingaman.

On July 14, as she was moving into her new office at the Justice Department, Bingaman read the letter from Metzenbaum, which would soon be circulating to the press. One paragraph stood out:

"I have been informed that the Commission intends to review the Microsoft case again later in July. I hope that the Commission will be able to decide what action to take at that time. However, if the Commission remains deadlocked, I would strongly urge you to refer the case to the Department of Justice's Antitrust Division for an independent review."

In fact, taking over the case should it once again reach a deadlock had been a bee in Bingaman's bonnet for several months. It had been buzzing about her auburn head since that lunch at the 701.

Earlier in the week, Microsoft's biggest competitors—Novell, Lotus, Borland, Sun, and Taligent—were lobbying at the FTC. On July 15, Bill Gates met with Commissioner Yao, who suggested possible remedies to curb Microsoft's predatory practices. The staff had surmised that Gates had been hanging around all week ready to settle with the commission if it sued. Instead, he began screaming at Yao, calling his ideas communist.

Gates met with Steiger and Steptoe on July 16. When Steptoe asked a question about beta programs and the disparaging code, Gates blew up and called her stupid. Bill Neukom watched impassively as Gates threw his fits. He and another Microsoft attorney then pulled Gates out of the meeting to scold him. Deborah Owen hit it off with Gates, as she had earlier. She admired him: Gates was thirty-seven years old and the richest man in America.

By July 22, the air at the FTC was like that of a funeral. The commissioners had emerged from their vote that day having reached another deadlock. The staff was mystified. Was the theory off? Facts off? Did they need more intent evidence? More effects evidence?

Before convening their meeting, Deborah Owen and Mary Azcuenaga wanted the case closed immediately, but a majority vote was needed to do that, and Yao and Steiger refused to close it.

Steiger and Steptoe had been surprised by the "Metzenbaum" letter, of which they had recently received copies, and were quick to note that no such "referral" process existed in the agency's rules. Behind the scenes, the scramble was on to find the smoothest way possible to move the case on to Justice.

Meanwhile, Owen was livid. She felt that "parliamentary rules" that govern the FTC had been violated. "A 2-2 vote does not mean a deadlock. It means that a majority did not find reason to pursue a case," she said. When it seemed that the case would not be closed, Owen demanded that the chair inform her of when she anticipated closing it. Steiger promised that it would be closed within thirty days.

All were now waiting for Bingaman to make a move. "We were walking on ice to see if she'd act within thirty days," said one staffer.

The three-and-a-half-year-long FTC probe was paralyzed, and Microsoft was overjoyed. It issued a press statement that day describing the stalemate as a "victory."

On July 30, while Gates and Neukom were addressing a gaggle of investment bankers and analysts in Seattle, back in Washington, D.C., a figure in a gray raincoat could be seen carrying carton after carton across the street from the FTC to the Justice Department. It was D'Artagnan. The Microsoft probe had been transferred, a scenario that FTC watcher Art Amolsch had previously described to the press as being as unlikely as "an asteroid hitting the earth."

The news came out in an article in the *Chicago Tribune* and was brought to Gates' and Neukom's attention during a question and answer session with analysts that day. "Is it true that the Justice Department is now investigating your company, as the *Chicago Tribune* says today?" an analyst asked. Gates and Neukom looked at each other in disbelief, unaware of the news story. They denied the allegation, but by the next morning, *The New York Times* and *The Washington Post* had both picked up the story.

Neukom issued a flurry of statements to the press. Meanwhile, Gates and Ballmer lashed out at Novell. They accused the company and its chairman and CEO, Ray Noorda, of masterminding the FTC and Justice probes.

Gates said the investigations were nothing more than sour grapes on the part of Novell because merger discussions Microsoft had initiated with them fell through. Noorda thought it an odd time for Gates to bring up that bit of history. Did he have a guilty conscience?

Meanwhile, Owen was fuming. She protested the case moving to the Justice Department and in a phone conversation told Bingaman so in no uncertain terms. Steptoe and others started referring to Bingaman as "the fifth vote," in effect the replacement for the recused Commissioner Starek.

Before being formally cleared to Justice, there was yet another battle, over whether the case should be closed at the FTC before being cleared to Justice, or cleared and then closed. Yao was insistent that it be cleared first, so that there was no misunderstanding about the fact that the case was only closed because of another agency taking it over.

Finally, by August 20, the Microsoft probe was fully in Bingaman's hands. She made personal phone calls to all the FTC commissioners, thanked them for their cooperation and asked them to share the reasons they voted as they did on the case.

"That was a natural thing to do," Yao said. "It was a matter of courtesy and also a matter of perhaps getting in on some people's viewpoints." He pointed out that the case would not have been

closed by the FTC if the Justice Department had not become involved. "Once Justice picked it up, even though that's something I
wish FTC were able to have completed, it made sense to close it as
a matter of fairness to Microsoft not having to deal with two agencies," he said.

Gates and Neukom still were complaining that this was like being
tried twice for the same crime. But there was no legal basis for their
complaint.

10

UPSTREAM

In the late fall of 1993, as the Justice Department got into the case record, Microsoft's market valuation had reached $24.0 billion, with $4.5 billion in revenues a year, about half in exports. Meanwhile, the antitrust ranks at Justice were being filled out. A trial lawyer was brought in to head up litigation for the case the feds were determined to file against Gates. A broader case, as outlined by Lotus Development Corp., was being weighed, and Anne Bingaman and her deputies were laying the groundwork for a coordinated effort with the European Commission. Meanwhile, Ray Noorda and his attorneys were not letting up. The complaint they'd filed in Europe was now bearing fruit.

Bob Litan was battling the current, as he did each morning at 6:00 A.M. when he climbed into his Swim-Ex. His new work life at the Department of Justice was much the same. He pulled fistfuls of water hand over hand. The current had been going against would-be antitrust enforcers for too long.

Following his swim, Litan made it a habit to walk to work. Each day now he approached the facade on Pennsylvania Avenue along one edge of the Federal Triangle between Ninth and Tenth Streets. He passed its Ionic colonnades and fluted pilasters, moving through to the interior, where stairways gave way to New Deal murals celebrating the role of law and justice in America.

It was November 1993, and the polished stone floors of the U.S. Department of Justice could be slippery. Justice could be a perilous place under the watchful eye of Congress and the American public. Anne Bingaman, Litan's pal of ten years, was beginning to gain control of the division: her deputies—including Litan—had just come onboard.

The third-floor hallways of the Antitrust Division were dim, and the building—built in the early 1930s—had that dusty smell that all federal buildings of its time seemed to have. Litan, a lawyer and an economist, had arrived from the Brookings Institution, where he'd been a fellow. Earlier he'd been a partner at Powell, Goldstein, the firm Anne had just departed to take her position at the Justice Department.

Both Litan and Bingaman had grown accustomed to the designer decor and fully computerized surroundings of their successful law offices. This place was quite a contrast. Luckily, Reno had recently donated $1 million from her discretionary budget to help computerize the sorely outdated division.

These days the staff was working long hours, and the office was beginning to feel like Litan's living room. At staff meetings, he and his boss were informal. Litan would rarely wear a jacket, and Bingaman would sometimes don slippers in the late afternoon. The staff could hear her coming a mile away—shuffle, shuffle down the salmon pink and gray stone floors.

Litan had never been so busy in his life. As regulatory deputy assistant attorney general, he oversaw all civil monopolization cases—an area where Bingaman was determined to crack down hard. Thirty cases had been started in recent weeks. "Anne's been here less than six months, and we're going to have some victories," Litan would say. He was certain of it.

Earlier that fall Microsoft's chief counsel, William Neukom, and some of his colleagues met for the first time with the Antitrust Division and were told of the seriousness of the new probe. Microsoft's market valuation was now $24.0 billion, and it enjoyed some $4.5 billion in revenues a year. About half of the revenue was in exports, making the company an important player in the global economy.

As Litan and his staff knew well, monopolization in and of itself is not illegal, and they knew how controversial this case was. Those lobbying on Microsoft's behalf protested that the government was merely taking potshots at a global star. A monopolist may not be doing anything wrong if, having obtained market power by legitimate means, it maintains its power by possessing superior skill, foresight, and "reasonable industrial practices." Monopolization is illegal only if it can be proved that there is a specific "intent" to monopolize, anticompetitive or predatory conduct directed at accomplishing this, and a "dangerous probability" of success.

In meetings with Section Chief Rich Rosen—a college roommate of D'Artagnan who focused on the computer industry and telecommunications—whose attorneys had been doing all the legwork on the probe since August, Litan and Bingaman had determined that Justice Department litigators would not have to go far afield or into innovative theories to bring their case. Bingaman had received the same impression from FTC attorneys. It was their analysis that had resulted in her sticking her neck out to take over the probe.

Now, while Bill Gates was in Las Vegas—having client dinners, giving his yearly speech to thousands of worshipers, and boogying at the Paladium and the Shark Club—Litan, Bingaman, and the staff at the antitrust unit were rejoicing: they'd won $4.7 million to beef up the joint. It was a budget increase of about 7 percent—unheard of in a time of government cutbacks. The trustbusters were back in business.

Congress had granted the increase largely thanks to the efforts of Bingaman. Almost immediately upon her arrival at Justice, she'd made a lightning tour, on Capitol Hill as well as making the rounds at the Office of Management and Budget, giving graphic presentations with big charts. She'd made her point well: the economy had more than quadrupled, but the size of the Antitrust Division had stayed the same since World War II.

Things were really moving along, Litan considered. Bingaman, who at one point found it hard to tear herself away from her home in New Mexico, was getting results. The Santa Fe señora was showing the world what she was made of: hot sauce, picante, southwestern salsa. (Her office, whose style could only be described as "federal drab," was festooned with her favorite southwestern artifacts.)

Litan was joined by hirees in three new positions: the economics deputy, Rich Gilbert; the international deputy, Diane Wood; and the merger deputy, Steve Sunshine. Having come from Brookings, he'd half-anticipated not being very stimulated by his federal colleagues. As it turned out, the new guard at the division was both erudite and experienced.

Shortly after her arrival, Bingaman had undertaken a major reorganization. When the staff presented her with the unit's organizational chart and decision tree, she'd been horrified. The number of boxes a case had to go through before a decision could be made was astounding. She decided to squash the vertical reporting structure that had made the top people late to get critical information in developing cases.

For more than a decade, Justice's record on anything but criminal cases had been abysmal. The FTC had at least outperformed it in merger regulation in recent years. Bingaman was intent on making the department's Antitrust Division a lively place once more.

Her deputies would be divided along functional lines: civil, merger, and criminal. She hoped the regrouping would ensure that important civil cases, like the monopolization probe of Microsoft, would not be upstaged by the megamergers occuring in the telecom and cable worlds. (It was also the division's job to police mergers and acquisitions.)

Litan and Bingaman had a full plate. In addition to their work at the division, they were both involved in an interagency legislative group under the direction of Al Gore. The group included the Department of Justice along with the National Telecommunications and Information Administration at the Commerce Department, the OMB, the FCC, and others, and was developing and formulating the administration's position on telecommunications policy. They would sometimes meet two or three times a week.

Washington antitrust pundits following the Microsoft case were afraid it would be lost in the shuffle, with much bigger deals coming down in telecom. The reorganization would solve that potential problem, as well as focus the DOJ's own efforts in the merger arena, which it had joint jurisdiction over with the FTC.

"The new structure cuts down on wasted work," Bingaman explained to her colleagues. "If there are developments that mean you don't want to bring a case, you stop it right there." In the case of Microsoft, the staff was seeking to enlarge the complaint to include violations the FTC had not fully pursued.

Litan knew that Bingaman, a self-described "crazy Croatian," would tolerate no stalling on Microsoft. At stake was Gates's ability to continue extending his control over what essentially would be the central nervous system of the digital future. Litan's staff had acknowledged that Microsoft had contributed greatly to the success of the software industry, but they had sufficient evidence to believe it had been maintaining its monopoly position through illegal means.

Bingaman had just hired Sam "Ziggy" Miller, a trial lawyer, as head litigator for the case. He would start on January 1—the day Gates was getting married on the Hawaiian island of Lanai.

Miller would remain based in the San Francisco office of the department, and commute regularly to Washington. Litan found Miller a great debating partner. He'd been wrangling with him over whether to bring a far-ranging case or to narrow the complaint in order to move things along. Miller was agreeable to pursuing—and intent on winning—any case the staff recommended.

To Litan, the curious thing was how inseparable Bill Gates the man seemed to be from the behavior of his company. All the stories in the industry were of "Gates doing this personally," "an edict from Gates," and "Gates was out to destroy us." The Justice Department attorneys, who had not yet met Gates, had heard about his arrogance and insults from their FTC colleagues. "I'm expecting to see Gates in my office soon," Litan said, with feigned dread, during a casual phone call in late December.

Back on August 11, 1993, between the time access to documents was given and full clearance granted, Lotus Development Corp., through its counsel Andrew Berg, had sent a letter to Anne Bingaman. He provided an appendix and numerous affidavits itemizing aspects of Microsoft's conduct that he hoped the investigation would address. At the same time, he pointed out, "We suspect Microsoft's conduct is far more widespread than suggested here."

Berg laid out a broad monopolization case, including how Microsoft leveraged its control of the operating system market for a clear advantage in the applications software market. He documented how Microsoft had misled software developers about which operating system—Windows or OS/2—was to be the focus of its development efforts, which would determine the standard graphical interface for the industry.

He rehashed what the FTC had pored over for years.

Microsoft had forced other companies to invest immense sums in displaced development efforts. It allowed Microsoft to exploit critical time to market advantages for Windows applications and forced others to be late to market in key Windows applications markets, Berg stated.

He argued that Microsoft's subsequent dominance in key applications markets stemmed from the fact that, when it brought Windows to market, it was the only company to have commercially available spreadsheet and word processing applications. Further, Microsoft used its operating system dominance to dictate technological standards in order to benefit its applications at the expense of its competitors'.

Microsoft's own programmers had unfair access to operating system information, Berg explained. They saw source code and could ask questions about operating system developments inside the company before new versions of the operating system was released. At the same time, Microsoft gave minimal answers to other companies about how best to develop applications software for the underlying operating system. It also used secret code that could benefit its own products and harm those of competitors.

Microsoft sold bundled products to computer makers. It priced the operating system so that its applications software cost close to nothing if bought along with the operating system. The same scheme was used to encourage systems integrators to exclude products of competing companies in the U.S. Air Force Desktop IV solicitation, which mandated the Windows environment.

Moreover, Microsoft offered predatory low prices to large customers through retroactive price reductions via bonus "credits," free lifetime upgrades in exchange for excluding products of competing companies, retroactive credits tied to the purchase of large quantities of Microsoft applications, large numbers of free copies, and no-charge trade-outs for competing applications.

Microsoft was blatant about its leveraging. "Since we own the operating system, we'll always be six to nine months ahead of" certain competitors, it said in public statements. In one case, Microsoft beat a major competitor for a large corporate account by claiming that its ownership of the operating system put it at an advantage with applications functionality and compatibility, despite competing products being rated on par with Microsoft's.

Berg's litany continued: Microsoft withheld promotional perks from companies selling competing products. It denied software companies promised promotional and marketing support, forcing distributors and dealers to exclude competitors from their promos. It denied competitors promised access to Windows user mailing lists and preannounced nonexisting products to damage sales of competing products.

During the fall and winter of 1993, Berg was spending much time with Bingaman's new staff in a last-ditch effort to make them realize that it wasn't just Novell's operating system market that had been damaged. Far more companies were slowly being drained by Microsoft's predation in the applications market, and that market would soon be lost if the division did not act fast.

But a massive monopolization case, as opposed to a "surgically specific" one, scared the hell out of Litan, Bingaman, and their colleagues. Nevertheless, their goal was to file a case that would allow them at least to kick the door in on Gates' methods. If they could get a settlement even on a narrower point, he'd be under scrutiny for some time. They could always go back after a broader case if the man could not take a hint.

Bingaman had redefined the jobs of her deputies, along with the reorganization, empowering Litan. Historically, the regulatory deputy at the Antitrust Division oversaw most of the litigating sections, but only on regulatory matters. This included mergers in regulated industries as well as all civil and criminal litigation in these industries. Bingaman's creation of a merger deputy position, to be filled by the former section chief Steve Sunshine, enabled Litan to devote most of his efforts to Microsoft and other nonmerger cases. Rich Gilbert and Diane Wood would help Litan evaluate the economic and global impacts, respectively, of pursuing a federal injunction against Microsoft.

Gilbert was a technology buff and an expert in industrial organization and intellectual property issues. He had started as an electrical engineer, working a four-year stint at the Naval Research Lab on integrated devices, only to emerge from Stanford with an economics degree. Most recently, at the University of California at Berkeley, he had taught regulation and antitrust, both in the business school and in the economics department.

Bingaman had not known him personally, but Gilbert had developed a reputation for his expertise in technology as well as his interest in high-tech markets and industrial innovation. He would provide critical input on the economic impact of Microsoft's behavior in the marketplace, and the ramifications of it being forced to alter its behavior. He would also analyze the economies of the computer industry and Microsoft's software licensing policies, along with a range of other practices.

Unlike those in the FTC's Bureau of Economics, which was infamous for working against investigations being pursued at the same agency's Bureau of Competition, the economists at Justice worked closely with the agency's attorneys. They also mutually agreed to dismiss cases deemed insubstantial.

Diane Wood, a University of Chicago law professor, had first talked with Bingaman about becoming her international deputy the previous June. By early August she had started on a temporary appointment, and she officially became international deputy in September.

Early on, Janet Reno, the Clinton administration, and Congress had been supportive of a new deputy position at the division that would focus on international markets. Wood, the first person to hold the job, hoped to coordinate a historic agreement on the Microsoft case between the European Community and the Department of Justice. While Wood would work closely with Litan and Gilbert to weigh the global implications of Microsoft's conduct, existing law prohibited a collaborative effort with the EC, which was embroiled in its own antitrust probe of the company. Wood and Bingaman were working on introducing legislation to enable such collaboration.

At about 9:30 P.M. on November 16, 1993, Comdex, the monstrous computer industry trade show, and the annual Chili Cookoff, was under way at the Thomas and Mack Center at the University of Nevada. The stadium was packed with industry pundits, CEOs, geeks, and groupies. Near the center of the arena, a bunch of computer industry executives was whooping it up over an armadillo race. (Yes, the geeks would bellow and squeal to encourage live armadillos to scurry as far as their little legs would go.)

About halfway across the stadium floor, to one side, a few figures stood quietly. A few steps farther into the center, whorls of bodies swept past. Some scrambled to refill their cups with beer or chili, while others wedged closer to the stage where some industry wise guys were making an attempt at music.

Not many noticed a small, white face, that hovered at the edge of the crowd, obscured by an oversized cowboy hat. Framed beneath an enormous brim, the face was slightly puffy, and almost childlike. He stood quietly, not speaking, and very still, although three men had drawn in around him. It was strangely silent in this small pocket that had formed at the edge of the crowd. Bill Gates, with light blue eyeglasses that one's mother might have picked out, looked so very tired.

135

Gates was vulnerable.

Not even the distractions and masquerades of Las Vegas could hide that. For a moment, Intel Corp.'s microprocessor guru, David House, gave him a brief greeting—something about seeing him in a few weeks. Gates nodded impassively. His small pale eyes opening and closing. The lashes looking as though they'd been rubbed away.

He slumped that evening like a man who had given up. He wasn't ranting here as he had last year when he bawled out Sheldon Laube. Gates had been more than mildly displeased that Laube's company, Price Waterhouse, was buying virtually no Microsoft products at the time, and had just committed to an enormous OS/2 order. Laube, with a get-off-my-case smirk, had just shrugged.

Now, as Laube joined the small group surrounding Gates, his presence was barely acknowledged. The handful of partygoers attempting to greet Gates were given little more than a nod or a word or two.

He was preoccupied, and seemed to be floating, almost in a dream-state; meditative, slumped.

Days before, at an industry awards dinner, the announcer had made a joke: "We asked our audience what they'd like to see the magicians Penn & Teller do this evening. They had only one request: Make Bill Gates disappear."

By December the Justice Department, however, was intent on the appearance of Bill Gates.

Anne Bingaman had just crossed around Janet Reno's desk, flung her arms about her, and squeezed. She had the attorney general in the grip of one of her famous bear hugs. The rest of the staff stood in awe and kept a polite distance. These were towering figures: the Justice giantesses. Reno was nearly six foot two, but some in the room noticed that Bingaman managed to envelop her.

The staff meeting had begun, as it usually did at 8:00 A.M. every Tuesday, and all the bigwigs were present: about fifteen of them including Reno and her assistant attorney generals.

Anne had left her third floor niche at the antitrust division to navigate elevators and fifth-floor corridors to Reno's office. Reno had been skeptical at first about Bill Clinton's virtually unknown antitrust appointee; she was pleasantly suprised to find in Bingaman a gutsy attorney with a flair for the workings of Washington. Indeed, Reno and Bingaman had developed a level of trust over the past several months. The party Bingaman had thrown at her Spring Valley home on October 17 in honor of the attorney general and her associate attorney general, Webster Hubbell, had only cemented their friendship. The event was deemed "an enormous success," according to a number of guests; it had given Antitrust Division attorneys a chance to get to know the people at the top.

On this morning, then, no one was overly surprised to see Bingaman—known to be direct, demonstrative, and aggressive—being so familiar with the attorney general. But that was not to say they always agreed. On this day Bingaman was engaged in a heated argument with her mentor about a certain ambiguous ethical rule regarding contact with represented parties. "Janet didn't expect to get an argument from anyone but Anne," said one staffer present at the meeting.

Bingaman wanted her staff to be able to cut through the bureaucracy. The press had speculated that it would take years for Justice to do anything with its Microsoft investigation. But Bingaman hoped to file suit against the software giant by spring. On this December morning, in law offices and living rooms from Georgetown to Spring Valley and back again—and in hotel rooms and corporate boardrooms nationwide—the groundwork was being laid for such an action.

Bingaman was about to give Bill Gates one of her famous bear hugs—in the form of an antitrust suit. Or so went the thinking of her staff.

While the feds were gearing up for action, Ray Noorda was unwinding in Orem, Utah.

"Did you get it stuck, dear?" he asked his wife, his eyes twinkling. Taylor Noorda—Ty for short—was fiddling with her newly re-habbed kitchen. Her head seemed to have vanished. But he knew it was there, obscured by the kitchen cabinet.

Noorda was trying to type his "memoirs." He had never learned how to type. Going through his files, he pulled out one of his poems, which he'd penned right after one of his infamous meetings with Gates, and read it aloud:

We sat together for
the fifth time,
and you brought four
though more than we
bargained for,
And I brought two,
and you still wanted more
than we bargained for
True?
The game's the same,
Pearly,
And you and I
can meet no more
together
Too bad!
This game is gone
we go on
to the next game!
ODI or no ODI
Oh my! Oh my!
And you still wanted more
than we bargained for

Moe, Larry, Curly, Pearly
and Straight Guy

The last two lines referred to Gates and four Microsoft executives who had accompanied him. ODI was not some nonsense term

Noorda had made up to get a rhyme. It, like a litany of other acronyms for technology under development, was a piece of technology that Noorda and Gates had been squabbling over. ODI was Novell's Open Data-link Interface protocol for computer networks, which rivaled Microsoft's NDIS, or Network Device Interface Specification. The two had been warring over the two standards.

Noorda had begun to think of his plans for after retirement. He was not about to disappear from Gates' universe.

Bradford had recently amended Novell's complaint against Microsoft to the EC.

Bradford wondered whether the ongoing battle bothered the sixty-nine-year old Novell chairman. "No, I like the excitement," Noorda would say. "It keeps my pacemaker going."

11

DISAPPEARING ACT

The unlikely tale of how most of the substance of the Department of Justice's case once again disappeared. Attorneys at Justice were revisiting the applications software market, where Microsoft was leveraging its market power and overtaking the leaders. But proving the software giant had a "dangerous probability of success" would be complex, given that it did not yet command a monopoly position in that arena. (It would, by the time Justice filed a lawsuit.) Slowly but surely, the suit would be whittled down to nothing, while Gates' power steadily mounted in new markets.

David Bradford was more drenched in legal theory than a ladyfinger in rum. The endless sentences in his legal briefs rivaled Proust's reveries over a madeleine.

It was clear, at least to Novell's chief counsel, that the European Commission had condemned practices similar to those Microsoft was using throughout the United States and Europe. Bill Neukom was being deluged. Now Gates' chief counsel had the EC to deal with. The complaint Novell had filed in Europe back in July was a mirror of Novell's complaints in the United States.

Reality *was* stranger than fiction. While the FTC probe had slipped through his fingers into the hands of the Justice Department, Neukom had helped Stefanie Reichel escape the advances of

Bill Gates. Meanwhile, Gates was preparing to unburden himself of Noorda once and for all, with his plans to make DOS completely obsolete with "Chicago"—which would become Windows 95.

Back on March 24, Gates had sent an e-mail message to Reichel apologizing for not repaying her the money she had spent on a trip to Amsterdam with him and assuring her of their friendship—despite her having finally spurned his advances for the attentions of Neukom. He also informed her of his forthcoming marriage.

Gates had seen Reichel riding around the corporate campus with another Microsoft employee in his Porsche, and it still made him envious.

Around the same time, Neukom had complained to his confidants that he felt unappreciated by Gates. He'd believed he was due a promotion after surviving all that FTC hell, but Gates was ignoring him. Months later, in January 1994, he confronted Gates and got his way. Sort of. Neukom stayed up all night writing his own press release announcing the promotion he'd been granted, without a raise.

Neukom's attempts to head off future FTC efforts had all been for naught. Before the July deadlock, his government-relations minions had approached the Washington senator Slade Gorton to ask if he would put a stipulation in the FTC authorization bill that forbade the agency's using any more money on the Microsoft investigation.

Things moved too fast to fret about the futility of his past efforts. Before Christmas, Neukom knew Gates and the operating system team were gearing up for an industrywide Windows software developers' conference to be hosted by Microsoft. He and his team had prepared the new nondisclosure agreements (NDAs). Noorda would be sorry he'd ever messed with Gates. So would all of Microsoft's competitors who had supported alternative standards, such as Wabi and OpenDoc, the same companies Microsoft knew had given testimony to the FTC and were now cooperating with Justice. Wabi and OpenDoc were open standards for developing Windows applications that would allow freedom from Microsoft's attempts to dictate the way software was developed. They would all receive "special" versions of the beta software and NDAs that would stop them in their tracks.

During the winter of 1994, the Justice Department litigator Sam Miller suspected that stuff was missing. Shortly after his arrival at Justice, he discovered that there were holes in the document record. There were big gaps in the new documents Microsoft had produced under Justice's subpoena.

On January 10, Janet Reno attended the Antitrust Division's sixtieth anniversary party and gave a speech in support of antitrust enforcement. Two days later Reno attended one of the division's "chiefs" meetings, where management issues were being discussed. "She supported us in lots of ways, and we're very grateful to her," Bingaman told her staff later. Miller reported to Bingaman, who reported regularly to Reno and her associate Webb Hubbell—till he had his own legal and political problems and was forced out.

In recent weeks Miller had phoned Norris Washington at the FTC, who felt evidence had been withheld throughout his dealings with Microsoft. Miller wanted to check the dates on the FTC's last subpoena and Justice's first. Both men knew, however, that in civil cases there was not much to be done even if evidence had intentionally been withheld. Stonewalling was difficult to prove without a whistle-blower inside the company. If this had been a criminal case, possible withholding of evidence would have been far more serious. Nonetheless, obstruction of a federal investigation was a criminal offense. And both Washington and Miller were alarmed. Bingaman also had a few sleepless nights.

It had been the week of December 7 that a group of the department's antitrust attorneys had set off for Lotus country—Cambridge, Massachusetts—to get a handle on the "evidentiary record." Section Chief Rich Rosen had kept Bob Litan abreast of developments on Microsoft. Among the group traveling with Miller was staff attorney Don Russell, a no-nonsense kind of guy. Miller had just begun to get into the case file.

Lotus' Andy Berg and Tom Lemberg, among other industry attorneys, had been frantically lobbying Russell, Miller, and the rest of the team to broaden their investigation. It was their last chance to make sure that the applications portion of the investigation would not be ignored. But developing that portion of the record was far more time-consuming and complex than the classic case of exclusive dealing and product tying that zeroed in on Microsoft's conduct in the operating systems market.

Berg had been heartened when Lotus received a subpoena from Justice that asked, among other things, for information on applications software market share—its own and those of its rivals. The department was also asking for recommendations on who at Microsoft should be subpoenaed. Depositions were being taken at Microsoft on a regular basis. Witnesses were also being interviewed at Lotus.

The technical expert Andrew Schulman spent two and a half hours in a hotel room being interviewed by the Justice entourage. Among other things, he was attempting to explain how Microsoft leveraged control of the operating system for technological benefits in the applications software market. There was no way of telling how much "sneaky code," like the AARD code, existed inside the millions of lines of code at the core of Microsoft's operating systems. Microsoft had created a technological smoke screen, and seemed to be confident that no one—the feds, or anyone else for that matter— could cut through it.

Justice grilled Schulman on topics such as interface management, standards, compatibility, undocumented interfaces, and potential remedies. The man's throat was becoming parched. The attorneys still offered no water, and the room began to grow dim with the waning daylight.

Schulman kept talking. The feds were taking copious notes. Finally, he reached over and turned on the lights. The guys had no social graces. They were a little like Bill Gates in that respect, he thought. Attorney nerds.

By late January 1994, while Gates was preparing to take the witness stand on another case, the buzz inside Justice was that Bingaman and her staff would be ready to file a federal injunction against Microsoft by early April, just before the early spring meeting of the Antitrust Section of the American Bar Association in Washington.

She had spoken to the FTC Bureau of Competition's director, Mary Lou Steptoe, whom she promised to keep informed on her progress—"I'll keep you posted. After all, you're the mother of it all," Bingaman had told her. Her original plan had been to file a case by February. But the debates among attorneys on how much the case should include had been fierce.

Some of the attorneys felt the FTC had handed them an almost fully developed case on a silver platter. But the commission's case focused on a limited aspect of Microsoft's business practices.

Miller would soon test the viability of a broader case in a moot court session held inside of Justice. Washington attorneys were digging out their old casebooks. Justice was wrestling with the same conundrum that had faced the FTC: to broaden or narrow the scope of their suit. After the regulatory deputy, Bob Litan, spent weeks debating litigation theories with Miller, it was decided that they would test the broader case in their own ranks and that it would be based on the notion of essential facility, a theory of antitrust that had not been visited in more than a decade.

The idea of essential facility had also been at the heart of the federal antitrust suit against AT&T, as well as the private MCI versus AT&T case. Although it was a controversial way to view the software industry, Litan and Miller at first were finding the case record promising. It also would be a way to address Microsoft's licensing practices, which they argued resulted in "exclusive dealing" and a range of illegal "tying" practices.

In addition, while antitrust laws restricted companies from using market power in one industry segment to gain an advantage in another market area, that theory of monopoly leveraging was far more controversial than the essential facility approach. The Supreme Court itself had upheld essential facility as a basis for bringing antitrust action, although during the Reagan years the definition of what constituted an essential facility had been greatly narrowed by the lower courts.

"Of course the government brought no essential facilities cases from the Reagan and Bush years," noted Robert Pitofsky, an antitrust expert who had served on President Clinton's Justice Department transition team and who would later become chairman of the FTC. "And I'm not surprised that a Democratic administration would [attempt to] open it up again." (Pitofsky would later do just that, bringing an essential facilities case against chip giant Intel Corp. in 1998.) Pitofsky and his colleague Michael Sohn, just prior to the FTC's second deadlock on Microsoft, had been hired by Novell to represent its complaints to Justice, replacing Sturge Sobin. They knew there was a well-established, fundamental basis in the law for arguing that when a company controls an essential facility, it has to deal with customers and suppliers on fair and nondiscriminatory terms.

Microsoft's competitors, under subpoena, had provided Justice with evidence that Microsoft indeed controlled a technological bottleneck through which all in the industry had to pass. The company withheld from the industry important technical information that it gave freely to its own applications developers.

In the latest round of subpoenas, the Justice Department sought to show conclusively that Microsoft's dominant DOS and Windows operating systems were essential facilities. As stated by law, proof of essential facility involved a four-part test: control of the facility by a monopolist, a competitor's inability to practically or reasonably duplicate the essential facility, the denial of the use of the facility to a competitor, and the feasibility of providing the facility to the competitor.

One Justice Department attorney argued, "It can be proven that Windows is an essential facility. I think it's something that downstream competitors essentially need to have appropriate access to in order to compete in the applications market."

Lotus' Berg was overjoyed at the thought that Justice might address the discriminatory ways Microsoft provided operating system access to competing applications software vendors. But broadening the case would cause big delays, and Bingaman wanted results fast.

Litan and Miller knew a settlement could be negotiated, but had to be prepared for trial if Gates wouldn't budge. They'd offer Microsoft the opportunity to sign a consent order, heading off a trial. It would be up to a federal judge, in the long run, to determine whether Microsoft had broken the law.

For its part, Microsoft seemed to be putting on a show that it had done nothing wrong. In Bill Gates' e-mail to one member of the press, collected under subpoena by the feds, he responded to the question of whether his company's policy of per processor licensing was anticompetitive this way: "Our [customers] describe [*sic;* Gates probably meant *decide*] the negotiation process and decision process they go through in deciding which volume level and which form of license they choose. A minority choose processor licenses." Gates knew that a handful of manufacturers represented the lion's share of computer shipments worldwide. There were tiny companies all over the planet that licensed small numbers of copies of Microsoft's operating systems. But the largest and most powerful companies were locked into per processor licenses. More than 60 percent, at this point in time.

Gates went on, "Of course when the government first started talking to us we reviewed all of our actions very very carefully. None of the law firms we engaged found anything they disagreed with. We did not change because we had no problem."

If Justice attempted an essential facilities case, it would be groundbreaking. Essential facilities for the most part had involved physical assets like railroad or phone lines, as opposed to an intangible asset like software technology.

Raising this theory as a way of viewing competition in the software industry could also have a dramatic impact on how competitive conduct would be weighed in emerging markets in the future. Although controversial, there had been precedent for success. The courts had upheld a nontangible asset as an essential facility for the purposes of Section II of the Sherman Act.

A 1988 case in the southern district of Florida, *BellSouth Advertising v. Donnelley,* had deemed "information" an essential facility. Donnelley wanted access to the list of phone subscribers in the BellSouth service territory so it could print a competing telephone directory. Donnelley argued that the list constituted an essential facility for antitrust purposes, and BellSouth filed a motion for summary judgment, claiming it did not. The court affirmed the denial of summary judgment, holding that this nonphysical asset could indeed constitute an essential facility. The order was upheld in the Eleventh Circuit Court of Appeals in 1991. This paralleled the type of information industry developers needed from Microsoft about the operating system in order to develop application software.

Meanwhile, during the first half of January, WordPerfect Corp.'s Ad Rietveld had approached Ray Noorda about a possible merger between WordPerfect and Novell.

Unbeknownst to Noorda, he had also stopped in for a visit with Jim Manzi. Rietveld had been entrusted with this fishing expedition by WordPerfect's founders, Alan Ashton and Bruce Bastian.

Rietveld had put on quite a show, but it was nothing like the show Bill Gates was putting on in federal court in Los Angeles.

Poor Bill sat on a hard wooden bench in federal court in Los Angeles on January 27, 1994, at 9:30 A.M. He looked at once vulnerable and defiant, like a naughty schoolboy. But instead of a slingshot, in his lap was a *Fortune* magazine. It rested there, on his knees. He had to keep his knees squeezed awkwardly together to keep its glossy surface from sliding off the dark blue-gray skin of his suit.

Gates looked about impassively.

The room was a mess. Along one grimy wall, cartons of depositions were stacked five high and four deep. Phone and computer cables were wound in a snarl and taped crudely with silver electrical tape that snaked through the center of the courtroom.

Gates was being sued by Stac Electronics for patent infringement. According to Stac president Gary Clow, Microsoft had used Stac's compression technology, called Stacker, in its DoubleSpace compression incorporated in DOS 6. Stac had turned down Microsoft's offer to license the technology because, according to Clow, Microsoft was offering to pay "virtually nothing," only the opportunity to "bask in the Microsoft orb."

Clow testified Microsoft had threatened that if Stac didn't give it the technology, it would do it anyway and put Stac out of business.

Beside Gates in the courtroom sat Bill Neukom, who turned to joke and whisper with him. Every now and again Gates furtively glanced down at that copy of *Fortune,* as if to reassure himself.

Gates now was worth almost $7 billion. He was the second richest man in America, having given up the "richest" spot to his pal Warren Buffett several months earlier. Gates had called Buffett to congratulate him. The fact of Gates' wealth was, however—at Microsoft's request—censored in this courtroom, where the jury trial of *Stac Electronics v. Microsoft* was unfolding. Judge Edward Rafeedie, balding and in his sixties, had agreed that Gates' personal fortune was irrelevant.

The history was laid out. In 1991 Stac began discussions with Microsoft about licensing its data compression technology for a forthcoming release of DOS 6. But when Stac began to address the licensing terms, it became aware that Microsoft expected to get the technology for a fee that hardly made it worth Stac's efforts.

Microsoft threatened that if Stac did not license the technology to Microsoft at the price the industry giant offered, it would put Stac out of business by incorporating data compression into DOS anyway. When Stac bowed out of a relationship with Microsoft in late 1992, Microsoft, as anticipated, incorporated data compression into DOS 6, through an alliance with another party.

Stac filed its lawsuit against Microsoft in January 1993. Microsoft responded with its own lawsuit against Stac, after searching out and buying a sixteen-year-old patent on which to base it.

A little-known aspect of the case focused on Microsoft accusing Stac of stealing trade secrets, undocumented features in the way DOS 6 used compression.

Stac discovered that Microsoft had incorporated third-party data compression in the kernel of the operating system. All computers list device drivers in a file called config.sys., and the operating system loads them from that file. Microsoft's "trade secret" involved having the operating system load the compression device driver before it processed config.sys. Stac, trying to mitigate the damage Microsoft had caused it by infringing on its patent and giving compression away with DOS, reverse-engineered the mechanism that allowed that to happen.

Stac claimed that Microsoft's use of an undocumented programming interface gave Microsoft—as the controller of the operating system—an unfair advantage over third-party utility suppliers. "They can preload their compression product, but we're not allowed to preload ours," Stac explained to federal attorneys later on. This put Microsoft in the position of having to defend its use of undocumented code—a practice it had alleged to the Justice Department did not exist.

The computer industry was buzzing, Washington was buzzing, and armies of Microsoft attorneys were scrambling. While their patent infringement trial proceeded and tiny Stac stood up to the playground bully and his mountain of cash, the Department of Justice was watching closely. Gates was being viewed as a scofflaw who needed reining in.

Indeed, he had become known for his apparent delight in "getting away with things"—getting cops to get his traffic violations dismissed, having two convicted felons handle his finances, repeatedly ripping off the work of tiny companies.

Gates was a trickster, Hermes incarnate. He liked stealing the fire of others, his detractors said. According to his foes, he had no boundaries. He was a predator, said the CEOs of scores of competing software companies: an ill-kempt, socially inept, scrawny, insecure, ruthless Lex Luthor.

On the other hand, Microsoft supporters would say, they were just green with envy.

They were ungrateful wretches whose very jobs had been created by *him*. If it wasn't for *him*, they'd be back in the Stone Age. Hadn't he single-handedly invented the computer software industry? It was *his!* Was it his fault that competitors were naive enough to show him their work? What right did they have to tell him what the rules were!

Oh Bill! Poor Bill! How could it be his fault that, only weeks ago, two of his security guards had illegally banned people from public parks and beaches on the Hawaiian island of Lanai during his New Year's Day wedding? The attorney general's office in Honolulu had launched a criminal investigation. On his wedding day! Fortunately, the Lanai Co. would take most of the heat. A visitor to the island couldn't possibly be expected to know that parks and beaches were public areas.

When his name was called as the first witness, Gates' face dropped. Looking pale, he stiffly rose, stumbled to the judge's bench, and stood awkwardly as the jurors—a group of six and two alternates, none of whom had much more than a high school education—filed in. All in the courtroom stood and waited. The room was musty, and it seemed to take forever for the judge to reach his place.

Neukom now gazed up at Gates, who was about to be raked over the coals, caught in numerous misstatements and contradictions by Stac's attorney Morgan Chu, a small dynamo of a man with jet black hair and a gentle but firm manner.

The jury was about to partake of the pleasures of e-mail from Bill. (This was a far cry from the warm and fuzzy Bill portrayed in his e-mail to *The New Yorker*!)

In an e-mail message dated March 6, 1992, from Gates to Brad Silverberg (with copies to Paul Maritz, senior vice president of the Systems Division, and Mac MacCauley, another Microsoft employee), Gates said, "I want QEMM functionality and Stacker functionality in order for it [DOS 6] to be exciting." (QEMM was technology developed by a competitor. He said that one reason he wanted Stacker functionality in Microsoft DOS was to "match the garbage that DR-DOS does."

Compression was a feature that was built into DR-DOS, but not available in MS-DOS. Gates was determined to add this to his forthcoming DOS 6.0 so that, among other things, he could raise prices to computer makers for the operating system.

The e-mail went on, "I don't know how your current Astro [a Microsoft code name for DOS 6] specification measures up to this. Maybe we should brainstorm some. Of course, since a lot of this is buying stuff, it is hard to know what is cheap but we should have PLN." (PLN meant plan, Gates explained.)

Essentially, Gates was saying that he needed to make sure the features of MS-DOS 6 could match what his competitors offered. He knew that the only way he could do this was to "buy," or in this case, copy, the technology from others. He had to get it "cheap" because he was intent on increasing his prices to computer makers while reaping a hefty profit from the royalty stream that would result.

Eventually, Stac would win its case, getting a jury award of $120.0 million in damages. Stac was one of the few small companies to have filed a patent on the technology it owned, and so was able to win a case against Microsoft. Stac was clearly the winner, although the jury also awarded Microsoft $13.6 million for its counterclaim concerning Stac's reverse engineering. Reverse engineering had long been a legitimate practice in the industry, but the jury granted Microsoft this small condolence anyway. The judge had issued a worldwide recall of DOS 6.

Sam Miller and Bob Litan had been fascinated by the trial between Microsoft and Stac Electronics. It might just shed the light the Justice Department needed to illustrate Microsoft's predation in the software marketplace. On the other hand, some might say it revealed nothing but the naïveté of a smaller company attempting to hold its ground when faced with the alleged bullying tactics of Microsoft. Justice Department attorneys considered that Microsoft may have put its foot in its mouth with the portion of the lawsuit alleging that Stac had misappropriated trade secrets.

Miller and Litan were watching. In the end, however, the issues were overly complex. The Justice attorneys determined that it would be too difficult to monitor Gates' predatory programming practices. Such situations, for the time being, could be remedied only by those who had the guts and the resources to bring private lawsuits.

Meanwhile, the staff was preparing for this scenario: Litan would call Bill Neukom and Bill Gates into his office and inform them that the division was preparing to sue. They'd be offered a consent order. If they refused to sign, within three weeks the Department of Justice would file a lawsuit in federal court. The case could take up to a year to get on the docket. If a consent agreement was reached, some negotiation on its terms would be expected. However, attorneys for Microsoft's competitors were perusing the details of the Tunney Act, which they hoped would ensure that the results would not be merely symbolic.

The Tunney Act, written by Senator John V. Tunney, set the procedure for public interest review of a proposed consent decree. It came about at a time when it was suspected that political payoffs were being made to get the Justice Department off companies' backs with the issuance of meaningless consent decrees. Because of the act, Justice must now file consent decrees accompanied by impact statements in federal court.

Third parties are free to file comments on a proposed consent decree. And all Microsoft's competitors were expected to barrage the court with their concerns.

Final approval of a decree could take months. Lawyers knew that even if Justice was able to get a consent decree signed by, say, May, it could be well into the summer before it took effect. It is noteworthy that no decrees have been dismissed as a result of the Tunney Act. But decrees have been rewritten after public input.

Washington antitrust pundits, as of late January, were betting that Microsoft would sign a consent order. "Gates would have to be nuts if he didn't," Rich Rosen said to his colleagues.

Bingaman's detractors believed that antitrust law was obsolete, that high-technology markets move too rapidly to be regulated. But Bingaman and her deputies had faith that the tools of antitrust, properly applied, are appropriate to analyzing high-tech markets.

Rich Gilbert pointed out antitrust tools are constantly being modernized and analytical approaches constantly being updated. "It's the same field of application. You know telephones are still telephones, there's just a heck of a lot more technology behind them," he said.

In response to those who want government to get out of the way and let markets take care of themselves, Gilbert argued, "I don't think that's really going to serve the economy. . . . Concentration can be a risk for innovations in some areas, concentration can be necessary for innovation in other areas. It's obviously our responsibility . . . to make sure we are familiar with both the facts and the economic issues, as well as the law, to make sure we reach the right decision on a case-by-case basis."

12

MAGNIFICENT OBSESSION

While the Justice Department's case was being painstakingly shepherded forward, the market was about to shift enormously. It was the age-old problem: markets move fast, law enforcement is slow, especially when it comes to antitrust. By the spring of 1994, two of Gates' competitors—WordPerfect and Borland—were ready to give up the ghost. A megadeal, with Novell subsuming the assets of both companies, was catalyzed by the notion that to play against Microsoft in the future, a company had to have its fingers in every pot. The applications software market was in the late stages of succumbing to Bill Gates.

D'Artagnan was holding forth at the Manhattan Club before a gathering of telecommunications executives in the heart of the Big Apple. It was now March 1994. Beside him sat his old college roommate, Justice Department Section Chief Rich Rosen, who was now as embroiled in Microsoft as his friend had been back at the FTC.

"Antitrust isn't everything. It's a pimple on the face of the economy," D'Artagnan said.

"I'd say it was more like a beauty mark," corrected Rosen. A burst of laughter rose from the group.

Economic forces—and markets themselves—seemed to be as uncontrollable as hurricanes; their courses often could not be plotted until after they'd unleashed their unpredictable impact on the landscape. By comparison, antitrust regulation was like a little blip on the rader screen. That had been D'Artagnan's point with the pimple analogy. Indeed, D'Artagnan had laughed when Rosen told him of the dartboard that hung in a Justice Department staff office, with Bill Gates' face in the center.

Now here sat two shepherds of the most controversial antitrust case since the breakup of AT&T. The market had already left them and their colleagues in the dust on more than one front. The telecommunications arena was turning out to be more fascinating than the computer industry. Everyone was getting a bit bored with figuring out the bits and bytes of Bill Gates. Gates himself had partnered with McCaw Cellular and would form Teledesic with Craig McCaw, hoping to have a piece of the satellite broadcast infrastructure of the future. There was a recognition by both the telecommunications companies and computer software companies that content, coupled with infrastructure, was king.

Convergence was the buzzword for mid-1994: computer companies, Hollywood content providers, phone companies, and media magnates were all mixing it up. The information age would see its true potential only when consumers could receive information in an entertaining way wherever they pleased.

Now, at the Manhattan Club, the telecommunications audience seemed to like this outspoken pair. Both Rosen and D'Artagnan had seen the law evolve during their long tenures with the government. The Federal Communications Commission was now wrestling with antitrust, trying to determine how to set boundaries between local and national competition as well as overlapping markets. What was more, new airwaves for the small computers and communications devices of the future were about to be auctioned off.

At Justice, staff attorneys were, as usual, still wrestling with the past. It was always that way. They were chagrined at the fact that Sam Miller and Bob Litan were still debating litigation strategies. There was so much evidence in the files.

D'Artagnan, meanwhile, had started a new, high-powered job at Kevin Arquit's firm, Rogers & Wells, making about ten times as much as he had as a civil servant. Yet he was demoralized. It rubbed him the wrong way to be on the side of the fat cats, which was where he sometimes had to be these days.

While Rosen and D'Artagnan debated in New York over the role of antitrust, across the country the computer industry was experiencing yet another tremor. A deal was being put in motion that would vastly change the competitive landscape.

In early March 1994, Josh Green was about to make history, yet all he could think about was getting home to have dinner with his wife and kids.

A year earlier, Green, an attorney with the Palo Alto, California, law firm of Brobeck, Phleger & Harrison, had been hired to represent the investment banker Morgan Stanley for the proposed initial public offering of WordPerfect Corp. In June 1993 hours before Green was planning to send the filing off to the SEC, the deal had been scrapped.

During work on the 1993 IPO, Green had gotten to know WordPerfect's management team quite well and had hit it off with Duff Thompson, executive vice president and general counsel, and the CFO, Dan Campbell. The IPO had been driven by the desire to obtain liquidity for WordPerfect stockholders. But the outcomes of a number of significant operational events remained unclear. For one, DOS 6 was just beginning to ship, and its degree of success was still unknown. WordPerfect Office 4.0 had only recently been launched, and market reaction was still uncertain. And WordPerfect 6.0 for Windows was scheduled to be released in October 1993.

The applications software market was also moving quickly, and WordPerfect, aware that it needed a suite offering, had made a pact with Borland to bundle the company's spreadsheet software with the WordPerfect word processor. "That plus living under the microscope of being a public company make things more complicated. Why put ourselves under that microscope?" Thompson had asked. IPOs were inherently risky; there was no sense doing this at a time when many things remained up in the air.

Now, in the spring of 1994, on a golf course in Phoenix, Thompson and Campbell had decided that Josh Green was their man.

The two had discussed the problem of using the law firm Wilson, Sonsini in the event of a potential transaction with Novell. Word-Perfect was in "play" to say the least, and it seemed to be involved in a game of musical chairs with two different partners. Thompson and Campbell were feeling increasingly uncomfortable with the thought of having Larry Sonsini—who served on both the WordPerfect and Novell boards—as well as being counsel to Novell—involved in any aspect of WordPerfect's strategizing.

"Larry shouldn't be involved," Thompson said, "regardless of whether we do a deal with Novell or Lotus."

On this day Green had watched as a whopper of a merger he'd been working on crashed and burned. A shame, but he was relieved to be done with it and looked forward to a little relaxation. Then, at 6:30 P.M., as he was heading for the door, his phone rang.

"Josh, you're never going to believe what I'm about to tell you," said Duff Thompson. Oh no, thought Green, there goes dinner. For the following two hours, Thompson related a serpentine tale of what had happened to his company since the previous June. The most recent events were juicy enough to make Green almost forget his dinner craving.

It was pretty much nonstop from then on: Green's family life went down the tubes again. But for the software industry this would be the deal of the decade. Or so he thought.

On March 16, 1994, a brushfire was raging in Bill Gates' office.

"Connie, I just can't believe how fucking stupid you are!" Gates ripped off his microphone and stormed out of the room, taking refuge in a small anteroom adjacent to it. He would not emerge.

Gates had been embroiled in an interview with the CBS television news star Connie Chung. *Eye to Eye* had turned into fist to fist. Chung had been questioning the CEO about Microsoft's performance during the recent Stac Electronics patent infringement trial. It was a touchy subject for Gates, who'd gone through a grilling with BBC television earlier that day.

Gates began hurling insults at Chung, seemingly offended by her line of questioning. Later, TV viewers would think he had been touched off by her pronunciation of DOS as "dose." It was not apparent that the tape had been edited to get rid of Gates' foulmouthed fit. The producers were thrilled with what they had on tape, and Chung had advised them to keep it quiet. She didn't want higher-ups, like the head of CBS, who was friends with Gates, to censor the broadcast.

Now Chung waited outside the anteroom where Gates seemed to have locked himself in. She had hung her coat in the room and couldn't leave until the enraged billionaire emerged.

Gates was under the gun. The press was restless, anticipating new developments with the Justice Department's antitrust investigation, and the recent Stac ruling had given Microsoft an ill-timed black eye, forcing the company to pull its best-selling MS-DOS 6 off the shelves to remove the infringing code.

But, all this adversity wasn't making Gates gun-shy. He'd just been on a whirlwind world tour, giving speeches about the leadership role Microsoft expected to play on the information superhighway. In Amsterdam, he virtually declared war on WordPerfect, which was far ahead of Microsoft's Word program in sales in the Netherlands. Gates would offer a Windows for Workgroups/Microsoft Word bundle in Amsterdam with steeply reduced prices, prompting a WordPerfect antitrust complaint to the EC in March.

Meanwhile, Lotus, WordPerfect, Borland, and Novell were not waiting around for the Justice Department to solve their competitive problems.

Jim Manzi, Philippe Kahn, Ray Noorda, and Alan Ashton and his gang were scrambling toward a megadeal motivated by the inevitable: Gates had leveraged into their markets and was stealing market share faster than anyone could measure. On the same afternoon that Bill Gates was having his tantrum with Connie Chung, back in Utah, Alan Ashton's cabin was being turned into the birthing room for a behemoth corporation aimed squarely at Microsoft's empire.

Manzi, Kahn, and Ashton had made their fortunes in applications software—spreadsheets, word processing, databases—that had fueled an explosion in the use of personal computers in businesses and in homes.

Gates had moved from operating systems onto their turf with Microsoft Office, a package that integrated all of what they offered. Lotus, Borland, and WordPerfect offered application "suites"—as these integrated products became known—as well, but believed Gates had an advantage in his control of the underlying operating system. His control of DOS and Windows allowed him to market everything in a bundle to computer makers, offering them price cuts on the operating system in exchange for also preloading Microsoft Office and other products. His competitors also believed he was better able to tailor his applications software to the underlying operating system because he controlled it and disclosed only select technical information about it to his competitors—leaving them in a disadvantaged position.

In combination, the companies might pool their resources to face the mammoth software leader head on. Any company that wanted to compete against Microsoft would have to be broadly diversified, they were realizing.

It was time to go.

Ray Noorda stood tall and pitched one last grand jab at his adversary. It was all going so quickly, more quickly than he had imagined. On March 16, 1994, an era was about to come to a close—for the industry Noorda was leaving and for himself.

At 9:00 A.M. on this day, Noorda found himself in Alan Ashton's "cabin," nestled on a peak of the Rockies. Surrounding him was a caucus of some thirty power brokers—a collection of CEOs, investment bankers, attorneys, shareholders, and corporate officers representing WordPerfect and Novell. The secret meeting here would ensure that the license plates of the cars sitting just outside would not give rise to suspicion. If the grouping had been seen in a WordPerfect or Novell parking lot, the cat would have been let out of the bag, it was thought.

All Noorda knew was that there was a vast, omnipresent enemy out there, a formidable foe. Leviathan. (Perhaps one of his Netherlander forebears had literally encountered one out in the North Sea a century ago. But now in place of the North Sea was this strangely

159

threshing marketplace. It would require the best of navigators, and the toughest of warriors.) This might be a last chance at summoning a competitive force that could truly make a difference.

Ashton aptly referred to the room in which they congregated as the Great Room. From its forty-foot-high rafters, a chandelier thirty feet in diameter hung over their heads—like the $1.4 billion merger deal that now dangled before them.

When informed of the meeting site, the attorneys and investment bankers involved wondered how thirty people would fit in a cabin. But clearly this was no ordinary cabin. This was a getaway built on the legacy of riches spawned by the early days of the software industry.

Ashton, cofounder of WordPerfect and co-owner of the still-private company, like his partner Bruce Bastian, had become a near billionaire since, two decades earlier, his company had offered one of the earliest word-processing programs. The software industry perhaps would never again see such meteoric success—that had also been enjoyed by Lotus, Microsoft, and Borland.

The world had changed a lot since those days. Noorda had taken a circuitous route to this meeting place. And he still had his doubts about bringing Novell—the leader in network operating systems—into the uncharted territory of the applications software business.

Yet here he sat, within shouting distance of WordPerfect's headquarters, literally on a precipice. On the Orem landscape, the 1,500-foot peak rose like a sudden thought. That was what the notion of this deal had first been to Noorda: a sudden and irrational thought.

When Ashton had approached him about a merger the previous fall, Noorda had dismissed the idea. "We're in the networking business," he'd said. Besides, Noorda at the time was engaged in serious talks with IBM about converging their networking businesses. There were thoughts of Big Blue spinning off a networking company and combining with Novell. But the IBM discussions had gone nowhere, and Noorda had finally been convinced by his colleagues to look at the market in a new way: the network was, after all, becoming the vehicle for delivery of groupware and applications suites. Here was an opportunity for him to use Gates' strategy: leverage his dominance in networking software, to deliver applications, a market he'd never participated in.

He was in no mood, however, for a contest with Lotus chief executive Jim Manzi, who had been aggressively courting WordPerfect for weeks. Unbeknownst to Noorda, Manzi and his corporate officers had only the day before chartered a Lear jet to Salt Lake City to give a multimedia presentation to WordPerfect portraying what life with Lotus would be like.

An all-out battle between Lotus and Novell for the number-two position in the desktop software industry was under way. WordPerfect had reasons of its own to hook up with either of these two companies. It could not compete with Microsoft's price cutting and bundling of application software in suites. It could no longer go it alone: not with Microsoft's operating system leverage, not with the suite wars driving prices to impossibly low levels. It was impossible to compete in the suite market without a spreadsheet offering of its own. A marriage with Lotus was enticing. (An earlier partnership with Borland to bundle the QuattroPro spreadsheet with WordPerfect's software hadn't solved the problem of more closely integrating and developing the two products—essential if the companies were going to keep up with Microsoft's own tightly integrated applications.)

Talks between WordPerfect and Lotus had been going on at a fairly rapid clip since the newly named WordPerfect chief executive, Ad Rietveld, had met with Jim Manzi during a press tour in Boston in January. Ashton had entrusted Rietveld to broach the subject with Manzi during that trip.

On January 21, Ashton also had a private meeting with Noorda. Noorda listened but was still dragging his heels. "We'd prefer to do business with you," Ashton said. Noorda laughed to himself. "I'll bet he says that to everyone," he told one of his colleagues. As it turned out, Ashton had meant it.

This was it. Noorda and Ashton, with their respective teams of attorneys, financial advisers, corporate officers, and shareholders

161

were here in the Great Room to see if a deal could be put together. Among those present were Ashton and Bruce Bastian, principal owners of WordPerfect; WordPerfect President Ad Rietveld, CFO Dan Campbell, Chief Counsel Duff Thompson, and Chief Technology Officer David Moon; Novell Chief Counsel David Bradford and Novell board member and counsel Larry Sonsini; and the Morgan Stanley investment banker Frank Quattrone.

It had been a long journey to this point. On June 19, Noorda would be seventy. Although Novell had announced to the world that he would remain at its helm even after a new CEO and president took control, Noorda hoped that by his birthday he could step down. If all went well, this day's deal would also be finalized by the time he blew out his seventy candles. Last week he had removed most of the contents of his desk at Novell.

The seeds planted in the fall of 1993 had begun to sprout by January 1994, and by March they were blooming in wildly unexpected ways.

Ashton and Bastian wanted to set WordPerfect free. They had become increasingly remote from the business and wanted to move on with their lives. At the same time, they wanted the fruits of their labors to be passed on to the industry in the most viable way. Hours before the IPO was to be filed the previous spring, Bastian, Ashton, and the company's executive officers had a revelation: independence was not necessarily the best way to exploit the technology and assets they had created. "If WordPerfect is really going to take on this Microsoft giant, we need to be hooked up with somebody with more resources," the thinking went, according to an insider present at the time.

By January 1, WordPerfect was actively seeking a merger partner. Ironically, Ashton's dream was for a Novell-WordPerfect-Lotus combination that would really knock Bill Gates off his feet. He would soon be wedged between Novell and Lotus, when an alliance with both was deemed impossible.

Ironically, Ray Noorda had suggested such an alliance with his "360" idea way back in 1990, after he discovered Gates' intentions in the network and applications markets. In the process of those talks, Lotus' Frank King had suggested that Lotus and Novell merge instead. As it turned out, that merger attempt failed because of vast differences in Manzi's and Noorda's management styles and arguments about control of the company. But it made WordPerfect want to keep its distance.

On March 4, 1994, Novell decided to consider its own merger discussions with WordPerfect. After being given a demonstration of WordPerfect Office, and inspired by the vision of the software engineer John Edwards and Chief Counsel Bradford, who were both enthusiastic about the potential for a Novell-WordPerfect combination, Noorda had finally given his "thumbs up."

That day a due diligence meeting was held between Novell and WordPerfect, and the meetings continued through March 9, when Duff Thompson and David Bradford drew up a formal letter of intent. Larry Sonsini had resigned from the WordPerfect board a couple of days earlier to avoid a conflict of interest.

Earlier March 9, in a meeting including Noorda, Bastian (present via conference call from Australia), Rietveld, Bradford, Thompson, and Ashton, all had agreed that a combination of the two companies would not make sense without a Windows spreadsheet product. Both companies then agreed to explore acquiring Borland's QuattroPro business.

WordPerfect made it clear that it would consider an acquisition by Novell *only* if QuattroPro was also acquired. "The WordPerfect guys felt that if you missed the next eighteen to twenty-four months being in the suite marketplace without a decent offering, you were never going to make it," Green explained to Novell. "You needed that as a bridge over the chasm, to get to the next level of applications software focused on productivity and groupware." WordPerfect paired with the Lotus 1-2-3 spreadsheet would have made a full suite of leading applications possible.

A Novell combination, however, had other attractions, not the least of which was the company's market strength and control of the leading network operating system. WordPerfect had not mastered selling in the market for office suites, and its old model for selling individual stand-alone software packages was not effective for the corporate marketplace. Novell had a strong presence in corporations, and a vast and effective reseller channel.

A deal, however, hinged on the ability to also acquire QuattroPro.

Philippe Kahn knew none of this. And Novell and WordPerfect were initiating acquisition discussions with Borland before they knew for certain that they had a deal with each other. That the deal hinged on the ability to acquire QuattroPro was a critical secret that would have given Kahn much leverage in his negotiations.

The first weekend of marathon meetings with Borland had begun the morning of Friday, March 11. A team of Novell and WordPerfect executives and their attorneys flew Novell's corporate jet to Borland's Scotts Valley, California, offices. Kahn and his clan were told that Novell was present because it would be involved in the financing of a broader deal between WordPerfect and Novell.

Duff Thompson, David Bradford, Noorda's assistant Ty Mattingly, Noorda, and Ad Rietveld who Kahn liked to describe as a "Dutch teddy bear," had entered the meeting room. There they found an entire welcoming committee—attorneys, investment bankers, marketing types, and Kahn himself. Among the delegation were the financial adviser Michael Price of Lazard Freres, the legal counsel Peter Astiz of Baker & McKenzie, and Chief Counsel Bob Kohn. The lineup suggested that Borland believed it was about to be acquired.

"Philippe is ready to be thrown on his knees and carried off into the sunset," said one attorney to another. This didn't surprise some Novell executives at all. Kahn had been courting Noorda for some time.

However, a discussion about the acquisition of QuattroPro ensued instead. Observers said they were amazed at how certain executives could speak all around an issue without stating what was on Kahn's mind: a buyout of the company, lock, stock, and barrel. Kahn was "waiting for someone to pop the question," said one executive present. But as the hours wore on, it was clear that Noorda was not going to rise to that bait.

By Saturday, the meeting had moved to the Palo Alto offices of

Brobeck, Phleger, legal counsel to WordPerfect. Separately, the Brobeck attorneys Josh Green, Steve Tonsfeldt, and Tom Villeneuve, and WordPerfect's Thompson and Campbell, discussed strategy related to both the QuattroPro acquisition and the simultaneous bids of Lotus and Novell. Finally, Villeneuve generated a purchase agreement, which was sent to Borland at about 5:00.

At 9:00 that evening, the Borland gang arrived at Brobeck to meet with WordPerfect, which was taking the lead with the Borland talks. The negotiations continued until at about 1:00 A.M., when WordPerfect attorneys sent the group packing. The Borland attorneys had wanted to continue negotiating through the night. Behind the scenes, Novell was kept informed of the progress of the negotiations.

From about 8:00 A.M. until about 1:00 P.M., on Sunday, Borland and WordPerfect continued their talks. Things were getting quite arduous, and there were wide gaps on major issues—not least the purchase price, inventory matters, future access to Borland tools, and source code. The gaps were still widening when WordPerfect abruptly ended the talks.

The Borland crew was not happy. The two camps parted very far apart in their thinking.

When the deflated Borlanders left the Brobeck offices, Duff Thompson and Josh Green confronted what faced them next: Lotus' Jim Manzi had requested a meeting in Salt Lake City the following Tuesday. He had chartered a Lear jet for himself and his top executives to make the journey.

Little did Kahn know the extent to which things were in flux. To put it mildly, WordPerfect was in play.

Late on the evening of March 13, Thompson and Campbell flew back to Utah, still unsure of the direction they were headed. By Monday, March 14, everything was relatively quiet, but for the twenty to thirty phone calls between Brobeck attorneys and WordPerfect. All were preparing for the Lotus powwow.

On Tuesday morning, Josh Green, Alan Ashton, Bruce Bastian and his wife, Melanie, and the company's five executive officers convened at WordPerfect's Orem offices for a briefing on the Borland negotiations and to strategize about the meeting with Lotus. A caravan of cars then departed for the noon meeting with Jim Manzi in Salt Lake. Manzi had arrived with his chief counsel Tom Lemberg and about a half dozen of his top executives.

The Hotel Utah, an ornate 1920s hotel that had been purchased by the Mormon Church, had been converted to the Joseph Smith Conference Center. It would be the site of an impressive show.

When the presentation was over, Manzi wanted an answer. It was clear that Lotus would be willing to pay a minimum of $900 million. No "formal" offer was made, because a number of major antitrust issues needed to be resolved before the companies could be combined. Both companies were skeptical that the government would approve the merger without Lotus scaling down its business somewhat, because of an overlap with WordPerfect products. Lotus would have to sell off AmiPro, the number-three word-processing program in the industry, and was prepared to do so if WordPerfect gave its thumbs-up on the larger deal.

Ashton and Manzi were starry-eyed about a suite combining Lotus 1-2-3 and WordPerfect. Yet there were longer-term issues at stake, and they would not be fully evaluated until the following day.

The WordPerfect contingent went off in a caucus. The assumption was that the AmiPro problem "would be taken care of" by Lotus. But Lotus would have to seek a buyer for the product without letting on that it was engaged in a potential merger agreement with WordPerfect. If that was known, Manzi would get "zilch" for the word processor.

When the caucus broke up, however, Manzi was told, "We can't give you an answer." The Lotus CEO was not pleased.

Ashton told Manzi, "We'll be in touch." Manzi and crew headed back to the Lear jet, leaving Lotus' chief counsel, Tom Lemberg, behind in case anyone needed hand holding.

The WordPerfect delegation drove back to Orem that night to prepare for the meeting with Novell that would commence at 9:00 A.M. the following morning. They discussed what they needed to hear. Basically, Novell had to prove that entering the applications business—in which it had no experience—would result in a strategic powerhouse with long-term viability in the marketplace. WordPerfect needed to hear how the two cultures would mesh, what would happen to its employees, and whether it would still have the creative freedom in product development that it had as an independent company. It needed to hear why it should overlook the immediate success it could have in the suite marketplace through an alliance with Lotus in favor of a longer-term view. And this had to be done with no mention of Lotus or its offering. WordPerfect had signed a nondisclosure agreement with Lotus and swore to keep their talks secret.

It was approaching noon on March 16. Elbow to elbow in the Great Room, the leaders of Novell and WordPerfect weighed the impact of their proposed marriage.

In this proximity, it was all the more clear that Alan Ashton and Ray Noorda were an unlikely pair. Company officers noted that the world seemed to have this stereotype that Mormons were all alike, that they all got along and stuck together with religious fervor. In fact, Noorda and Ashton were about as different as two people could get. Noorda's style was the "tough guy," whereas Ashton was all softness and compassion.

Now Novell's John Edwards was holding forth, making his pitch about his company's vision for a combined applications-networking business: "The network will become the delivery vehicle to corporations and customers." At that early date, no one knew that the vision of such a network would eventually be fulfilled by the Internet, a pipeline that would not be controlled by a single company—unless Bill Gates succeeded in leveraging his power there. The idea was powerful. At the time, Novell was adding more than a million new "seats" of Netware a month worldwide. The network would be a mechanism for delivery of suites and a future Novell-WordPerfect groupware line of products. This would arguably be Novell's most important sales pitch of the decade. The power structure of the industry was at stake.

Noorda glanced about the room. There was what's-his-name: the financial adviser Frank Quattrone from Morgan Stanley. Noorda's mind was as sharp as a knife, but his short-term memory was failing him. He was at a loss, at moments, to come up with the names of his closest advisers, now surrounding him.

Morgan Stanley's Quattrone, in his presentations this day, would make "lemonade of lemons," as one executive put it. Lotus' pricing was overinflated, Quattrone would say. "It's trading at eighty times the value of next year's earnings." With Novell, however, there was much upside. The company had been languishing and had lots of room for growth. Quattrone was great at this stuff—highlighting a company's strengths—noted some attorneys present.

Bastian, unlike his counterpart Ashton, was a tough guy, Noorda thought, as Bastian played devil's advocate with each of Novell's points.

"What makes you think you can fight in the trenches of the applications market, where the bullets will be flying over your heads? You've got your nicely pressed suits on, and have been comfortably successful in networking. But there's a war going on in our market. Are you willing to get yourselves dirty in an all-out battle?" Bastian liked to stir the pot.

Indeed, some recalled Bastian's confrontation with Noorda earlier that morning. In a private meeting in a back bedroom with Noorda, Sonsini, and Ashton, he'd challenged Noorda. "You're leaving anyway in June, Ray," Bastian had said. Noorda had growled back with his tough-guy act: "I'm not going anywhere anytime soon."

Now Edwards continued. WordPerfect knew about selling software to a single user out of a box. The world didn't work that way anymore.

Noorda listened. He'd only recently been sold on the idea of entering the applications business himself. The discussion was getting heated. At moments like this, time tended to hold still.

Noorda found himself reflecting back rather often these days. The mirror of the present brought up a thousand other vivid images. At his age, life was rich, a palimpsest whose text had been engraved and reengraved over its surfaces, refining and retelling itself. This moment was, oddly, like the one a couple of years back when he had taken that spill. Noorda had found himself tumbling headfirst over the handlebars of his bicycle. On the way to the ground, it occurred to him that he was not as young as he once was. The silly pup had gotten spooked and run in front of the bike, making a human projectile of his master.

Amazingly, Noorda had ended up with only some cracked ribs. But he'd had to give up his running and other activities for a while. And he'd wake in the middle of the night nauseated, get up, and pass out. The bike accident led to the discovery that his heart rate had been maintained by the level of exercise he'd been accustomed to. He'd be in for a pacemaker operation soon thereafter.

That spill seemed to mark a turning point. Novell was facing a turning point as well. Now Noorda and David Bradford were reviewing the WordPerfect-Novell merger agreement and evaluating its risks. Between the lines of the document lurked the specter of the Leviathan. "The market for operating systems software, including network operating systems and client operating systems, has become increasingly problematic due to Microsoft's growing dominance in all sectors of the software business." The men continued their discussion. Everything could be up for grabs if Microsoft kept on its current course.

While the industry dallied, dawdled, and dozed, Microsoft was getting fatter and more powerful. "We're all a bunch of sissies. We need to stand up to him," Noorda would say time and time again of Microsoft chairman Bill Gates. Noorda had a magnificent obsession, yet he was not without a sense of humor about it all.

In the filings to the SEC, they would explain to federal regulators the rationale as well the risks of the acquisition of WordPerfect and the purchase of Borland's QuattroPro. "Microsoft is increasingly dominant . . . and may enjoy competitive advantages with respect to the development and sale of application programs . . . as a result of access to information not documented or shared with independent vendors . . . in a timely manner."

The strategic concerns were further spelled out, "Microsoft may have a significant competitive advantage in preloading products because of its control of the DOS and MS Windows operating environments."

Noorda could see his target coming up as clear as day. Microsoft—an enormous, sharp-toothed Leviathan, with the pathetic face of a man young enough to be his son—had taunted Ray Noorda one too many times.

Sunlight was streaming into the windows of the Great Room as Noorda listened to the voices around him. His chief counsel Bradford was at his most inspired, and board member Larry Sonsini was expressing caution about the potential difficulty of accomplishing the QuattroPro piece of the deal, with everything else going on.

Just before lunch an intense debate had broken out about the direction of the software industry. For how long would software suites be important in the marketplace? Where was groupware headed? How could WordPerfect help fill out Novell's knowledge of the applications software market? How might Novell help WordPerfect reach corporate customers? WordPerfect had been selling its Office groupware for about nine months, but was still uncertain about the most effective distribution. The conversation would regularly come around to Microsoft and its dominant role in the industry, and how Novell and WordPerfect might combine their resources to face the software giant head-on.

The WordPerfect delegates began to recognize that while a Lotus-WordPerfect combination would result in a powerful suite offering, longer-term strategic issues came down to operating systems. Ultimately, any company that wanted to play against Microsoft would have to have its fingers in every pot: applications, user interfaces, client-server software, and network communications. WordPerfect allied with Novell would be in a stronger position to compete with Microsoft in the long term.

WordPerfect was concerned about how the company would be run, and Novell proposed that it be a separate division, with Rietveld reporting directly to the soon-to-be announced CEO of Novell, Hewlett-Packard's Bob Frankenberg. With Lotus, WordPerfect would be joining an organization that had its own strong ideas about applications development. With Novell, WordPerfect would be calling most of the shots in terms of applications development. The WP people would be relied upon as the experts.

By about 3:00 that afternoon, the discussions were winding down. Josh Green pulled aside Larry Sonsini, Frank Quattrone, and David Bradford. "We at WordPerfect are in decision-making mode," he said. "We haven't talked about terms, and this is not intended to be an auction. All I can say is, we're not going to tell you, 'That's not good enough.' "

Bradford, Sonsini, and Quattrone listened. "Don't hold back," Green went on. "Now is the time to put your best deal on the table. I can't tell you about anything that's happened with Lotus. But we're not going to come back and ask for more. When you leave, we're going to make a decision."

The trio disappeared for some ninety minutes, to caucus with Noorda and the rest. When they returned, they presented WordPerfect's Thompson, Ashton, and Bastian with an offer. Novell was willing to pay $1.4 billion in a nondilutive stock offering. Ad Rietveld would report directly to CEO Frankenberg, and WordPerfect would be run as a separate division, with a measure of autonomy. The sum was about two times WordPerfect's sales, which some believed to be a fair offer. Numerous Wall Street analysts would later view the amount as excessive.

After departing the Great Room at about 5:30, Noorda and the Novell delegation split up to drive back to Provo or take the corporate jet back to California. Now all they could do was wait. Nine key members of the WordPerfect contingent stayed on at Ashton's cabin to strategize.

The group settled in. Green created a list of seven priorities by which a deal with Novell versus Lotus would be weighed: (1) the ability to remain "creators"; (2) the fate of WP employees; (3) the ability to have a strong suite offering with a Windows spreadsheet presence; (4) long-term viability; (5) the ability to retain a presence in Utah; (6) price; and (7) the fate of the executive officers.

The group debated for about two hours.

Their decision had to be made that evening, so it was determined that a secret ballot would be taken. Seven individuals would vote: the shareholders Bastian and Ashton, and each corporate officer. Finally the group broke up, and each individual went into a separate corner to meditate on his vote.

The decision was unanimous. All had voted for a merger with Novell, on the condition that QuattroPro be acquired from Borland.

Josh Green called Larry Sonsini with the news at about 9:30 P.M. Thompson called Bradford, and Rietveld called Noorda. Lotus' Tom Lemberg, who had been hanging out in a Salt Lake City hotel room since the previous day, got the news from Thompson, and Rietveld called Jim Manzi back in Cambridge.

Manzi was not amused. Now he would be battling not just one behemoth in his applications market but two: Microsoft and Novell. Bill Gates would surely write him off as dead meat.

On Thursday, March 17, a marathon began. WordPerfect, Novell, and Borland were in a sprint to come to agreement on the nitty-gritty terms of their alliance. Everything had to be final in time to make a public announcement before the stock market closed on Monday, March 21.

Although the previous weekend with Borland had been intense, no progress had been made. Insiders said that Kahn was holding out for a very high price, in excess of $200 million for the Quattro-Pro business alone, never mind the licensing of the Paradox database and other technology. WordPerfect was asking for sell-through data on QuattroPro—including predicted and existing sales— which, although Borland is a public company, was not broken out publicly in its numbers.

There were battles about the escrow amounts, money that should be set aside for outstanding claims against the business. Borland's attorneys, Bob Kohn and Peter Astiz, were perceived to be playing

Jim Cannavino, head of IBM's PC division at the time the FTC began its investigation, found that his room was bugged just prior to a critical strategy meeting with Microsoft. To blow off steam, Cannavino was known to hit the road on his Harley.
Photos by Laura Wilson

FTC attorney Steve Newborn, known to his pals as D'Artagnan, was instrumental in the Microsoft probe being wrested away from the FTC by the Justice Department, a development that antitrust pundits categorized as being as unlikely as an asteroid hitting the earth.

Kevin Arquit, head of the FTC's bureau of competition, at one of his FTC press conferences. Arquit was responsible for overseeing the FTC's case against Microsoft. Later, when he left for the private sector and the law firm of Rogers & Wells, he served as outside counsel to Sun Microsystems, a competitor of Gates'.

Bill Gates and Stefanie Reichel at Michael Caine's London restaurant
during the time Microsoft offered inducements to get Vobis chief Theo Lieven
to promise that he'd never ship another copy of a rival product.

Andrew Berg, D.C. counsel to Lotus
Development Corp. at the law firm
of Akin Gump, spent years
documenting for the FTC allegations
of Microsoft's anticompetitive acts in
the applications software market.
In its 1994 settlement, the Justice
department failed to address these
concerns, but would finally return to
them in 1998. Berg had attended
Harvard at the same time as Gates.
Photo by Michael Schumann

ABOVE: Robert Litan, deputy assistant attorney general at the Justice Department, along with antitrust chief Anne Bingaman, threatened Microsoft with a major antitrust lawsuit in 1994 that was settled after drawn-out wrangling sessions with Gates and Neukom. The settlement put an end to per-processor licensing, but left most of Microsoft's predatory activities intact.

BELOW: FTC attorneys Steve Newborn and Mary Lou Steptoe with Department of Justice attorney Steve Sunshine and Department of Justice antitrust chief Anne Bingaman, interrupted by the author at a D.C. restaurant, toasting the Sherman Act, just before Bingaman made her move to take over the Microsoft case from the FTC. *Photos this page by Michael Schumann*

FTC attorney Marc Schildkraut, along with his colleague Norris Washington, were responsible for beginning the investigation of Microsoft back in 1989, which eventually led to the series of antitrust suits filed against the software giant by the Justice Department.
Photos this page by Michael Schumann

FTC Commissioner Dennis Yao, in the spring of 1993, was urging the Commission to file an antitrust suit against Microsoft. The FTC ended up deadlocked.

Michael Sohn, Novell's D.C. counsel at Arnold & Porter, and antitrust scholar Robert Pitofsky, also of Arnold & Porter, who had been on Bill Clinton's short list to fill the position of antitrust chief at Justice. The men were caught by the author in Sohn's office in the spring of 1993. Sohn was at the time reviewing the antitrust complaints filed against Microsoft with the European Commission, and would play a key role in Justice's first settlement with Microsoft. Pitofsky would later become chairman of the Federal Trade Commission.

LEFT: Anne Bingaman, assistant attorney general in charge of antitrust at the Department of Justice, met with the author after her arrival at her D.C. office in July 1993. Bingaman stunned the business world and antitrust pundits alike when she made the unprecedented move of taking over a deadlocked case from the FTC.
BELOW: Department of Justice section chief Steve Sunshine in his D.C. office, prior to the DOJ's suit blocking Microsoft from acquiring Intuit Inc. Sunshine was instrumental in the probe that led up to the suit. *Photos by Michael Schumann*

Ray Noorda, chairman and CEO of Novell Inc., retired from Novell in 1994 to form a number of small companies, including Caldera, which bought DR-DOS from Novell. Caldera then filed a massive lawsuit against Microsoft, seeking damages that went back to the early days of the DOS market. The issues comprised a pattern of predation that had continued clear up to the Justice Department's and states' 1998 lawsuits, though these most recent suits addressed new markets. In 1994, Gates had sent an e-mail to his top executives blaming Noorda for the federal probes of his company, and seeking retribution.

In 1998, Steve Hill, a long-time outside counsel to Novell hired by Caldera, was pursuing witnesses all over the globe, documenting Gates' predation in the operating system market as part of the Caldera suit.

He and his colleagues, Ralph Palumbo and Steve Susman, had accumulated hundreds of thousands of pages documenting Microsoft's behavior. Among those they would subpoena in their case were former Vobis chief Theo Lieven, and former Microsoft Germany account manager Stefanie Reichel.

Ken Wasch (left), head of the D.C.-based Software Publishers Association, polled his members—hundreds of software companies of all sizes—to determine what remedies the Justice Department should seek in its case against Microsoft. Wasch provided important background information on the industry to Justice Department attorneys. Microsoft, which was also a member of the SPA, threatened to cancel its membership.

Jerry Kaplan disclosed Go Corporation's plans for a pen-based operating system to Gates and his executives under a nondisclosure agreement, after Gates expressed an interest in possibly developing applications for it. Internal documents collected by the feds showed that Microsoft sought to gather operating system information to create its own version of the software. The feds could not share their evidence with Kaplan.

Microsoft executive vice president and sales honcho Steve Ballmer, one of Gates' closest confidants, was grilled by both the FTC and the DOJ about Microsoft's alleged use of "sneaky code" to disparage competing products. *Steve Ringman*/Seattle Times

Juergen Huels, head of Microsoft's OEM accounts for Central Europe, attending a Microsoft OEM meeting in Stockholm in December 1991, around the time Microsoft was trying to get Vobis to cease shipments of DR-DOS. Microsoft managers had a "Viking party" during the meeting, feasting and drinking beer.

ABOVE: Joel Klein, head of the Department of Justice's antitrust division, finally had the opportunity to show that antitrust regulation had teeth at the close of the century with his massive antitrust suit against Microsoft.

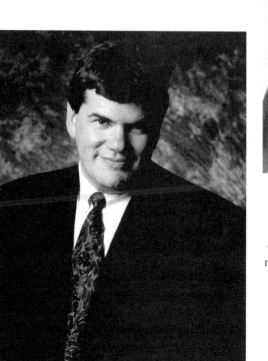

Philippe Kahn, chairman and CEO of Borland International, a bitter rival of Gates, sold his flagship product, QuattroPro, to Novell Inc. when he was unable to keep up in the face of Microsoft's aggressive presence in the applications software market. He later formed Starfish, a new company in a market niche that sidestepped Bill Gates.

good cop–bad cop, with Astiz drilling away dutifully at the deal while Kohn diverted attention by "yelling and screaming about this and that being onerous and unfair."

Needless to say, the WordPerfect attorneys were not looking forward to continuing their wrangling with Kahn. Yet the entire deal hinged on the acquisition of his QuattroPro business.

By Thursday evening, all were intensely reading an eighty-page merger agreement draft in preparation for the final negotiation meetings, which would begin the next day and continue around the clock through the weekend.

On Friday, March 18, WordPerfect and Novell convened at the law offices of Wilson, Sonsini to begin going over the document. Two negotiations commenced simultaneously—for the $145 million QuattroPro portion of the deal and for the $1.4 billion Novell-WordPerfect merger.

WordPerfect attorneys led the Borland negotiations, picking up where they had left off on the previous Sunday. By 10:00 Friday night, Borland's counsel, Bob Kohn, and Peter Astiz were still at great odds over the business terms being presented by WordPerfect and its attorneys. Meanwhile, progress was being made separately on the big $1.4 billion contract between Novell and WordPerfect.

But tempers were beginning to flare in the Borland-WordPerfect camp. Philippe Kahn had been in constant phone contact with his representatives. He would join the meeting on Saturday but depart later to fly to Phoenix for an industry conference.

By Saturday the Borland talks had been passed over to Novell. By evening Novell and WordPerfect were on common ground, and the handshakes were going around. But Borland wasn't budging.

At around midnight, Bradford flung his pen across the room. Things were going nowhere fast.

Philippe Kahn was surrounded by darkness, high above the fracas unfolding on the Palo Alto terrain. It was 3:00 A.M. on Monday, March 21. He hoped his attorneys had made some progress. These WordPerfect guys were being greedy as hell. After all, what was an extra $50 million when you were doing a $1.4 billion deal?

Kahn was behind the controls of his plane, coming in for a landing. He would return to the fray after a brief dinner in Phoenix at an industry conference where he had talked freely about his pals at Novell and WordPerfect. Meanwhile, his pals and he were getting further and further apart in their understanding of this acquisition. Since 7:00 A.M. on Sunday, there'd been barely a break in the meeting. Kahn had kept in touch by phone. Ironically, this little $145 million piece of the package was holding up the show. The night before, Novell and WordPerfect had all but dotted the *i*'s and crossed the *t*'s on the big merger. Now everyone was waiting for Kahn to get with the program.

He knew that timing was becoming critical. They had to finish this QuattroPro business in time to make an announcement by midday. When Novell finally received the actual sell-through data from Borland, its attorneys had hit the ceiling. It appeared that Borland had been inflating its valuation. Based on the data, the price would be negotiated closer to the $110 million that Novell finally signed off on.

In the end, after twenty-five hours of wrangling, the companies would come to an agreement just in time to brave the light of the next business day.

The agreement was only fifteen pages long but was more tortuous than any of them could have anticipated. WordPerfect and Novell needed to make sure they had access to Borland tools, which required code that was shared with other Borland products. "It was a lot more than just buying the assets and picking them up at the loading dock the next day," said one executive present in the meetings.

The phone kept ringing all weekend long. Ad Rietveld and other WordPerfect executives were getting repeated calls from Jim Manzi and his chief counsel, Tom Lemberg. Things were moving too quickly, Manzi was said to have protested, promising a better deal. Rietveld was said to be at his wits' end. He, like everyone else, had been operating for six to seven days on about three hours of sleep.

By daybreak Monday, WordPerfect had not been distracted. The merger agreement was final, and even Kahn had signed off on the acquisition of QuattroPro. The QuattroPro spreadsheet line would be acquired for about $110 million in cash. Novell would also get a nonexclusive license to certain Borland software products and source code, development tools, and related technology; and, for an additional $35 million, a bundling arrangement for WordPerfect, QuattroPro, and Paradox that WordPerfect had entered into back on April 5, 1993. Novell also offered to employ about a hundred Borland employees involved with the QuattroPro product line. In the event the merger failed to satisfy government requirements, Novell would loan Borland $50 million. If the merger failed for other reasons, Novell would pay Borland a breakup fee of $10 million cash within ten days of the termination.

Ray Noorda was glad that Borland and WordPerfect would survive. At least for the time being.

It was clear that Wall Street didn't like the deal. Within days of the merger announcement, Novell's stock dropped to a low of $15 a share. The conventional wisdom was that Novell had overpaid. But there was nothing conventional about this deal. "It was a vision thing," said one company insider. "It was not for short-term profit." Noorda did not balk at the market's reaction. The company's value had fluctuated in recent years between $10 and $15 billion. He recalled being offered the opportunity to own 35 percent of what was then called Novell Data Systems for a mere $125,000. That was almost as good a deal as Bill Gates had gotten for Q-DOS! Well, almost.

June 19 was coming up fast. Noorda would be let loose with his free time, and he had big plans. He was eyeing personal investment in a number of new ventures that he felt would contribute to the health of the industry—and kick some dust in Gates' face.

His most immediate project was to purchase from a small company in Virginia some technology that would enable a product code-named Expose and give it to Novell. The Novell board was set to make a decision on the matter, and the new CEO, Bob Frankenberg, was said to be excited about what Noorda described as an "in your face" product that would be Windows compatible and run on any computer platform. Noorda had hopes that the product would be commercially available by fall. In the lab, Novell technology buffs were getting a kick out of watching the system run many of Microsoft's Windows applications.

Noorda viewed this product as an alternative to Microsoft Windows, which he planned to virtually give away to the marketplace, just as Gates had done with Windows to undercut his competitors and gain market share. But all technical interfaces to Expose, and its upgrades, would be given to the public—an approach vastly different from what Noorda perceived as Microsoft's Windows "dictatorship."

Meanwhile, Noorda was well aware that the "special meeting" scheduled in mid-June by WordPerfect officers and shareholders left the opportunity for the merger to be called off at the last minute. The buzz was that Lotus' Manzi was still trying to stick his nose into the deal—and there could be plenty of opportunity should Novell's stock take another beating.

Noorda had flung his last harpoon this time, and with a weakened arm. The new guard was filtering in. In some ways, Frankenberg was what had clinched the deal for WordPerfect. "We needed a visionary to pull this off. We had the utmust trust in Frankenberg's ability," said a WordPerfect insider. But Frankenberg would later quit, and his reign would be a disaster.

Novell faced the formidable task of integrating the companies. Its track record in acquisitions had not been promising: it had still not effectively put to use the assets it acquired in its purchase of Digital Research Inc., and its attempts at integrating other small companies it had purchased had not gone well.

As Noorda removed the last vestiges of his days at the helm from the corporate offices of Novell, the company was working out the convergence of its workforce. A lot of fat needed to be shed before the new Novell would be primed for its next journey.

Consolidation in the computer industry had taken a bit longer than Noorda had anticipated. "I expected this all would have happened back two to four years ago," he would tell Bradford. "It was inevitable. There's always one big guy that everyone has to team up to fight." He predicted, "In three years there will be a superior guy to Gates leading the industry." Indeed, James Gosling had started work on a new technology called Java, and a tiny company known as Netscape had been founded to create a way for the masses to browse the Internet.

But eventually they would be put on the "treadmill" as Microsoft executives called it, an endless loop intentionally created by Microsoft to keep them losing market share—no matter their initial success—because of Microsoft's continued ability to leverage its dominance into new markets.

Novell's challenges remained immense. Noorda said, "We have a difficult time inside our company right now because we can't all understand what the network is. Four or five years ago it was a different entity, and knew what its functions were supposed to be." Noorda predicted that the network would need to do what the telephone does: provide all different kinds of services, regardless of supplier.

He told his colleagues, "You can buy a service from MCI that goes through AT&T that is delivered by somebody else. And Bill Gates knows that. He knows that has to happen, so he wants to get every part of it.

"That's what we hope will happen," Noorda would say, "recognizing that getting that all to happen means we have to get lots of partners. In the meantime, Pearly is moving ahead, trying to do it with all his own stuff—and he's got a lot. He wants to keep all of those applications people out."

During April and May, as the Security and Exchange Commission and the Justice Department were reviewing Novell's merger filings, antitrust attorneys at Justice were interviewing potential witnesses at WordPerfect in preparation for an antitrust action against Microsoft. The software giant was under the gun, with the Novell-WordPerfect-Borland gang on its tail and Justice scrutinizing its every move.

These activities seemed to mark an odd new chapter in the computer industry. Wall Street hated the Novell move, and consumers were uncertain about how it would all shake out. A fierce political battle was being played out, not only in the press but in congressional offices, based on the activities of the new regime at Justice.

On Thursday evening, April 7, 1994, Department of Justice antitrust chief Anne Bingaman stood outside the ballroom of Washington D.C.'s Shoreham Hotel in a black velvet suit. Freshly tanned, she'd just arrived back from a two-week vacation in Costa Rica. At the moment, she could barely remember being on vacation at all.

"It's a blur!" she said, speaking with one of her colleagues. A few lingerers were being corraled into the ballroom for the annual dinner of the antitrust section of the ABA.

An hour earlier, the who's-who-in-antitrust were collecting in the Garbo Room of the hotel for a cocktail party thrown by the law firm of Jim Rill, the former antitrust chief under President Bush. Rill admired Anne, although he sometimes thought she went too far.

Sipping cocktails or sparkling water in the richly paneled room, there now was Rill himself, and Bingaman's section chief Rich Rosen, and FTC chairman Janet Steiger—under whose watch the Microsoft probe was begun. There was Schildkraut, the former FTC attorney who had originally brought concerns about Microsoft to the FTC's attention, long before a formal probe was initiated. There was Anne's international deputy Diane Wood, and FTC Bureau of Competition director Mary Lou Steptoe. There was platinum blond Deborah Owen, now strolling toward the bar in a slinky suit.

Close on Owen's heels was the demure Commissioner Mary Azcuenaga, whose second "no" vote on Microsoft had resulted in the case being deadlocked 2–2 at the FTC. Over against the opposite wall, one could see Roscoe Starek, grinning and nodding to his acquaintances in the crowd. Starek and "recused" had become synonymous. If not for that, the Microsoft case would have been decided one way or the other more than a year earlier.

Yet another entourage was weaving itself through this cocktailbrandishing clan: the private-sector antitrust attorneys from Washington D.C.'s most influential law firms, many of whom were representing the concerns of Microsoft's competitors to Justice.

Among them were six-foot-four Andy Berg, counsel to Lotus Development Corp.; and Ed Glynn, Taligent's antitrust expert. Taligent was an ill-fated joint venture between Apple and IBM, which had hopes at one time of offering a new operating system that would show up Bill Gates for good. The product never got off the ground—computer makers could not budge from their contracts with Gates—but Taligent provided reams of evidence to the feds, under subpoena.

The fact was, this week most antitrust watchers wanted to grill Anne. Every now and then, throughout the parties going on this evening, one could hear murmurings of "Microsoft."

Was the drawn-out investigation of the software giant about to emerge from the shadows, or would Chairman Bill's Microsoft Corporation, with all its power and influence, somehow find a way to wriggle out from under the government's microscope?

The antitrust horde eventually filtered into the ballroom, to dine and laugh over the antics of a comedy troupe known as The Capitol Steps. By the next morning, it was Bingaman's turn to take her place on the dais for her big speech on the state of antitrust enforcement.

In the ballroom of the Shoreham, Anne waited for one of her colleague's to finish his introduction. In his colloquy, he joked that Anne had just informed him that she'd dotted all the i's and crossed all the t's in her speech. "Hmmm," he said to the audience. "What words have *i* and *t*? Well . . ." A litany of possibilities poured forth. Finally he exlaimed, "Microsoft!" Laughter from the crowd.

A week earlier, her head of litigation, Sam Miller, had issued a new batch of subpoenas to Microsoft and other software developers. It would be months more before she would be ready to file a lawsuit.

By May 1994, Bill Neukom and Stefanie Reichel had set off together for a little vacation at Pebble Beach, and for the meeting of the Association of General Counsels.

Over the months Reichel had confided in Neukom all of her experiences with Gates. On their first date in the United States, months after their meeting in Europe, Gates had invited her to the gatekeeper's house on the grounds of the luxury house he had been building for years. She did not know until later that his close friends knew that that was Gates's favorite place to bring his female conquests.

Back in September 1992, Reichel had confided in Neukom that she was confused and worried that if she did not respond to Gates' advances she could lose her job. Neukom took on the role of her protector, and by late fall of 1992 had become her lover.

Reichel had transferred to the U.S. headquarters of Microsoft. Now she was on Pebble Beach with Neukom and the phone had continually been ringing. The Justice Department had a lot to say to Neukom. But Neukom could do nothing without the approval of Gates.

Reichel mused over the phenomenon that was Bill Gates. There was something very likable about him, and something very confusing.

Gates had asked her to accompany him to Amsterdam at the time Neukom had urged her to disengage herself from the Microsoft chairman back in September of 1992. When Gates called to make arrangements to meet her, she told him she could not afford the trip. "You promised you'd show me around Amsterdam," he said. "I'll loan you the money." So Reichel agreed to meet him and vowed to inform him that their relationship was over.

Upon her arrival the two headed for the luxurious Hotel L'Europe. Reichel was very nervous. At the reception desk, Gates went all out, reserving the Presidential Suite, the entire upper floor of the hotel, assuming that Reichel would be staying with him. Meanwhile, Reichel had taken out her credit card to book her own room. Unbeknownst to Gates, Bill Neukom was paying for it. He had insisted that Reichel hold her ground.

Gates told Reichel that he was enormously disappointed but he understood and would be glad to be her friend. They dined at various restaurants together over the next couple of days, and Gates expressed a desire to find the red-light district. He was curious about this culture's legendary openness about sex.

Along the narrow streets, small, square windows glowed with red light, and the near naked figures of women lounged in those windows, as if they were brightly designed packages displayed on a retail shelf. It was amazing. Commerce was going on!

Reichel and Gates eventually relaxed in a café bar, where they indulged in "space cakes," a hashish delight that was legal in that country. They drifted together in reveries, far from the world of deal making, contracts, and quarterly reports.

Settling into the obscurity of a dark Amsterdam bar, Bill Gates finally had drifted off for a few hours of boyhood.

13

SETTLEMENT

Bill Gates knew Novell's number was up. In a memo to his executive committee just after Novell announced its acquisition of WordPerfect and Borland's QuattroPro, he evaluated the deal while recognizing that Ray Noorda was trying to beat him at his own game. But Gates' strategies worked like a charm. And his evaluations of Novell's weaknesses were right on the money. Nevertheless, Gates was finally being called on the carpet by the Justice Department. Yet his predation continued right through settlement, requiring the feds to bar him from the use of contracts that resulted in restraint of trade. Gates, however, shrewdly manipulated the feds into agreeing to some precise wording in a settlement that would leave him free rein to leverage his market power far into the future.

Ray Noorda knew how to get Bill Gates' goat.

The Microsoft chairman could now be heard braying and wailing in memos and e-mail messages across the company in reaction to Noorda's recent acquisitions.

Gates was trying to put on a good face while seething with competitive ire. In memos he asserted that he was flattered Noorda should copy his strategy—recognizing that only a fully integrated suite offering could compete with what Gates was doing.

After all, Gates was paranoid that Noorda would succeed in mak-

ing the network the delivery mechanism for all types of software—
and would leverage his networking dominance as Gates had leveraged his operating system control.

In a memo addressed to the executive staff, Gates wrote that the
Novell-WordPerfect merger and acquisition of QuattroPro changed
Microsoft's competitive framework substantially. He noted that
Novell had adopted his own strategy of integrating products, point-
ing out that Lotus had done similarly through its acquisitions and
Notes strategy. Gates thought it great that competitors were "fol-
lowing our strategy" as long as Microsoft executed a lot better, he
said.

Gates then went on to itemize the key impacts of Novell's move on
each area of his business. His concern was how the merged company would impact Microsoft Office, Microsoft's office productivity
suite, fretting that Novell could turn its own office suite into "a serious contender which could force price and volume cuts in our Office business."

As had been clear with the case of DR-DOS, Gates was particularly keen on the fact that increased competition meant he would
not be able to maintain high prices. He acknowledged that the combined companies would be better able to integrate QuattroPro and
WordPerfect, and reverse their "fading strength." (Both products
had been losing market share to Gates' Microsoft Excel and Word—
which were the spreadsheet and word processing packages included in Microsoft Office.)

Gates, oddly, was still concerned with DR-DOS, though its market share by now was almost nonexistent. "Novell could do some
strange pricing by bundling their Office suite with Netware like
they have bundled DR-DOS," he wrote.

He seemed to be thinking out loud that Novell might beat him at
his own strategy of "strange pricing," as he called it, that involved
offering customers price incentives for taking a nondominant product with the dominant one. Netware was Novell's network operating
system, the leader in the industry and one of the only areas where
Gates did not dominate. He feared that Novell would start giving
away its newly acquired applications software with Netware in

order to cut into Gates' own market share—which Gates had gained, in part, by using the same tactics.

Gates then went into a discussion of "financial scale," exhibiting his acumen in such topics as global marketing, customer presence, and brand awareness. "The Novell brand can become an umbrella for a wide range of activities," he wrote. That had been Microsoft's own highly effective strategy.

The memo was like a primer in many of Gates' strategies and showed how he would have gone about taking advantage of the synergies of the new Novell corporation.

Perhaps most interesting was Gates' pondering the ability of a market leader to control standards—something he had done with amazing results. He appeared to be worried.

"Initiatives to promote anti-Microsoft platforms/API's/object models become easier to coordinate because fewer companies are involved," he wrote, and he considered whether Novell would now be able to set more standards for workgroup, document management, image systems, and "all of the 'services' they have been moving towards."

He then went on to itemize what he believed to be the business unknowns, things that stood to put Microsoft in a position of advantage. For one, all those employees involved in the acquisition would be diverted for the next six months. At the same time, "QuattroPro developers are being excised from the barbarians world to a completely new company." (Gates considered anyone to be working for Philippe Kahn a "barbarian.")

Seeming to read Jim Manzi's mind, who, unbeknownst to Gates, had vied for the partnership with WordPerfect himself, Gates said, "Novell and Lotus should become major rivals fighting over the non-Microsoft parts of the application business."

He then turned his thoughts to technology unknowns, noting that, unlike Microsoft, Novell never had a central "technical agenda." Long term, Novell needed a database strategy, as its rights to Borland's Paradox database package were limited. At the same time, he worried that Borland, unburdening itself from the QuattroPro business, "becomes a pure competitor to the products in our Developer division. The $145M eliminates their cash problem." Microsoft and Borland had been fierce competitors in the area of programming languages and tools, and now the company would be more focused.

Finally, Gates spelled out "Actions" to his executive committee that he was urging in response, and the need to "win" in the area of e-mail software and corporate environments. To ensure winning, Gates suggested that Microsoft buy up all remaining small companies in the "mail" arena, for one.

It merely continued a longtime strategy of his to purchase great products and technologies in any areas in which Microsoft was behind.

Gates viewed Windows NT—the more robust version of Windows that he'd been trying to make acceptable for corporate mission-critical environments—as an area where Microsoft could not afford to lose. He was still way behind Novell in that area.

"NT has [to be] viewed as a major success or Novell will thwart our Workgroup efforts. We should consider increasing our sales investment in these 2 products including buying the installed bases of remaining mail companies," he said. Mail was an important application within corporate computer networks, and a key component in the hot category of workgroup computing.

"We need to take a harder look at the product, acquisition and sales efforts to gain scale in Mail/Workgroup," he said.

Finally, Gates advised his minions of the need to develop a plan "for recruitment at WordPerfect and QuattroPro." Gates would be quite successful in this goal of going after WordPerfect and Borland employees. Philippe Kahn would later sue him for preying on his workforce, and would win a settlement.

Other executives inside the company picked up on Gates' missives, shooting off staff memos throughout the company, urging managers and sales representatives to get on the phone to customers to put the Microsoft spin on the Novell merger. One, sent on March 24, 1994, stated that the tone of their message should seem "humble," but nevertheless should make a number of points.

For countries where WordPerfect had a large presence, it was a perfect opportunity for Microsoft to convince WordPerfect/ DOS users that "there has never been a better time to switch." (The Netherlands was one such country where WordPerfect still had a dominant share, and WordPerfect would soon file a complaint to the EC against Microsoft for predatory pricing.)

The memo spelled out what Microsoft's "public response" to the merger should be, emphasizing that it must validate that Microsoft Office was ahead. Competitors that were lagging in the integration race were consolidating to catch up, the memo acknowledged, and "Keeping the top talent will be challenging for them." The memo didn't mention that Gates had a plan to raid these personnel from his competitors himself, as his more narrowly distributed e-mail stated.

Interestingly, Microsoft recognized internally that it had taken over the applications market, but to federal investigators was portraying itself to be behind in market share. The fact was, "Lotus now clearly [is] a distant third in size and resources. Microsoft leads the OS and applications, Novell has the network," it stated.

Prophetically, Microsoft's evaluation of the situation would turn out to be right on the money. In a matter of months, Novell would unload WordPerfect to Corel Corporation for a fraction of what it had paid for the company itself.

The words of Gates' memo and those of his managers echoed throughout the company and eventually through the analyst community.

———————

Back in Provo, on Friday, April 22, 1994, Ray Noorda was at home with his wife working on his memoirs. Hewlett-Packard's Robert Frankenberg had just been named CEO at Novell, and Noorda was spending less and less time in his office. (He'd also evaluated Sun's Scott McNealy and the former IBM executive George Conrades for the CEO job.)

Also on this day the proxy statements for the WordPerfect-Novell merger and the acquisition of Borland's spreadsheet division would be filed. Things were moving along quickly. WordPerfect's chief counsel, Duff Thompson, was in Hawaii on a vacation, and his No-vell counterpart, David Bradford, had likewise taken the day off.

Philippe Kahn hadn't quite been able to have his cake and eat it too. He still was virtually begging Novell to acquire Borland out-right. The company had already taken a pounding and was suffering more with Microsoft's latest invasions into the ranks of its engineers.

While Noorda lounged at home on this afternoon, Kahn was fuming. He and his four-and-a-half-year-old son were in his car on their way to see *White Fang II*, a story about a wolf. Kahn was delighted with the companionship of his son, but was in a huff about business matters, and took a moment to return a phone call. "They're gunning for our top engineers, and promising huge signing bonuses," he said.

At about the same time that afternoon Gates' top publicist, Pam Edstrom, was frantic. "Get Gates! Get Gates!" she yelled across her office.

On the phone with a *Financial Times* reporter, she had just calmly denied charges that Microsoft had been unfairly restricting competing software companies from receiving needed technical information on "Chicago," the merged DOS and Windows product that would become Windows 95. The Justice Department had just brought the matter to Microsoft's attention.

Having denied the facts, she privately turned and shouted to her colleagues, "*FT* has the story! *FT* has the story!" She thought the reporter had put her on hold, but the reporter had instead pushed the mute button and was listening to the havoc now breaking out in her office.

Under subpoena by the Justice Department, WordPerfect, Lotus, Novell, Borland, and others had shown federal attorneys that Gates was attempting to restrain trade by restricting access to essential operating system specifications to software developers making applications programs for Chicago. Microsoft would not provide access to any company developing products for standards not owned by Microsoft.

The company had forced software developers to sign nondisclosure agreements that stated if they did not support Microsoft's data transfer system, called OLE, they would be barred from receiving information on Chicago. Several companies, including WordPerfect, Lotus, IBM, and Apple, supported an alternative standard called OpenDoc, and WABI—or Windows Application Binary Interface, which Sun, Novell, IBM, and others supported.

David Moon, chief technology officer for WordPerfect, had testified in affidavits to the Justice Department that Microsoft was pushing the industry by illegal means to adopt its proprietary OLE standard. Moon said, "It's pretty heavy-handed . . . for them to try and dictate what kind of functionalities are in our applications. If [Microsoft] is going to start prohibiting anybody who has anything competitive from access to the industry-standard operating system then that's pretty dangerous for the industry."

Along with WordPerfect, Borland, Novell, Lotus, and Sun Microsystems had complained to the software giant, and to Justice, that they had been given incomplete code, forced to accept restrictive licenses, and barred by Microsoft from attending supposedly open development conferences.

In late April, after Microsoft hadn't responded to complaints from WordPerfect Corp. and others, when Microsoft was made aware of newspaper reports on its restrictive contracts in the *Boston Globe* and *Financial Times*, the company made a rare about-face and issued a public statement that it would cancel such restrictions in certain contracts. The Justice Department would later bar the use of such contracts in its settlement with the software giant.

Weeks earlier Bill Gates had declared war on WordPerfect in Europe. He was also after Ad Rietveld's top sales executives there. At Nijenrode University in Amsterdam, Gates gave a speech in which he credited Rietveld's nationality with the fact that WordPerfect had a 90 percent market share in Holland. He was determined to move in and immediately slashed prices, bundling Windows for Workgroups with Microsoft Word for an impossibly low price. It was clear that Gates was out to gain market share, even if he temporarily lost money doing it. In response, WordPerfect shot off a letter to Microsoft threatening to file a complaint with the EC for predatory pricing.

On June 2, 1994, Bill Gates was deposed by Department of Justice litigator Sam Miller, with Microsoft's outside counsel Steve Holley present. At the beginning of his deposition, he was confronted with the government's Exhibit 17, a collection of Gates' handwritten notes, including the "purge email" note that Norris Washington had discovered amidst his documents years earlier at the FTC.

Gates was asked by Justice what purge e-mail meant. Before he could answer, Holley interrupted, instructing Gates that he did not have to answer if the answer involved advice he received from his attorneys. Gates then told his questioners that he didn't have anything to say. He was then asked by the Justice Department if written guidelines existed within Microsoft regarding e-mail destruction and deletion. He replied that yes, guidelines did exist.

Gates was asked if he knew what these guidelines were. No, Gates replied.

Did Gates have a copy of the guidelines, he was asked. No, he again replied. Who within Microsoft would have a copy then? Gates replied that this would be handled by Bill Neukom.

Anne Bingaman's hair was in an upsweep, as if anticipating gales.

While Gates' competitors had taken their competitive predicament in their own hands, the feds—after years of study—were finally preparing to take some action against Gates. The Justice Department informed Microsoft that it was preparing to sue. It was June 21, and Bill Neukom and Microsoft's outside counsel Richard Urowsky were due to arrive at the Antitrust Division to engage in the first round of settlement talks.

By this time, Neukom had been given a deadline of July 14 to settle with the Justice Department and the European Commission. Both were talking tough, but it was a game of chicken, he knew. Neukom had already advised Gates that they had to settle, but he was sure they could get off easy.

189

Bingaman and Litan greeted Neukom and Urowsky in the division's main conference room. Next to a conference table, Bingaman had arranged on an easel the written outline for a comprehensive consent decree.

It prohibited various licensing practices used by Microsoft for its operating system products, MS-DOS and Windows, including "per processor" and "per system" licenses, as well as "minimum commitments"—deals in which a computer maker made a minimum dollar payment under a license agreement in exchange for authorization to ship a specified number of Microsoft operating system products.

Bingaman's decree also limited the duration of Microsoft's licenses with computer makers and regulated pricing of operating systems by prohibiting or limiting volume discounts. It prohibited lump-sum licenses—which authorized computer makers to ship unlimited numbers of Microsoft operating system products in exchange for a lump-sum payment—and exclusive dealing contracts. Neukom protested that Microsoft had never used the latter two types of licenses.

The decree also placed limitations on nondisclosure agreements Microsoft entered into with companies who received early test copies of new Microsoft operating system products so that companies and personnel were not unduly restricted from working on applications products designed for non-Microsoft operating systems.

The meeting that day was followed up in the same conference room on June 27, with a meeting of Neukom, Urowsky, and Bingaman. Also present was Seth Waxman, an aide to Bingaman. The two sides began wrangling over a compromise involving the duration of Microsoft's licenses, the types of licenses Microsoft offered, and whether Microsoft's licenses were "requirements contracts." Justice Department attorneys noted Neukom's habit of debating nit-picking issues that to them were obvious. Also in play was the nature of Microsoft's per system licenses and their relation to the economic relationship between Microsoft and its OEM licensees, the use of nondisclosure agreements, and the duration and nature of any settlement Microsoft might reach with Justice.

Toward the end of the meeting, Neukom suggested that Bingaman coordinate her settlement with the EC's DG IV, which had a separate antitrust action under way based on the complaint Novell had filed with the EC in the summer of 1993. Microsoft had to do business on a consistent basis worldwide, he explained, and if the company reached an understanding on licensing issues with Justice without assurance that DG IV would concur, Microsoft might be subject to different, and possibly conflicting, requirements relating to a central part of its business.

"Let's see if we can have a joint discussion between Microsoft, the DOJ, and DG IV to see if a global solution is possible," Neukom had suggested.

"I'll see if the DG IV is interested," Bingaman said.

She then left the room and phoned Claus-Dieter Ehlermann, director general of the DG IV. He agreed to consider the idea and respond after he had spoken with others.

Janet Reno commanded focus in any room she entered. On June 30, Neukom found himself eye to eye with the attorney general, who had joined Bingaman, Waxman, Neukom, and Urowsky to discuss the final issues underlying the Justice Department's investigation of Microsoft.

Bingaman informed Neukom that he was to be in Brussels, at the DG IV's offices, on the morning of July 4 for a detailed settlement discussion that would involve Microsoft's predatory practices in the United States as well as Europe.

On June 30, while Reno educated herself on the action her antitrust chief was about to pursue, the DG IV sent to Microsoft a draft of a statement of objections—its preliminary complaint—in the case filed by Novell. In the draft the DG IV stated that various Microsoft licensing practices—primarily per processor and per system licenses, together with minimum commitments—had the "effect of economically tying the licensing of MS-DOS to . . . Windows and thereby limiting the market for competing products," such as DR-DOS.

For the previous two weeks, Justice attorneys had repeated the same message to Microsoft: If you refuse to sign a consent order, the department is going to sue. Those fourteen days were filled with around-the-clock talks among Sam Miller, Neukom, and Bingaman. Meanwhile, Microsoft was denying press reports that a Justice Dept. lawsuit was imminent.

It was a calm summer evening in Brussels on July 4, and the lobby of the Stanhope Hotel was all but empty. Bingaman and Ehlermann had dropped by for a brief meeting with the two men representing Microsoft in an attempt to prepare them for the next day.

Neukom was given a two-page summary of the joint position of the Justice Department and the DG IV with respect to Microsoft's licensing practices. It included a specification of the points of concern and their proposed remedies.

Some new items related to product tying had been added to the Justice complaint and were also included in the DG IV's case. It now prohibited contracts that, in combination, foreclosed competing operating systems and conditioned the sale of Microsoft operating systems on licensing of other products or services. It also barred "bundle pricing" for multiple operating system products and required separate pricing based on actual sales of each product.

Bill Gates was not going to be happy.

On July 4, after its meeting with regulators, Microsoft responded with a two-page statement of its own. Regarding the tying issues, Microsoft agreed that the settlement would include "contracts for MS-DOS 6.22, Windows 3.11 and Windows for Workgroups 3.11 and their successor replacement products, including 'Chicago,' or Windows 95." The company agreed that the prohibitions would involve "OEM contract terms that . . . foreclose competing operating system products."

Neukom added, "Microsoft will prohibit conditioning the licensing of any stand-alone Microsoft product on a customer's agreement to license another Microsoft product. Microsoft will continue to develop integrated products like Chicago that provide technological benefits to end users."

Meetings continued daily in Brussels from July 4 to July 8 in an attempt to negotiate a settlement that would satisfy all parties. Neukom was joined by William Allan, a partner of Linklaters & Paines in London who provided advice on European Union law, and Urowsky. Bingaman was assisted by her deputy economist, Richard Gilbert, and attorney Mark Schechter. On the DG IV side was Ehlermann with Helmut Drabbe and Fin Lomholt, two senior staff members at the DG IV.

The final meeting convened in Ehlermann's Brussels office on the evening of Friday, July 8. On July 5, Justice and the DG IV had produced a first draft of a settlement arrangement. It made clear that, from the outset, the two contemplated that the "product code-named Chicago" would be a successor to Microsoft's current operating system software products, MS-DOS and Windows, and would be covered by any undertaking.

On July 6, Neukom had presented Ehlermann with a statement of position in response to the July 5 draft, which showed Microsoft's agreement to the provision provided that it applied only to the specified products and "successors to those products that were made available to [computer makers]."

Microsoft appeared to be qualifying its acceptance of the proposal based on defining *tying* as limited to conditioning the licensing of one "stand-alone" product offered in the OEM channel to the licensing of another such product, and not extending it to integration of products that resulted in a new product offered to OEMs as such. After all, Gates was planning to tie DOS and Windows together irrevocably by making them one product: Chicago.

No agreement was reached in Brussels. By the morning of July 9, the parties were at odds on a number of significant issues, including Microsoft's continued use of minimum commitments, the nature of permissible volume discounts, the terms on which Microsoft could continue to offer per system licenses, and the duration of any settlement arrangement.

Bingaman informed Neukom that he should tell Gates he had a deadline of July 14 to settle, or a lawsuit would be filed.

Great heat was being generated in a conference room in the federal triangle on July 14 and 15, where an all-day and all-night war had been waged.

"I will not be two-timed by Bill Gates," Bingaman wailed at her colleagues during a break. Gates had repeatedly tried to undo every bit of progress the antitrust attorneys felt they were making with Neukom. Litan described the process as an intense roller-coaster ride. "It was clear to us that the lawyers were going back and asking Gates for authority and direction," he told his colleagues afterward.

Bingaman insisted that the only way to resolve the problem would be to bring Gates into the talks. Neukom and Gates were being read the riot act. "If you want to settle this, now's the time," Litan said. He then itemized the extent of the case he and Bingaman were ready to recommend to Janet Reno.

As discussions proceeded on Thursday, July 14, Bingaman decided to let the deadline slide. After all, Neukom was finally at the table drafting the language.

On July 13 a draft of an antitying provision intended to satisfy Justice and the DG IV had been prepared as part of a comprehensive internal draft of settlement terms. It read: "Microsoft shall not enter into any License Agreement in which the terms of that agreement are conditioned or depend upon the license of any other Covered Product, Operating System Software product or other product (provided, however, that this shall not be construed to prohibit Microsoft from developing integrated products which offer technological advantages)."

"Remove those last four words," Gates barked to his chief counsel, who sat beside him, stone-faced.

It was after 10:30 P.M. on July 13, and Neukom had phoned Urowsky, with other Microsoft lawyers present in a conference call. The group now debated the substance and wording of various provisions set forth in the consent decree, especially the impact of product integration, given Gates' plans with Chicago. The lawyers dared not proceed further without Gates' reading on the situation.

Gates wanted to eliminate the words "which offer technological advantages" on the ground that Microsoft would not accept limitations on its right to design new products, in particular, limitations that involved application of vague or subjective criteria.

Gates insisted that Microsoft had to have the right to develop "any integrated products" or it would lose its ability to innovate. (Later, it would become a bone of contention whether Windows 98 offered any technological advantages by integrating Internet Explorer other than to steal the market from Netscape.)

Neukom and his assistants, acting on Gates' orders, revised the antitying provision to read: "Microsoft shall not enter into any License Agreement in which the terms of that agreement are conditioned or depend upon: the licensing of any other Covered Product, Operating System Software product or other product (provided, however, that this shall not be construed to prohibit Microsoft from developing integrated products)."

On the morning of July 14, in Bingaman's conference room, Neukom and Urowsky faced off against Bingaman, Litan, Gilbert, Schechter, Drabbe, and Lomholt. It would not end until Saturday, July 16, when Janet Reno stood up before the press to announce what she believed to be a victory for her antitrust cops.

Neukom opened the meeting with a preliminary statement, then circulated copies of his revised decree. After much page turning and mumbling, Neukom walked the regulators through his document, highlighting issues and his proposed language changes, inspired by Gates.

When he reached Section E, Neukom pointed out that Microsoft had added a proviso to one subsection in order to make explicit that the company retained the absolute right to offer "merged products" or products embodying "integrated technology." He noted that nothing could be construed to limit Microsoft in the area of product design. "This has been our position last week in Brussels," Neukom reminded his investigators. "Therefore, this is not a substantive change."

Following Neukom's review, the meeting adjourned, and Bingaman and her colleagues compared notes on the issues that remained open. Bingaman was furious. "I will not be two-timed!" she told Litan again. "He is not going to undo everything so that it's meaningless! No more concessions after this!"

That evening, Neukom again sat with Bingaman and the DG IV negotiators, with Ehlermann intermittently present by phone. Bingaman insisted that Gates also participate by speaker phone.

Neukom and Gates were now facing a united front: the European Commission and Justice were threatening the same lawsuit. It was certain that Microsoft would have to enter into a stipulation with Justice agreeing to entry of the consent decree and an undertaking with the DG IV that was essentially identical to that decree.

Flanking Bingaman were Litan, Gilbert, and Schechter, joined by David Seidman, a staff lawyer in the Appellate Section of the Antitrust Division. The DG IV's Drabbe and Lomholt were present, with Ehlermann communicating by phone.

The negotiations resumed late in the afternoon of July 14. Again the draft decree was reviewed item by item. Finally Litan declared that the proviso proposed by Microsoft in the morning was agreeable to Justice and the DG IV, subject to a language change making it clear that, while the proviso removed "integrated products" from the strictures of Section IV(E)(I), it did not exempt Microsoft from review under the Sherman Act and the Treaty of Rome. Things were left precariously so that "integrated products" were neither prohibited under the consent decree nor permitted under statutory law. No attempt at defining an "integrated product" was made.

Microsoft counsel Urowsky noted, "While I'm certain that Microsoft and the DOJ had different views on what limitations the Sherman Act placed on high-technology product design, we do not have to resolve the issue this evening. The law will govern." (The issue indeed would come up again when Bingaman's successor Joel Klein filed his monumental lawsuit in 1998.)

Bingaman realized she had at least gotten her foot in the door; she could perhaps file other cases to keep Microsoft in line.

The meeting broke up, and additional drafts were drawn up, with all parties recognizing that they'd be camping out at the Justice Department that night.

By 10:30 P.M., Justice had produced a new draft for yet another review by Neukom and his colleagues. The language regarding product tying now read: "Microsoft shall not enter into any License Agreement in which the terms of that agreement are expressly or impliedly conditioned upon: the licensing of any other Covered Product, Operating System Software product or other product (provided, however, that this provision in and of itself shall not be construed to prohibit Microsoft from developing integrated products, or necessarily to permit it to do so)." The draft was then shortened before being placed in final form. In the wee hours of the morning of July 15, the group disbanded.

Later that morning the talks resumed, and agreement was reached on additional terms and language. By dawn, on July 15, Bingaman was at the end of her rope. She'd spent eleven months investigating Microsoft, and had one of her attorneys stationed in Salt Lake City to file the lawsuit against Microsoft in Novell country should Gates at the last minute refuse to settle. Justice Department attorneys thought Gates and Neukom would get a kick out of their choice of venue.

But on July 15 at about 6:00 P.M., the DG IV undertaking was signed by Microsoft. At the last minute, with Gates agitating on the phone to Neukom, the language of that critical Section IV (E) in the Justice Department's stipulation was again scaled back. The last version removed the words "or necessarily to permit it to do so." Neukom said he merely wanted to eliminate unneeded and potentially confusing wording, as opposed to changing the substance of the item. It would be of critical substance, however, later, and a far cry from being unneeded wording. The clause now stated that Microsoft would be allowed to create integrated products with no doubt cast on the fact that doing so could in some cases be anti-competitive.

Gates' shrewd negotiating skills had come over the line as clear as day. He knew the strategic importance of keeping people locked in via this integrated approach. He was about to ship Windows 95. And his new online service, the Microsoft Network (MSN), was about to be integrated with Windows 95.

That was before he'd gotten the religion of the Internet.

By 8:00 P.M. Neukom had signed the consent decree and agreed to stop licensing Microsoft's operating systems by the number of processors sold rather than the number of operating systems bought. In addition, Microsoft agreed to drop restrictions connected with testing its software and to stop tying the sale of one software product to another. In the lawsuit it was prepared to file, Justice stated that "Microsoft's monopoly power allows it to induce PC manufacturers to enter into anti-competitive, long-term licenses under which they must pay royalties to Microsoft not only when they sell PCs containing Microsoft's operating systems, but also when they sell PCs with non-Microsoft systems."

The decision to narrow the complaint to licensing issues, product tying, and the testing contracts was a pragmatic one. While they knew Microsoft seemed to have been guilty of other antitrust violations in the applications market, Justice Department lawyers had decided to go after a case they thought would be an easy win. They would continue to monitor Microsoft's behavior on other fronts.

Bill Gates told reporters after the decision that he didn't anticipate any "adverse financial impact on Microsoft" and had "not changed internal forecasts for sales of DOS, Windows, or subsequent versions of those products."

Bob Litan found Gates' and Neukom's statements odd indeed, given that they had fought the decision tooth and nail. "If this was so easy to comply with, why didn't they settle years ago?" he asked his colleagues, who along with Bingaman were shocked at how the settlement was received by the industry.

It was being portrayed as a meaningless slap on the wrist. Industry analysts noted that Gates had gotten off without paying restitution to its competitors or to the government, without dividing up the company, and without admitting guilt. It was a sweet deal indeed.

IBM was about to test the effectiveness of the settlement. It was planning a price war. Novell and IBM sales reps were calling computer makers, reminding them that they were now free to accept other contracts. But they slowly realized that Gates still had the industry in his pocket. Everyone was afraid of being cut off by Microsoft if they turned to its competitors.

Novell's David Bradford got on the phone to WordPerfect's Duff Thompson and to Philippe Kahn's chief counsel, Bob Kohn. Private lawsuits now were being weighed.

Summer had slipped over the landscape, its lull softening the edges of what had once seemed solid.

In his Washington, D.C., office, Lotus' counsel, Andrew Berg, was packing up the files on Microsoft. Although the Justice Department's settlement would be up for review under the Tunney Act, and outside parties could contest it as meaningless, Jim Manzi's chief counsel, Tom Lemberg, had instructed Berg that Manzi did not want to waste a minute more on the effort. The army of lawyers who had represented the applications software companies were throwing in the towel. Their issues had not been addressed, and they believed their market was all but lost.

By mid-August, Ray Noorda had resigned as chairman of Novell. He was scheming about how to use his free time in a new effort to restore competition to the information age.

14

HARDBALL

As the Tunney Act proceedings unfolded before Judge Stanley Sporkin, everything seemed up for grabs. The Justice Department's settlement was thrown out, and the feds were in the odd position of taking Microsoft's side in demonstrating the validity of the consent decree to an appeals court. Subsequently, Sporkin's ruling was thrown out on procedural grounds and the decree reinstated, ironically just as antitrust chief Bingaman was beginning to get the full picture of Microsoft's intent while reviewing the software giant's bid to acquire Intuit Inc. As the consent decree was being entered to address a market in which competition had long been dead and gone, a swarm of companies in a range of new markets came forward to protest the business practices of Bill Gates.

Bill Neukom arrived at the federal district court by cab on January 20, 1995, and made his way to Courtroom 6 on the second floor.

The calm of the Hay-Adams Hotel had been replaced by camera crews on the courthouse steps. An unlikely mob now snaked in a disorderly line just outside the courtroom of Judge Stanley Sporkin.

The Tunney Act proceedings were about to begin. This was the third in a series of hearings that had grown increasingly contentious. Reporters, Wall Street analysts, and lawyers from the private sector and the government had shown up for the occasion.

While the crowd settled in, Anne Bingaman stood scribbling frantically on an oversized chart at the front of the courtroom.

A hush fell over the room as Judge Stanley Sporkin entered, wearing his eyeglasses on his forehead. This was the same man who had overseen the savings & loan case between Charles Keating and the government, reprimanding Keating's lawyers, "You're not going to strong-arm this court." He'd received the nickname Attila the Hun during his time as an aggressive enforcement chief at the Securities and Exchange Commission.

Under the Tunney Act, the public had a certain amount of time—usually sixty days—to file comments on consent decrees before they were entered by a federal judge. In the case of Microsoft and the Department of Justice, only five comments protesting the decree had come in from small companies.

Now the formalities began, with the introduction of counsel: Bingaman, followed by Richard Urowsky, Microsoft's counsel (with Bill Neukom and a group of Microsoft attorneys also seated at the counsel table); and Gary Reback, a former lawyer of Philippe Kahn's, now with Wilson, Sonsini, Goodrich & Rosati, who had filed a brief for three of Gates' competitors only ten days earlier, causing quite a stir. Also present were Jeff Jacobovitz, of IDEAssociates, a tiny company that had been harmed by Microsoft and protested the settlement, and John Chapman, for the Computer and Communications Industry Association. The rest of the industry, in complete disgust, had stayed away.

Bingaman began. "We are here today in the final chapter, we believe, and it should be the final chapter of a six-month Tunney Act proceeding of a case filed July 15."

The judge wiped his nose.

Bingaman went on, pointing to diagrams on her chart. "The Court is required under the D.C. Circuit standard . . . to approve the decree if it is 'within the reaches of the public interest.' It is a very broad test," she said.

In her two previous sessions before Sporkin, it had been clear that he considered the consent decree weak because it did not address numerous allegations of Microsoft's predation stated in published reports he had read.

Bingaman continued, "The court is required to conduct the public interest assessment in the least complicated and least time-consuming manner possible."

Sporkin, impatient with her reading the laws back to him, shot back, "Can I use my own pen to sign the decree, or is the government going to supply that? I mean, I got to have some role here."

Tension had been mounting between the court and federal lawyers ever since that Reback brief had come in. Gary Reback had included with it a few samples of Gates' predation in memos that Kahn had passed on to him from an earlier dispute with Microsoft.

Sporkin and Bingaman were by now shouting at each other, and Bingaman was on the verge of tears, shaking her finger at the judge and defending her prized consent decree. "We did it in eleven months. . . . We sweated blood. What else can we do?"

Sporkin retorted, "I spent twenty years investigating white-collar crime. I come up with a different conclusion. When you get internal documents saying we're going to do it to hold off others . . ." Ironically, Sporkin had not even seen the stuff Bingaman had in her files.

Suddenly, Reback bolted up from his seat. Months earlier Bingaman had invited him to file a white paper with the Justice Department explaining the competitive impact of Microsoft's proposed acquisition of a tiny company called Intuit, the leader in personal finance software. Now Reback was looking like a traitor, criticizing her work as having been incomplete. Yet the Intuit merger review was still in progress, and Reback was supplying the Justice Department with much data and economic analysis from the industry.

Bingaman eyed Reback's standing figure, and waved her arms to shut him up. "I'm not interested in you coming up here," she scolded.

The sparring continued, as Bingaman told the judge, "You're in a dogfight if you're in a suit with Microsoft. These guys aren't stupid. I know why [computer makers] don't like 'em."

And then, with bravura, she added, "I sorta like suing these guys."

Bingaman went on to give her history of events. Sporkin sat chewing on something and rocking back and forth, like Bill Gates.

Things were getting outrageous, and the crowd of spectators in the court were erupting in laughter. Sporkin shouted at Bingaman, "I think I'm having more trouble with you than I had with Microsoft!"

When Reback finally got his chance, he fueled Sporkin's doubts, feeding him juicy tidbits. As an example of one area that Justice had ignored, Reback stated that he had earlier handed documents to an FTC attorney himself, and then to Sam Miller at the Justice Department, showing that Microsoft made companies provide confidential information in order to get operating system support. It had been just the previous spring that Miller had told him this was "a smoking gun," yet the witness was never interviewed by the Department of Justice.

By the end of the day, Sporkin had had his fill. But a month would pass before his decision.

Back in Germany, Theo Lieven felt he had been ignored. Why hadn't the Justice Department ever bothered to contact him? Only a few weeks earlier, in December, he had sent Bingaman a letter.

Lieven really would have preferred playing his piano. But this Microsoft problem had become a recurrent thorn in his side. He'd read about the Justice Department's consent decree being reviewed by a judge named Sporkin, and had made public Vobis' own problems with Microsoft. All during the investigations in the United States and the EC, he simply could not believe that no one from either organization had contacted him. After all, he was head of the largest computer manufacturer in Germany. The largest in Europe for that matter.

He had had enough and penned a personal letter to Anne Bingaman. It began, "As you may know VOBIS Microcomputer is a German based manufacturer and retailer of PCs. The total quantity of PCs shipped in 1994 will be more than 550,000. . . ."

Vobis was currently in the midst of yet another dispute with Microsoft, regarding its licensing practices. Lieven explained that Vobis' present contract with Microsoft was a per processor license agreement for DOS and Windows for Workgroups.

The problem was that, since November 20, 1994, Vobis had offered its customers a choice between "Windows-Only" and "IBM OS/2 & Windows" computers—a choice, Lieven said, that was "highly appreciated by our clients."

IBM's OS/2 was paid for by a per copy license agreement with IBM. Since OS/2 could be installed on top of Windows and "upgrade" the operating system, this made sense. However, "after introduction of Windows 95 in the market there will be a conflict between both operating systems. The customer then has to choose either OS/2 or Windows," Lieven wrote.

"We think that only a per-copy license for the Microsoft Windows can be the right solution: The customer may make his choice and Vobis will pay both IBM and MICROSOFT only for used licenses (i.e., on a quantity discount basis)," Lieven said.

But Microsoft would provide per copy licenses only at prices that more than doubled the cost of the operating system. It was using "per system" pricing, which the government had not forbidden, to accomplish the same thing it had accomplished with per processor licensing.

Under the terms of the current per processor contract, Vobis paid $28 per DOS&Windows license. "Microsoft's offered us for DOS&Windows under the terms of a per-copy license $23.50 for DOS and $39.95 for Windows. This increases our cost by $35.45. Obviously we cannot agree to these prices, as we consider these price increases to be a penalty for not accepting per system licenses," Lieven said.

After negotiations Microsoft offered a new per system contract, including the same pricing as the per processor license ($28 for DOS & Windows). The per system contract seemed to comply with the Justice Department's final judgment. "We had to define the 'systems' that will be shipped with DOS and Windows. After discussions with our product managers we recognized that again we have to license *all* systems for DOS and Windows," Lieven said. After choosing any specified system to be defined with DOS and Windows, the license fee had to be paid to Microsoft for all systems with the same hardware configuration, whether or not the customer wanted DOS and Windows. "In addition we believe that the customer should have the possibility of choosing any hardware config-uration with or without DOS and Windows," he said.

The solution suggested by the final judgment's Section IV G was "Choose separate free systems," Lieven noted. That is, these would not have to be shipped with DOS and Windows, and would be avail-able to run OS/2.

The problem, however, for computer makers like himself, was "If any system we produce shall have a chance in the market it also has to be offered with the Microsoft operating system. Windows has and will always have a significant market share. If we want to give a choice to the customer one of these choices has to be Microsoft."

That meant Vobis had to produce any system in two versions, Lieven explained, one for customers who choose Microsoft Win-dows and a version for those preferring IBM's OS/2. But this results in "at least 30 to 50 percent higher volume of products that have to be stocked simultaneously," Lieven explained.

It also resulted in higher financing costs and increased the risk of products becoming obsolete in a highly innovative market.

"Because we—and as we think all manufacturers—cannot take the above mentioned risks in this highly competitive market we would have to decide to ship our PCs only with Microsoft operating systems. In our opinion the per-system license means in effect the same as the per-processor license," Lieven said. "We believe that the majority of manufacturers will avoid the above described risks and license all their systems exclusively for Microsoft. As a result no other operating system will get a chance in the market."

The Department Of Justice's elimination of per-processor licens-ing was meaningless, Lieven was saying, since Microsoft was ac-complishing the same thing with per-system licenses.

What's more, after the consent decree was entered, Vobis entered into a contract with IBM to license OS/2. Immediately afterward, Microsoft audited Vobis' books, an unusual move seeing that both Vobis and Microsoft were already aware of the balance that was due Microsoft.

The audit, which was invasive but a permissible procedure stip-ulated in Microsoft's contracts in cases where the software giant felt a computer maker was not providing accurate shipment reports, was done for Microsoft by Deloite and Touche. Vobis believed that Microsoft subjected Vobis to the audit for retribution. Indeed, under oath in a deposition Lieven later stated that he felt the audit was done to punish Vobis for doing business with IBM.

The only area that Lieven believed the Justice Dept.'s settlement had a positive impact in the market was in its banning of minimum commitments. He said having a per processor license was like being in chains, and the per system contracts did not correct the situation. Minimum commitments likewise had restrained trade. "If you're a grocery store and prepay the milkman for a two-year supply, you won't buy someone else's milk." Microsoft used prepayments as another way to lock computer makers in. At least those things were now banned.

By Valentine's Day, Sporkin had made his decision. He rejected the settlement, filing an extensive legal brief explaining his decision. Basically, the Justice Department had not done a thorough job, he said, leaving much of Microsoft's predatory conduct intact.

Anne Bingaman now was allied squarely with Microsoft; both filed an appeal stating that Sporkin had gone too far.

The U.S. Court of Appeals in Washington, D.C., was packed to capacity on April 24, 1995. The court was hearing oral arguments in the Department of Justice's appeal of Federal Judge Stanley Sporkin's decision to throw out the agency's antitrust settlement with Microsoft Corp.

Now on the bench, Judge Laurence Silberman took the lead, with his colleague Edwards beside him and the mostly silent Buckley on the other side of Edwards. Overall, the tone of the hearing was one of skepticism concerning the merits of Judge Sporkin's unusual reversal. Indeed, the judges seemed to have already made up their minds: Sporkin had overstepped the authority given to him under the Tunney Act.

Nonetheless, Silberman and his colleagues posed a few questions—most of them seeming rhetorical—to the parties before them. Joel Klein, Anne Bingaman's new regulatory deputy, did all the talking as Bingaman sat in the courtroom among the throng from the Justice Department, dressed in lavender and looking tense.

The court told Klein that "it [was] a problem" that Justice had agreed to add concessions suggested by Sporkin to the settlement but abandoned those changes when Microsoft would not agree to them. In particular, Sporkin had recommended that a "special master" be assigned within Microsoft to assure that the software giant was complying with the terms of the consent decree. (Bingaman, in the February hearing before Sporkin, had agreed that she would be willing to add that requirement to the consent order.)

Silberman also pointed out that since Sporkin would be weighing future actions related to this antitrust settlement, "it seems to me we are having problems on the question of the methodology by which the decree was implemented." He went on, "How can we simply accept the decree as negotiated between you and Microsoft, and say, 'Well, you know, the district judge legitimately raised this point, even though the government was willing to accept it, nevertheless, we are going to ignore all of that on appeal?'"

The banter continued. Klein said, "The question is whether the [agreement] we negotiated is reasonable, and the answer to that is yes." He was in the odd position of standing up for Microsoft. But he hoped to rub it all in Microsoft's face when an opportunity came to show that the settlement had teeth after all.

Silberman shot back, "I think you basically preempt the role of the district judge in the Tunney Act proceeding."

During the hearing, it was pointed out that an error in the settlement was that no restrictions were placed on Windows NT. It seemed all too obvious that Microsoft was using its control of the operating system market to slowly but surely establish an entrenched position with NT.

It could not have been said more clearly than by John Chapman, an attorney representing the Computer and Communications Industry Association that day. Chapman told Judge Silberman, "In a statement filed with the SEC signed by Microsoft's Chairman Gates . . . NT has a migration strategy. It is here in their SEC filing with NT. It is the leverage of monopoly power, from the operating systems marketplace."

Chapman was fervently trying to impress upon the court the inadequacy of the settlement with Microsoft. He then read from Gates' signed statement, which spelled out that Windows NT provides for the "automatic migration of information from previously installed versions of Windows." In fact, Microsoft could not have been clearer about its intentions with NT when it addressed Wall Street. "The end point is NT, we've been told," said Rich Edwards, an analyst with Robertson, Stephens & Co. "Everything will lead to it."

But the issue remained unaddressed, and the court reinstated the consent decree. Bill Gates was once again off the hook.

Anne Bingaman and D'Artagnan had become chums over the months and had begun a diet together. In personal phone calls the two often compared notes about the big antitrust cases in progress.

Bingaman had spent months collecting evidence for a lawsuit blocking Microsoft's proposed merger with Intuit Inc.

In one phone call, Bingaman, who had been shocked over the uproar surrounding her consent decree, told him, "I'm just beginning to understand how Gates operates."

Later in the week of that appeals hearing, she filed suit.

Gary Reback had made his points well in his white paper. So had numerous witnesses interviewed by Justice. She noted to D'Artagnan, in amazement, "Gates still has not gotten the fear of Sherman."

Most companies sued for antitrust violations by the government became more careful about acting fairly in the marketplace. Gates, however, seemed to have only become more arrogant, and more aggressive in his predation.

Microsoft, as expected, appealed the Justice Department's suit, intent on taking over Intuit and leveraging itself into the personal finance market, which would open up vast new areas of commerce—including electronic banking and transactions of all sorts conducted via the Internet as well as private networks all over the globe—to the software giant.

Reback had divided the market into layers, explaining to the feds Microsoft's leveraging strategy.

The software giant had succeeding in forcing the market to migrate to a new operating system, Windows, via its dominance with DOS. It thereby inserted a new layer, the "graphical user interface" (GUI) between the operating system and the applications software. Using its leverage in the operating system and the GUI, it became dominant in applications software.

Microsoft's larger strategy was, in addition to controlling individual personal computers, to gain control of the intrabusiness "server" market, the backbone of business.

Internal documents and statements made publicly by Microsoft executives showed that Gates expected 300 million servers would be operating in the business world, running all manner of electronic devices, including phone systems, copy machines, and cash registers. He had a parallel vision in the home market, with consumer appliances and electronic systems throughout homes being controlled by a version of Windows.

"If a single company controls all business server markets and applications, that company has far greater market power in various sections of the economy than . . . mere control of the desktop would bestow," Reback reported to the Justice Department.

The home-to-business server market, which at the time, for the most part, did not exist, would emerge quickly with the Internet as its backbone. It would enable home banking, home shopping, online delivery of the news, travel bookings, and all types of commercial transactions.

Microsoft's approach was based on linking the layers within the same market—such as linking DOS to Windows on the desktop—and creating technological links between layers in one market and corresponding layers in another. That is, it would link Windows NT, its answer to Novell's NetWare, to the Microsoft Network and Internet Explorer, linked to Windows 95 on home computers.

Overall, Microsoft was pursuing a leverage strategy from markets in which it is dominant, to markets in which its position was weak.

Gates was shrewd. In addition to marketing tactics, he would create technological links to new markets from established monopolies.

———————————————

Gates seemed as carefree as could be. It was May 1995, and he was certain that his bid for Intuit would be approved on appeal. After all, hadn't they gotten that crazed Sporkin out of the picture?

Now he stood with his left arm resting awkwardly on his hip while his right gesticulated wildly as he spoke before almost 3,000 attendees of the Microsoft Interactive Media Conference in Long Beach, California.

The basketball giant Shaquille O'Neal had joined him on the stage at the Long Beach Convention Center just as Gates looked up Shaq's page in a demo of Microsoft's Encarta encyclopedia, with links to new content on-line.

Gates clicked on the icon for Microsoft's Shaq page—known as Shaq World—on the Microsoft Network, Gates' new on-line service, aimed at the likes of America Online and CompuServe. The celebrity appeared, towering beside him.

"I need a favor. Can I get a loan?" quipped O'Neal. "I'll play you one-on-one for the network."

After his speech Gates made a beeline for his limo and was gone.

It had been only a few days since the software giant had commenced manufacturing of Windows 95, and Gates seemed to be a mixture of elation and nerves.

"You may have noticed we've had some good publicity about Windows 95," he had said, in perhaps the largest understatement since a Microsoft attorney had conceded to a federal judge the previous winter that "Windows is successful."

Newspapers worldwide had played the product announcement as page one news. When had a company's product announcement—unless it was a scientific breakthrough, which Windows 95 was not—ever been played as front-page news?

Well in advance of its availability in the marketplace, Windows 95 seemed to have received more press attention than the presidential campaign. Still, it remained unclear to Joel Klein, who had launched a new probe of the company, whether Windows 95—and the Microsoft Network—would be a slam dunk for Gates, Shaquille or no Shaquille.

Microsoft directors had been selling off their shares in droves all summer. The inside buzz was that the Win 95 operating system would not live up to the hype.

Fearful of what the feds would make of his plans to include MSN in Windows 95, Gates designed a "switch" in the software with which he could easily eliminate MSN if the feds forced him to. But he never needed to use it. After much wrangling Justice did not file suit to prevent Gates from bundling MSN in Windows 95.

The fact was, Gates still hadn't gotten the right model for on-line transactions. It had nothing to do with a proprietary, closed system like MSN. It had to be totally open and Internet-based. In a few months it would become clear that the net was exploding faster than anyone had anticipated.

By May, Gates' play for Intuit had opened up a Pandora's box filled with the swarming competitors of his future.

In a federal district courtroom in San Francisco, on Monday, May 8, 1995, shortly after 9:30 A.M., what can only be described as the Intuit Follies had begun.

The courtroom was bristling with barely suppressed outrage, and Judge William Orrick's eyebrows seemed to have risen almost to his hairline.

After an extensive investigation, the Department of Justice had the previous month filed suit in federal court here to block Microsoft's proposed acquisition of Intuit. Armies of attorneys had shown up to protest what they viewed as an outlandish request: Microsoft wanted access, for its internal counsel and other company executives, to confidential documents its competitors had turned over to the Justice Department under subpoena in its investigation of the software giant's deal with Intuit Inc.

Now these competitors came scurrying forth like a bunch of aphids from under a rock, to explain to the judge the competitive damage that would result from granting Microsoft's request. The software giant itself had made sure its prolonged litigation with Apple Computer had been conducted under a protective order that prevented its archcompetitor from gaining sneak peeks at its competitive information. Mike Bailey, Anne Bingaman's new regulatory deputy, whose former firm, Brown & Bain, had represented Apple in that litigation, surely recognized the irony in Microsoft's current stance.

Many in the courtroom looked around in wonder: it seemed that all those who had been subpoenaed by Justice during its investigation of the merger were present.

There was Prodigy Services Co., Apple Computer, NationsBank, and CompuServe. Moreover, there were lawyers and executives from the investment broker Charles Schwab & Co., America Online, Computer Associates, Bank of America, Sunsoft Inc., and Visa International. Rounding off the pack, among the sea of suits sat attorneys for Wells Fargo Bank, U.S. Bancorp, Lotus Development Corp., Novell Inc., Banc One Corp., and the Software Publishers Association.

After all, among them they had turned over hundreds of thousands of pages of documents to the Justice Department over five months. Novell had provided—under subpoena—no fewer than 9,000 pages of documents in the course of Justice's investigation of the proposed Microsoft/Intuit merger. U.S. Bancorp had produced 2,600 pages of documents, including financial services budgets, customer profiles, analyses of revenues and expenses, past and future sales, and the company's expectations about future plans of competitors of Microsoft and Intuit. (The bank officer Linda Parker had been interviewed three times over five months and been deposed under oath by federal attorneys on April 20 in Seattle.) Apple had produced more than 1,000 pages of documents for its review of the merger, and Wells Fargo had given up almost 4,000 pages.

On March 31, Prodigy had been subpoenaed by Justice. NationsBank Corp., for its part, had disclosed under subpoena details of the development of its own PC-based home banking software, codenamed the HBS Product, which would compete with Quicken and Money. Like others, NationsBank had been subpoenaed early in the year.

On April 3 it was the turn of John Meier, vice president of marketing, planning, and development for CompuServe, to be subpoenaed. And on April 17, Charles Schwab & Co. had been subpoenaed by Justice.

If anything, this courtroom crowd provided a visual demonstration of how broad Microsoft's competition promised to become. Far from the typical members of the software community—the Lotuses and Novells of the world—here were banks, investment brokers, credit card companies, and on-line service providers.

Microsoft's Bill Neukom presided over the defendant's counsel table, accompanied by his company minions as well as outside counsel from four prominent law firms. All had convened because of Microsoft's last-minute objection to Justice's proposed confidentiality order limiting access of third-party documents to outside litigation counsel for Microsoft and Intuit.

No one present could have anticipated that little more than a week later Microsoft would announce it was abandoning its attempted acquisition of Intuit. That would be after the judge granted the restraining order restricting Microsoft execs' access to its competitors' confidential information. Had the order not been issued, the software giant would have received a gold mine of information covering technical specs for competing products, confidential market research and analysis, and contracts and negotiation strategies between banks and software companies.

But, from what followed this day in court, focusing on such a routine matter such as discovery procedures, it was clear that this was only a taste of the major battles to come.

The might of Microsoft's legal machine was not lost on Judge Orrick, who remarked at one point, "I counted—just for something to do—the number of lawyers on the defendants' side, which is twenty-seven."

The crowd in the courtroom represented the gamut of new markets and competitors Microsoft was now facing in new forays that the public mostly knew nothing about.

In his declaration in support of his company's application for a temporary restraining order preventing Justice from turning over its confidential information to Microsoft, Edward Bennett, CEO of Prodigy Services Co., said,

> It is profoundly disturbing to Prodigy that Microsoft's law and corporate affairs vice president . . . Neukom has been reported to believe that the opportunity presented for users of the Windows 95 operating system to access online services would fill customer demand for those services. This Microsoft officer, who publicly opined on market demand and strategy for Microsoft's proposed competitive online service, is the same officer whom Microsoft proposes be one of the Microsoft officers entitled to receive confidential competitive information produced by Prodigy. . . . Mr. Neukom is responsible for significant business operations at Microsoft.

Bennett then cited a January 31, 1994, press release issued by Microsoft in which Gates described Neukom as having "led Microsoft's efforts to establish, distribute and protect its intellectual property rights throughout the world." He also presented a February 24, 1995, *Washington Post* article in which Neukom discussed Microsoft's market strategy in providing "beta" software to competitors, pointing out that the company would give beta versions to others only when doing so would serve Microsoft's business interests.

"The prospect of disclosure of Prodigy's trade secrets to a person involved in market strategy casts in high relief the dangers presented by the production of trade secret documents by a third party such as Prodigy," Bennett said.

CompuServe identified areas of information provided to Justice that, in the hands of Microsoft, would cause it irreparable harm. "CompuServe studied the potential profit that it is thought Microsoft would earn, based on public information, when it enters more fully into the markets in which it apparently is headed," said the company's counsel William Farmer, who also represented America Online at this hearing. "We compared that to our own profit structure, and have identified the areas . . . we think are most profitable for us to go into and to continue pursuing." Farmer concluded, "If the places where we've identified the gold in these markets . . . [are] turned over to Microsoft's internal personnel—even Mr. Neukom—it's like handing Goliath a submachine gun."

To close the hearings, Gary Reback introduced Hank Gutman, outside counsel for Lotus Development Corp. "This was a delicious moment," said Gutman to his colleagues when it was all over.

Reback and Gutman had been archrivals in the ongoing legal battle between Borland and Lotus. Clearly, standing up to Goliath was occasion for even the fiercest of former enemies to stand arm in arm.

Gutman represented to Judge Orrick that "Lotus . . . views Microsoft as its biggest, fiercest, most significant competitor." One Microsoft counsel had earlier that day apologized to the judge for appearing in informal clothes because his suit pants had not shown up with his suitcase. Gutman joked that had Microsoft not sought to derail the protective order, "I wouldn't have had to hide Mr. Warden's pants on the airplane last night, and then he and I wouldn't have had to make the trip out here."

The judge replied, "That's what's called playing hardball in my court."

Throughout the day faxes arrived in the judge's chambers. During the lunch break one had arrived from Citibank, also protesting Microsoft's motion. "Is there anyone else? I'm concerned about going back to my chambers because when I went back last time there was another fax," the judge said before winding up the day's proceedings.

In a conference call with the press Neukom brushed off Microsoft's failure to file the most basic of legal documents in the case with "It's common to miss filing dates." Justice attorneys found this most unusual.

In the teleconference, Neukom seemed to bristle with annoyance as he made his statement. Gates appeared more nervous than usual, swallowing several times between words. Could it be that Microsoft had more to lose by airing its business strategies in court than it had to gain?

The agency had every reason to rely on evidence it had collected over the course of its scrutinizing of Microsoft to exhibit the software giant's pattern of anticompetitive behavior—and potential parallels between its impact in the PC market and the emerging online and personal finance worlds.

In a matter of days came the coup de grâce: the two Bills proclaiming to the world in a teleconference with the press and analysts that their reason for dropping the Intuit merger was the government's unfortunate habit of dragging its feet.

Déjà vu.

Joel Klein was embarking on yet another probe of Bill Gates. On Wednesday, June 21, 1995, the Justice Department issued another round of civil investigative demands to Microsoft. On June 23, Microsoft responded by filing a motion to quash in the Southern District of New York, asking the court to deny the invasive information request.

This filing too was a repeat performance for the software giant. It had quietly made a similar move just as Justice was about to enter the second phase of its antitrust investigation of the company in the spring of 1994. The press never picked up on that filing as the government and Microsoft quietly began settlement talks.

Filing such a motion is a routine practice of corporations seeking to stall federal investigations. During the first round, Neukom bragged to insiders that that motion to quash was what had scared Justice into settling.

Once again, the move would effectively stall the department.

15

LAST RITES

While Bill Gates was pushing into new markets, his competitors in the applications software market were dropping like flies. Jim Manzi and Lotus Development Corp. would be next, succumbing to Gates' market power as well as to Lotus' own organizational inefficiencies. Digital Research had been snuffed out, as had WordPerfect. Borland had lost its lead to Microsoft, as had Lotus. Gates had horizontally leveraged his advantages across the applications market, and no one could keep up. His own applications products were tightly tied to the Windows operating system, and soon they would be tied to the Internet as well.

The horse was sent hurling into space, and down went Cannavino tumbling over so that earth was a green blur and the solid brown of the horse had become a wave, no longer solid but as if made of sound or heat.

It was the summer of 1995, and IBM's chief strategist had taken a spill near his countryside estate as markets continued to tumble to Bill Gates.

Cannavino had recently received an urgent call from his friend Jim Manzi, and the two would meet in Cambridge for dinner and a heart-to-heart talk.

Cannavino had been wryly observing Microsoft's antitrust battles, thanks to *The Wall Street Urinal*, as he liked to call the great gray lady. Meanwhile, he'd read that Philippe Kahn had stepped down as head of Borland and his company was almost dead; Ray Noorda had retired; WordPerfect was gone. He knew that Lotus was about to succumb to his own big boss, Lou Gerstner. Jim Manzi was about to be eaten by IBM. It was perhaps an act of mercy.

Cannavino himself was in the midst of wrangling with Gerstner over his severance package; he was throwing in the towel as well. The Lotus chief needed some consoling, and some guidance.

Cannavino's horse, one of many in his stables, did not survive the fall. The fifty-three-year-old Cannavino sadly picked himself up; except for a sore back, he was as good as new after a quick visit to the emergency room.

Manzi had had quite a ride with Lotus over some twelve years. He couldn't have dreamed that its end would be so precipitous.

Jim Manzi's eyes had become large, brown saucers that rolled around in his head as if knocked loose by the force of events.

At least the Lotus chief would no longer have to think about Bill Gates: Lotus was unexpectedly in play.

Manzi was tired after all. Now his deep, mournful eyes roved from face to face, as if studying for the last time the visage of his minions, arrayed about him for a final night of mischief.

It was Thursday, June 8, 1995, the eve of the closing scene of what had started out as a corporate nightmare. It would have been so for any CEO: a hostile takeover was under way, and there was nothing anybody could do about it. Since April 1986, Manzi had spent what seemed to be a lifetime viewing the world from the top spot at Lotus Development Corp. He had overseen the company's rapid rise and subsequent decline. Tomorrow a deal would be all but nailed, and the empire would be lost. Tonight, however, this private dining room in Manhattan was his.

Manzi was administering a type of raucous last rites for the company. His confidante Kc Branscomb, senior vice president of business development, gazed at her pal: There went those eyes of his, rolling in his head, up and back in mock woe. A slight smile played about his lips.

"Louie! Louie!" the cry went up from the table. That was a Bronx cheer meant to honor Lou Gerstner, the unlikely corporate raider who had made a $3.3 billion preemptive bid for Manzi's empire just three days before. Manzi's pal Cannavino had warned him about Gerstner's strange habits, but he'd never expected this. Manzi and his cohorts roundly mocked Gerstner and his fat, slow-moving empire—despite the fact that it was about to make them all quite wealthy.

The Lotus culture, which in many ways embodied the baby boom generation, was about to be sacrificed to the prototypical corporation of the 1950s.

Stationed beside Manzi was his chief counsel, Tom Lemberg, who was usually cautious, intelligent, circumspect. The man had been admirably stoic during all those years the feds had grilled him about Microsoft, only to do nothing about the applications market. It was no wonder this fiasco was taking place. For this evening Lemberg had removed his normally unmoving mask to laugh uproariously with his chief. Joining in were CFO Ed Gillis and Russ Campanello, vice president of human resources.

The dinner at the Four Seasons was an elaborate one of many courses. It would be the last enjoyed by this group of corporate officers. In a matter of months, the Lotusians around the table would be history. Gerstner was about to swallow them all in a huge act of corporate faith. Some of the group had virtually grown up together as the corporation had grown, from its founding, to public offering, to the hostile takeover now under way. But, hell, the shareholders would make out like bandits. The wine flowed, and the plates were piled high. "Louie Louie," went the cry. Lumbering Louie and his plodding mammoth.

With the hostile bid, the week had progressed from an air of doom to the current giddy acceptance. But big questions remained: Who had won what? Was Louie about to be taken for a ride?

The words that had come sputtering out of Jim Manzi's fax machine on Monday morning, June 5, were somewhat unreal. "Because you have been unwilling to proceed with such a transaction . . ." That sentence, in the letter Gerstner faxed to Manzi at 8:30 A.M. announcing his hostile intentions, still made Manzi's blood boil.

Before receiving the fax, Manzi had gotten a phone call from Gerstner warning him that an announcement was about to be made. At the same time, IBM had its lawyers file suit in Delaware to rescind Lotus' poison pill, which it had adopted back in 1988. It also filed papers offering a $60-a-share cash bid to shareholders and appealed to them to replace Lotus directors with IBM candidates. It was a full-court press.

IBM's attack was the culmination of a secret May 12 meeting at which Gerstner and his top executives set June 5 for making their hostile bid. Gerstner insisted he was forced to take such strong action because Manzi had earlier spurned friendly talks in discussions with IBM Senior Vice President John Thompson.

What an outrageous notion that was to Manzi. To his thinking, Thompson—that "IBM weenie," as some of Manzi's cohorts liked to describe him—had only weakly hinted of anything suggesting a merger. Manzi recalled that over dinner on January 31, 1995, Thompson had said in the midst of an informal conversation, "Why don't we buy some equity in your company?"

"Go ahead," Manzi responded. "You can buy up to 15 percent, but be careful. There's a poison pill."

Thompson cryptically answered, "Well, Jim, what if we wanted *all* the equity?"

Manzi's eyes widened. "What the fuck does that mean?" he asked. "Why don't you just buy dinner instead?"

The subject never came up again, Lotus insiders insist.

Gerstner's outlandish idea that Lotus had rebuffed his offers to buy the company had left Lotus open to "the Mongol hordes," as one attorney described the "off-the-wall" shareholder lawsuits that came pouring in on June 5, only two hours after Lotus had received the IBM bid. Manzi spent most of the day in a state of shock, conferring with attorneys and confidants—including Richard Braddock and Roger Klein, his old buddy and former boss from McKinsey & Co.; the management guru Michael Porter; and, most important to Manzi, Gershon Kekst, one of his closest advisers and mentors.

By Tuesday morning, Manzi was quaking with rage. He wanted more information from the Street to plan his next move.

Bushy, bristly, and somehow elegant, Felix Rohatyn knew one thing: poison was a game. As one of the highest paid investment bankers on Wall Street—he had made at least $7 million the previous year—Rohatyn was an expert in the cagey business of takeovers, and every shape, size and color of that corporate takeover defense phenomenon known as the poison pill.

Rohatyn and his colleague Jerry Rosenfeld—a whiz on financial analyses of such deals—had been hauled in by Manzi on June 6. Rohatyn was sheepish. About a month earlier Manzi had come to him in a tizzy after he'd been tipped off that IBM was thinking about a hostile takeover of Lotus. "Don't be crazy," Rohatyn had told him. "It would be overkill. That would be the dumbest thing they could do. Don't worry—if they wanted to take over the company, you'll at least receive a letter first."

Now all Manzi's fears had materialized. He returned to Rohatyn, who, despite his embarrassment at not foreseeing IBM's move, was still the best Wall Street had to offer. Rohatyn, sixty-six years old, would play the ultimate adult, the voice of reality and a salve to Manzi's wails of existential angst. Manzi was "ballistic," according to those around him, and wanted to lay out a battle plan.

"I haven't had an original idea in twenty years," Rohatyn pronounced to the surprise of Manzi and the Lotus advisers and attorneys gathered in a conference room at the Manhattan office of Lazard Freres. After all, there is a mystique surrounding takeovers and takeover defense, Rohatyn went on, sounding more like a Tibetan seer than a Wall Street investment banker. These things have a life of their own. Sometimes they are unstoppable.

Manzi listened in disbelief, his lieutenants watching clouds of emotion evanesce across their leader's face. He was still looking for a way out that afternoon. "I can call AT&T, Olivetti, and I can call

Andy Grove at Intel. I can see whether Larry Ellison at Oracle can figure out how to scrape the money together," he said, according to his confidants. Manzi did make the calls to feel out his prospects, but he quickly concluded that they were long shots, and that he would not be able to hold his organization together long enough for the fight.

Rohatyn—along with Braddock, Klein, and Kekst—would slowly but surely bring Manzi around to reality. You can fight to your heart's content, he was told, but you've already lost the hearts and minds of your shareholders. Times had changed, and IBM—and Microsoft's unquestionable dominance—was ushering in a new era in the industry. The arbitrageurs and the large institutional investors now took priority. Hostile takeovers, once thought impossible in the software industry, would be accepted practice.

In an all-cash bid such as the one on the table, the bottom line was that, even if the poison pill held up, all a company could buy for itself was time. Manzi came to the realization that a battle with IBM would be difficult if not impossible. At the same time, he was intent on sticking it to Gerstner. He told his colleagues, "Gerstner wants to read the headline IBM BLITZKRIEG BAGS LOTUS. We're going to make him pay for that headline. We're going to make him do this deal so fast that he won't know what hit him."

Later that day, without consulting his advisers, Manzi called Gerstner. "You dropped a bomb. Do you know what you did?" he said. "Let's sit down, and let me hear what you have to say."

That night Gerstner and Manzi dined together in Gerstner's hotel room at the Sherry-Netherland in Manhattan. The food was atrocious, Manzi reported to his colleagues. He had ordered a hamburger medium, which came up to the room raw.

As the two men talked, Gerstner kept repeating that Lotus would retain its independence.

"Don't say that again. I'm not that stupid," Manzi said. "You wouldn't be spending $3.3 billion if you wanted to keep us totally independent." Manzi was making it clear to Gerstner that he was not dealing with a man who would hang on every word the IBM chief had to say.

Gerstner remained steely as Manzi passionately protested his tactics. Manzi confided he was "pissed" that Gerstner had made out that the two companies had been negotiating this for months. Gerstner obviously didn't give a shit how Manzi was feeling, the Lotus chief realized, according to his colleagues. That was OK. Manzi knew he'd nail him in the end.

Manzi's directness was not without its impact on Gerstner. His eyes widened when the Lotus head irreverently told him he was interested in only two jobs at IBM: "Thompson's and yours." Manzi later told his colleagues that the man seemed to have no sense of humor; the only jokes he laughed at were his own.

During the course of the dinner Manzi indicated he was willing to play ball. "I don't know why we can't have this done by this weekend," Gerstner replied. To Manzi, Gerstner was playing right into his hands.

After returning from the dinner, Manzi reported, "Lou is going to use money as a vehicle to get this done. We're going to get every penny we can."

Jerry York had let it drop that he was carrying a pistol. Not that Big Blue's cold-blooded CFO intended to use it. Today he didn't need a gun to be persuasive. It was Wednesday, June 7, and a break had occurred in the proceedings at First Boston Corp.'s offices, where a legion of investment bankers, attorneys, and corporate officers for IBM and Lotus were gathered.

The executive and legal teams of both companies were face to face for the first time. On the IBM side, Gerstner and York were surrounded by their lieutenants: Larry Ricciardi, Big Blue's new general counsel; John Thompson, in charge of IBM's software efforts; Brian Finn, investment banker for First Boston; Lee Dayton, general manager of business development; and Alan Finkelson, a Cravath, Swaine attorney and IBM's outside counsel.

Manzi sat with his own henchmen: Hank Gutman and Ken Siegel, attorneys at outside counsel Baker & Botts; Tom Lemberg, Lotus' chief counsel; Braddock; Rohatyn and Rosenfeld; Gillis, the Lotus CFO; Manzi's adviser Klein; Branscomb; Robert Weiler, executive vice president; Jack Martin, vice president of the communications products group; and the Wachtel attorney Barry Bryer, counsel to Lazard.

Rohatyn had opened the meeting by saying, "I'm surprised I'm still here as Jim's banker. A month ago, when Jim told me about this, I told him not to worry, that IBM wasn't that stupid. It was stupid then, and it's stupid now. You're going to have to pay to make it not hostile." The world's dean of investment banking was telling the chairman of IBM that his maneuver was pure idiocy.

The air in the room was thick. For relief, some light chatter had broken out. Rohatyn and everyone else knew Manzi was cornered. Gerstner, authoritative and stiff as usual, left no doubt about who was taking control of this meeting.

As the meeting continued, Gerstner and York made quite an impression. At one point York had made one of his infamous pronouncements, causing the blood to drain from each face around the table. "Organizations are resilient. They grow back," he said, waxing eloquent about the "efficiencies" of the corporate enterprise. Everyone knew what that meant.

Manzi sat impassive at the table. Having gotten past his initial shock and rage, he had a barely perceptible yet unmistakable smirk of defiance on his face.

York was about to officially set the price at the original offer: $60 a share. Just outside, in the reception area, a hulk of a fellow shifted in his chair. On the way in one attorney had whispered to another, "Must be Lou's bodyguard."

"No, it's York's," the other corrected. Indeed, the lug belonged to York, who could raise his own pants leg to reveal an ankle holster. "The guy has a sock pistol!" irreverent members of Lotus' senior management ribbed each others for days about that one. After all, York—five feet eight, 140 pounds, and balding—could boast of having fired 100,000 from the ranks of Chrysler. "If you'd fired as many people as he did, you'd need a bodyguard too," one member of the Lotus team quipped.

This mammoth deal, as it turned out, would be York's last performance for IBM. He would soon leave to join his old raider buddy, Kirk Kerkorian, as vice chairman of Tracinda Corp. When the man spoke, people trembled. This time York was plainly posturing—it was a role he had perfected. "Sixty dollars and not a penny more," he said.

No one believed that.

The first formal meeting between the two companies had been tense. "It was like kings and courts," said one of the participants. "Only Gerstner and Manzi had speaking roles. We were looking at all the chess pieces. The kings spoke—everyone else took notes."

The large meeting then was divided into groups and scattered to offices throughout the city. One group was charged with figuring out the legal terms and conditions. Another focused on what the price should be. Lotus CFO Gillis headed up this group, along with York, Rohatyn, and Rosenfeld. Also present was Brian Finn.

The third group homed in on how to maintain Lotus' structure and cultural integrity. Braddock, of the office of Clayton, Dubilier & Rice, the New York leveraged buyout firm, headed up this group. A Lotus director brought in as a turnaround consultant, he functioned as Manzi's second in command. Previously, Braddock had served as president and COO of Citicorp, and CEO of Medco Containment Services Inc. He was also on the board of Eastman Kodak Co. and had been a finalist for CEO there.

From Wednesday through Friday, Manzi and Gerstner sat in a room with a list of items to resolve from the various groups. The cultural stuff was the most problematic: how to make it work, and improve the level of trust between the two companies.

There was also a discussion of severance arrangements, to make sure Lotus people would stay on to give it a chance. At his insistence, the specifics of Manzi's role were not discussed until after the deal was done. He didn't want there to be a hint of a trade-off of shareholders' and employees' interests for his own.

When Manzi made observations about the divergence in culture, Gerstner countered that the three IBMers present—himself, York, and Ricciardi—were the only ones who still wore jackets and ties to the office. "But I have a beard," said Ricciardi, who was former chief counsel of RJR Nabisco.

Ricciardi was a pleasant surprise as the newest member of IBM's ranks. Whereas Gerstner and York were in blue suits and white shirts, he showed up at the meetings in a cream-colored sport coat, desert boots, and sports slacks. His beard and curly hair further distinguished him from the IBM mold. "Ricciardi appeared to be the one person there that will make decisions, and quickly," noted one member of the Lotus team.

In the end it came down to Gerstner saying, "As long as you perform, it's your company." All agreed that Lotus would remain in Cambridge and would be run by Manzi. They also agreed it would be a "private Lotus for the next two to three years."

On Thursday morning, Gerstner arrived at Manzi's room at the Four Seasons Hotel in New York City. Manzi still had dollar signs on the brain; he had to play on Gerstner's willingness to whip out the cash. Before the two left the room, Manzi "accidentally" side-swiped Gerstner so that he bumped into a small telephone table. On the table was a pad of paper on which, in Manzi's handwriting, were scrawled the names and phone numbers of several Japanese Gerstner knew—wealthy men capable of interfering with this deal.

Manzi could now perhaps milk another quarter of a billion dollars out of Gerstner. The IBM chairman had no way of knowing that Manzi had already been turned down by his Japanese friends. No one wanted to tango with IBM.

"And not a penny more," York had stated then left the room, to give Gerstner the freedom to go back on his CFO's word. It was Friday, June 9, and the two sides were still wrangling over terms. The bid would be sweetened to $63 a share.

Manzi and his backers had reason to be exhausted. They had spent the night before carrying on over dinner. Manzi had been at his acerbic best. And now the price tag was being inflated. Lotus' stock price had already doubled on speculation that IBM would raise its bid.

As the deal makers made their way to First Boston that morning, they were convinced they were being followed. Reporters and arbitrageurs had been hanging out in the lobby of the Four Seasons Hotel, where most of the Lotus group were staying. Now a group of Japanese businessmen were also waiting for the elevator.

The next day Lotus executives were tickled to discover that the press was speculating that a group of Japanese investors was vying for control of Lotus—apparently on the basis of the presence of the Japanese group in the lobby the previous morning. Manzi also had coyly hinted to a few members of the press that there was some interest from some Japanese investors.

Things would get sweeter still when Ray Ozzie, the technical genius who had created Notes, arrived on this day to meet with Gerstner. Lawyers and investment bankers on both sides were star struck. They asked to be introduced.

Ozzie entered the Manhattan office looking like a rock star in a black cashmere sport coat and blue jeans. A quiet and unassuming man, he seemed somewhat surprised to be in the limelight. Unlike both Manzi and Gerstner, Ozzie had not a trace of ego about him. According to one of his colleagues, he possessed a strong work ethic and "unbelievable commitment to the product."

He would prove to be the $3 billion man—the linchpin of the deal. Everyone present—including Gerstner and Manzi—knew Ozzie had enough money to do what he wanted. No one wanted to piss him off.

Gerstner and Ozzie disappeared into a room for a number of hours. According to insiders, when they emerged the price had been increased to $64 a share. It was a gesture of friendship and respect by Gerstner.

Manzi and Ozzie were very close and deeply respected each other. It was agreed that if Ozzie was to stay, Gerstner should hold on to Manzi. By the end of the day, the details of the agreement were all but ready to present to the Lotus board for a vote on Saturday.

Later Friday, Gerstner called Manzi to discuss the terms under which he would be willing to stay with the company. Manzi, who was at the Wachtel law offices, told him he'd call him back in a couple of hours, then went to see Klein and Kekst for some last-minute advice. While he was out, Gerstner called repeatedly. When the two finally talked, he asked, "Where were you?" Manzi paused. "I went to St. Patrick's," he said, remembering the facade of the cathedral just two blocks from Wachtel's offices. It was another of his jokes.

To an attorney, the conference room at Wachtel in Manhattan was cause to drool. The room could seat at least forty and was equipped with an enviable teleconferencing system. Tiny microphones were built into the light fixtures above the table, then hooked into the phone system. Some of the investment bankers and attorneys gathered for this occasion on Saturday, June 10, were paranoid that the mikes were on all the time, and that their asides and whispers could be heard.

Felix Rohatyn was about to perform for the Lotus board. The man was a master showman, presenting all considerations of the deal without seeming to be leaning in any particular direction. However, by the end of his presentation, only a madman could have voted against it. Rohatyn and Rosenfeld—presenting the financial details—were convincing indeed. Articulated by the rise and fall of his outlandishly bushy eyebrows, Rohatyn had mastered the rare art of persuasion that purports not to be reaching any conclusions but merely to be presenting facts.

A handful of lawyers then gave their spiels. Hank Gutman, the Lotus attorney known for his cleverness in the courtroom—he would be handling Lotus' dispute with Borland pending before the Supreme Court—presented his view of the merger, and Barry Bryer, Lazard's counsel, did his own presentation. Piping up also were Ken Siegel, a colleague of Gutman with the calm, unruffled surface of a Zen master, and Tom Lemberg, who was famous in some circles for having coined the term "head-fake" to describe Microsoft's snookering of the industry with respect to Windows development.

Bryer and Gutman spoke to the board's legal duties, and the standards by which they would be judged if their decision was reviewed after the fact.

That evening the Lotus board approved the deal. But there was still some mischief afoot. IBM's board would not be meeting until

Sunday, and early Sunday morning Lotus attorneys decided they weren't going to tell IBM that a decision had been reached.

It was more a matter of etiquette in the mergers and acquisitions community than anything else. The protocol, after all, was that the buyer approves first. The Lotus board had only approved the deal subject to IBM's own approval. It also was another perverse twist of Manzi's humor. Word filtered back to Gerstner that Lotus had not yet given an answer, and he interpreted this to mean that Lotus had rejected the deal.

"He went off the planet," said an IBM insider. Gerstner had quite a fit. "I thought we had a deal!" he screamed at Manzi.

Gerstner eventually calmed down, the IBM board met at the offices of Cravath, Swaine, and the deal was approved. Lotus then acknowledged its acceptance.

On Sunday a press conference was held during which an overzealous Gerstner whispered to Manzi, "Tell 'em about St. Patrick's." Lotus insiders subsequently got an enormous kick out of the fact that *The Wall Street Journal* reported Manzi's little white lie as fact. Manzi had never gone anywhere near the cathedral. As usual, no one but Manzi's initiates ever got his jokes.

After the press conference, lunch was held in a drab conference room. Manzi and his cohorts later had a few guffaws at Gerstner's expense. But as things wound down, the shell shock was general, "and the lunch sucked," said one worn-out attorney.

When you have a thermonuclear bomb lobbed at you—which is how Manzi described his experience of the hostile takeover bid— it's not surprising to feel a bit giddy at having survived the ordeal. Perhaps this explains Manzi's behavior the day after IBM announced to the world that it had closed the deal with Lotus.

In keeping with the spirit of his "last supper," Manzi decided to send a signal to IBM. He intended to remain independent, and he intended to get things done, despite the lumbering elephant whose shadow he would now be under. On Monday, June 12, Manzi ran a two-page ad in several newspapers and magazines that sported the Lotus logo on one side, the IBM logo on the other, and a slogan suggesting that Notes had brought the two companies together. "IBM and Lotus in Spiritual Harmony," the ad read. He didn't bother to get IBM's approval.

The companies were still in the process of getting FTC approval for the deal, and some Lotus attorneys were pulling their hair out about Manzi going ahead with the ad. The deal was signed, but the cash hadn't even passed hands yet. They told him, Hey, it looks like you're scrambling the eggs before the government has approved the deal.

"Fuck it, I'm doing it anyway," Manzi said.

Predictably, IBM was in a furor over the incident. "Things were quaking in Armonk," said one observer. "That kind of thing doesn't happen in the IBM culture. At that point I was thinking, This may never work out, but Jim was doing his best to show that he takes the independence notion seriously."

Manzi sent framed copies of the ad with personal notes to all his investment bankers, lawyers, and senior management. Defying the IBM bureaucracy tickled him to no end.

Gerstner was willing to put up with Manzi's high jinks, at least for a time, if that was the cost of acquiring Lotus and getting his hands on Notes. For the most part, he seemed to ignore Manzi's advice.

Over dinner in August, Manzi gave the IBM chief a software strategy document he had prepared. It suggested that keeping IBM and Lotus separate was a bad idea. "I'm prepared to smash the two companies together and run things," Manzi told Gerstner.

Gerstner replied, "Remember, Jim, I'm always going to ask you for one thing: time."

"Fine," Manzi replied. "Just remember one thing, Lou: There is not time."

Thompson, aware of Manzi's proposals, told Manzi three times that he was willing to step aside and allow Manzi to take over the combined software business.

"Lou had the opportunity to give Thompson another job. He could have made him CFO or head of the PC company. It was clear this wasn't going to happen by the end of the year. That's why Jim left. He wasn't willing to hang around waiting," said a Manzi confidant.

Meanwhile, Gerstner was bringing in executives from American Express and Boston Chicken, people cut out of his own mold. Manzi griped to his colleagues, "All they talk about is brand management and advertising. It's insane." Manzi had sat through just about the last meeting he could stand concerning "brand personalities for the AS/400," said one insider.

Notes was a critical part of Gerstner's overall plan for IBM's revival. He had become almost "spiritually" sold on the concept of Notes and what it could do for his notion of "network centric computing." In fact Gerstner's philosophy was what the likes of Novell's Ray Noorda and Sun Microsystems's Scott McNealy had been spouting about for years. With the Internet explosion, the concept that the network is the computer was beginning to resonate with the masses.

Gerstner believed Notes could tie together IBM's disparate computer systems and help solidify its role as the computing solutions provider for the corporate enterprise. Notes would become one of IBM's strategic weapons with which to break Microsoft's hold over the desktop and its growing influence in the server market.

At the same time IBM was acquiring Notes, however, doubts began to surface among the pundits over the future of Notes in an Internet-centric world. Many of the groupware capabilities that had been available only on Notes were now being offered on the Internet from a variety of companies at a much lower price. The possibility that Gerstner had paid billions of dollars for a technology past its prime was becoming more real as 1995 came to a close.

Regardless of the challenges, Manzi was anxious for a chance to head up the combined software operations of the two firms. But in a meeting with Gerstner, Manzi was told he couldn't be given a larger job within IBM because he just didn't "know the IBM organization." Manzi protested that his track record was superior to IBM's: "I just sold my software business for $3.5 billion!"

Inside Lotus, employees had been taking bets on whether Manzi would make it until Thanksgiving. After being denied the opportunity to head up IBM's $11 billion software business—the biggest piece of the pie—Manzi quit, with $78 million to show for his 12 years with the company.

Thompson held the job Manzi coveted. Some within Lotus argued that he was a lackluster wimp whose only aim was to please his boss, that he didn't have an original thought in his head. Other IBMers described Thompson as a superb executive.

"Manzi decided he would stay only if he could make a difference," said one of his confidants. "He overestimated Gerstner's ability to deliver."

Manzi's departure came around the same time as the exodus of other Lotus executives, including Bob Weiler, Tom Lemberg, Ed Gillis, and Kc Branscomb.

By February 1996, when a stream of talent at the company was expected to depart, Lotus stood to lose as much as 25 percent of its workforce. When Gerstner had been sweetening the deal for Lotus, Manzi got him to agree to a bonus—10 percent of their salary—for 1,000 key employees if they agreed to stay through December. During November, insiders say, scores of these employees were calling Manzi for moral support about their decisions to leave after Christmas.

Longtime IBM watchers said that Gerstner had not changed the company's sluggishness. "They've put a new head on but have not changed the body. That body can resist anything," said one Lotus insider. The personality of IBM had not profoundly changed despite a sprinkling of newcomers like Ricciardi.

Manzi, on the other hand, had invested much of his life in Lotus. His colleagues said his key problem was that "he wants to move too fast." Jim Manzi within IBM was like "a sixty-mile-an-hour car slamming into a brick wall." But Manzi critics pointed out that he was also responsible for slowly driving Lotus into the ground. Embracing IBM's tender offer, despite the personal affront it represented, would be his most noble deed, they said.

In his farewell letter to Lotus employees, Manzi wrote: "I am most proud . . . not of what we've accomplished, but in how we've accomplished it. As an organization, we've developed a commitment to the human spirit and tried to create a 'soulful' environment. . . . Through it all, we tried not to take ourselves too seriously, and always to laugh out loud with one another."

Manzi's employees responded by hanging a banner across the building that faces Lotus headquarters in Cambridge. In mid-November it still hung there, with the words "Jim: For all of what Lotus has been . . . both body and soul. Thanks."

Earlier that month, in a patch of woods in the Adirondacks, one could have caught sight of the tousled brunette head and slim figure of Jim Manzi, alone, indulging in a bit of 1980s-style, Lotus-like self-actualization. Manzi was camping—something he's always wanted to do and never had time for—and anticipating a trip to Tuscany for some world-class cooking classes. His plan was to do nothing until the first of the year, then to focus on his next move.

Times had changed. The "new-age" culture of Lotus was long gone. The biggest merger in the history of the software industry had ushered in a world in which hostile takeovers are a practical necessity, not an act of barbarism.

Software companies now had to get out of the way of Bill Gates.

16

BOMBS

Netscape was redefining the competitive landscape through its software for accessing the Internet. The tiny company had Bill Gates in a frenzy as he sought to leverage his Windows monopoly into Netscape's turf. Justice was on his trail again, sending out subpoenas to Gates and his new competitors. As Netscape soared, convincing major computer makers like Apple to adopt its technology, Gates was about to stage a little coup, killing many birds with one stone. Apple had quietly threatened him with another patent infringement suit, but his little-known alliance with Steve Jobs turned the tables on the company.

Roberta Katz, the forty-eight-year-old chief counsel for Netscape—the only woman to hold such a position in the industry—had just moved the last mountain of evidence off her desk. The Justice Department's San Francisco attorneys seemed to have been crawling all over Silicon Valley in recent weeks.

It was August 1996. Joel Klein, via his high-tech attorneys in the valley, was about to lob another round of subpoenas at Microsoft, as well as its new competitors in the Internet commerce space.

Back on December 7, 1995, Pearl Harbor Day, Gates had made a point of the change in his strategy. The chairman, in a speech at an

Internet strategy workshop and before several hundred analysts and reporters, marked a turning point in his public position regarding the role of the Internet. "The Internet is pervasive in everything that we're doing," Gates said. "For Windows, it's very simple. We want to be the best Internet client. . . . A major way we'll do that is through integration."

Gates went on, "We'll take what we do as a stand-alone machine or as a machine that works on local area networks; we'll tie that into the ways that we embrace the Internet, taking the best of the local case and the Internet case and bringing these together."

The day of that speech, the stock of rival Netscape Communications Corp. dropped 17 percent, and it never recovered. The world knew Gates usually got any market he went after.

Gates' view of the Internet had slowly changed shape.

To the Justice Department, Bill Neukom later portrayed Gates as having switched his focus to the Internet in December, based on that speech. In fact, the chairman had been obsessing over how to beat Netscape for some time. On May 26, 1995, Gates wrote a memo to his executive staff that Microsoft also leaked to the press. His memos to top executives were often informal, and often never seen by his secretary.

Entitled "The Internet Tidal Wave," the memo described the Internet as "the most important single development to come along since the IBM PC was introduced in 1981. It is even more important than the arrival of graphical user interface (GUI)."

In the same memo, Gates recognized the threat browser technology posed to Microsoft's dominance: "A new competitor 'born' on the Internet is Netscape. Their browser is dominant, with 70% usage share, allowing them to determine which network extensions will catch on. They are pursuing a multi-platform strategy where they move the key API [applications programming interface] into the client [browser] to commoditize the underlying operating system."

Gates' top executives were likewise obsessing over the threat posed by Netscape and Navigator to Microsoft's operating system monopoly. These were the same men who had helped Gates keep control of the operating systems market in the early days of DOS and Windows. Now they were helping him orchestrate a plan for snuffing out Netscape.

Brad Silverberg, senior vice president for the Internet Platform and Tools Division (IPTD), who had schemed with programmers on how to keep the public from knowing about the code they had created in the beta version of Windows 3.1 targeted at sabotaging DR-DOS, now offered his ideas. On April 25, 1996, in his presentation to other Microsoft executives and programmers at a meeting of his division, Silverberg said, "The Internet Battle: This is not about browsers. Our competitors are trying to create an alternative platform to Windows."

Other executives spelled out the nature of the battle as they saw it. Following the lead of Gates and Silverberg, a few months later, on June 22, 1996, in a document titled "Winning @ Internet Content Marketing Plan," Andrew Wright, manager of advanced authoring tools, said,

> The rise of the Internet has been driven by the success of a series of "platforms" that utilize [Internet protocols such as HTTP] at their core and provide a set of APIs for ISVs [independent software vendors] to develop on top of. By far the most successful platform to date has been Netscape's, with Netscape Navigator on the browser and Netscape Suite Spot on the server. The core threat for Microsoft is the potential for this platform to abstract the Win32 API. For example, if Netscape continues its success in getting ISVs and ICVs [independent content vendors] to develop applications for Netscape's client/server API's, these API's could be the most important API's in the future putting Win32 and Microsoft's platform position in jeopardy.

Months earlier, on February 22, 1996, another top executive and Gates confidant gave a presentation explaining the strategic importance of the browser market to the future of Microsoft. Paul Maritz, group vice president of Microsoft's Platforms Group, could not have

236

been more to the point, describing "The Problem: Browser Market Share."

He said, "[Web] pages become applications; Netscape/Java is using the browser to create a 'virtual operating system' [that is] no longer a browser, now an environment. . . . Windows will become devalued, eventually replaceable?"

On April 4, Microsoft worldwide marketing managers were instructed to worry about browser share "as much as BillG[ates]" and "go for maximum browser share."

Brad Chase, vice president of developer relations and marketing in the Platforms Group, in a memo titled "Winning the Internet Platform Battle," noted that although the browser is a "no revenue product . . . you should worry about your browser share, as much as BillG because: we will [lose] the Internet platform battle if we do not have a significant user installed base."

He went on, "The industry would simply ignore our standards. Few would write Windows apps without the Windows user base. At your level, if you let your customers deploy Netscape Navigator, you [lose] the leadership on the desktop."

Clearly showing Microsoft's predatory intentions in giving away free products, Chase instructed his colleagues, "You should be able to break most of Netscape licensing deals [with Internet service providers] and return them to our advantage because our browsers are free."

The master contract negotiator Joachim Kempin, who had done such a brilliant job in Germany and all over the globe locking computer makers into DOS contracts, then Windows contracts, and further into bundling deals with Microsoft applications software, now also was fully aboard the Internet bandwagon, driven by Gates' clear mission.

Later in deposition testimony, Kempin acknowledged the immense threat to Microsoft if other companies were allowed to succeed in the browser market. He said that by adopting a non-Microsoft browser interface, computer users "might not know if they are on a Unix machine, or a Macintosh, or a Windows machine anymore. Because the next browser might have a totally different interface, and it just can't be in our interest to promote that other interface. . . . I mean if the user gets used to a totally different metaphor, he might not buy a Windows machine anymore. He might just say, oh, now I can buy a Mac, I can buy a Unix machine, I can buy a Nintendo machine."

As had been true historically, Gates' concern was not making great products but keeping the world locked into using his products.

While Gates and his top executives were scrambling for leverage on the Internet, the competitive landscape was about to be redefined once again. Gates had always been attentive to paradigm shifts. Windows had come about because of his recognition of the superiority of Apple's user interface on its Macintosh computers—which required only one click on graphical icons to accomplish tasks, instead of using arcane character-based commands like DOS.

Back in February 1995, after seven years of wrangling, Apple's copyright infringement suit against Microsoft had been dropped, following an appeal by Apple to the Supreme Court. Apple had lost. The case had gone through three judges, and during the time it was being litigated, copyright law had evolved in Microsoft's favor. Pundits speculated that had the case been tried sooner, the law might have evolved quite differently. Ironically, it had taken all those years for Gates to finally catch up with Apple, imitating most of its operating system functions with Windows 95.

Now, in the spring of 1996, Apple chief counsel Ed Stead had a few cards up his sleeve. Over the years, he had been building up Apple's portfolio of patents—for offensive and defensive purposes. He was not going to make the mistake of his predecessors, who attempted to protect the company's intellectual property rights through copyright law versus patents. These days, copyright cases were much harder to win than patent infringement cases. In the future he would make Gates pay dearly for any attempt to steal Apple technology.

According to his colleagues, Stead was convinced that it was Microsoft's massive public relations campaign that had swayed the courts. The software giant, whose resources and sophistication in such matters dwarfed Apple's, to Stead's thinking, had mounted a massive "disinformation" campaign, portraying Apple's case as bad for the industry. (Later, Microsoft would launch similar massive PR efforts to combat Joel Klein's antitrust suit.)

Now Stead and newly named chief technology officer, Ellen Hancock, had dropped a quiet little bomb at Bill Gates' feet. Hancock, appointed by her friend Gil Amelio, now Apple's chairman and CEO, had been a previous colleague of IBM's top strategist, Jim Cannavino. She'd just come off a thirty-year stint at IBM.

This wasn't the first legal problem in the past several months between the companies. Back during the Sporkin circus, in February 1995, Stead had filed a lawsuit against Microsoft for stealing Apple code and using it in Microsoft products as well as distributing it to other companies and on the Internet. He had won an injunction against the software giant, forcing it to stop distributing the code. But this was something bigger.

Apple believed numerous attributes of Windows 95 as well as Microsoft Office were infringing on a range of Apple patents.

Little did Stead and his colleagues know that Steve Jobs would come back into the picture, take control, and give everything away once again.

Ironically, at least according to Neukom's account to his friends, Steve Jobs had helped Microsoft in that troublesome copyright suit. But if such help ever occurred, neither Stead nor any other member of Apple's executive office ever knew about it.

Back in the fall of 1993, there had been an engagement party for Gates held in San Francisco, at the home of Microsoft board member Dave Marquardt. Now appearing as Eliza Doolittle to his Henry Higgins, Dave Marquardt's wife had once been a stewardess—he had fallen in love with her on his many business flights. She and Marquardt had invited their guests to come in costume.

Henry Higgins and Eliza Doolittle had meandered across the

room, followed by Maid Marian and Robin Hood. The man dressed as the hero who took from the rich and gave to the poor was none other than Neukom, and the Maid of course was Stefanie Reichel.

Gates' old flame, Ann Winblad, had strolled across the room with another woman and a man. The threesome came in the guise of a ménage à trois from the 1960s.

The Great Gatsby and Daisy had been toasted by all. The former was one of Gates' favorite characters, and he and Melinda French had played the couple well.

The party was followed by another fete to Gates, following his wedding, in January 1994, at the home of Microsoft's Chris Larson.

This time Steve Jobs sat, amid champagne glasses, across the table from Neukom and Stefanie Reichel, among other guests. When Jobs had strayed away from the table, Reichel nudged Neukom in the ribs with her elbow. "What is *he* doing here?" she asked, her eyes popping at the sight of Jobs, who she had believed to be an enemy of Gates'.

"Oh, of course he's here," Neukom said. "He was of great help to us in the Apple suit."

Now, in 1996, in a series of meetings with Microsoft, Stead and Hancock were coming on like Robin Hood and Maid Marian. Stead and Apple staff attorneys explained to Microsoft executives— including Gates and Greg Maffei, that this was serious business, and they wanted Gates to offer a solution. Stead thought he had a case that would prevent Gates from continuing to ship Windows 95 and Microsoft Office. Gates had already had to do a worldwide re-call of DOS 6.0 when two years earlier the judge in the Stac trial had ordered him to stop shipping the code he'd stolen from Stac. Given all his problems with litigation lately, and with the feds, they were sure he would not be thrilled with another huge lawsuit with Apple.

The talks continued for months, but no resolution seemed forth-coming. Apple was in a precarious position and had been losing market share steadily. Meanwhile, Gates was paranoid. It didn't matter that by the end of 1996 his personal wealth had swelled to $23.6 billion.

Gates wanted Apple's commitment to his Internet Explorer, and to his version of Sun Microsystems' Java technology. He was paranoid, not only because Apple had chosen Netscape as its default browser but because of Apple's future operating system plans. He'd heard that it would be running on Intel processors, the foundation on which he'd built his own empire. (Apple had historically used a totally different processor architecture, based on chips from Motorola.)

Meanwhile, Hancock's head was spinning. While Gates ignored Apple's new claims and focused on revising his operating system strategy radically in response to the threat of the Internet, Apple was confronting its own operating system future.

Upon her arrival at Apple in July, Hancock had been thrown into the midst of solving a crisis. She was quickly realizing that a project code-named Copland, which was the essence of Apple's future and had been designed as Apple's answer to Gates' Windows 95, was about as viable as Cannavino's maimed horse.

Copland was dead despite the fact that the company had invested years and millions of dollars in its creation. It had been killed by gross mismanagement on the part of Apple.

By September 1996, Amelio and Hancock had put together a secret team to shop the industry for a technological epiphany. Apple's future depended on it.

———————————

In early November the rolling hills outside Doug Solomon's window hung with fog. Banks of mist were shifting as if about to draw clarity out of the haze.

Plate glass caught his reflection. Solomon, Apple's senior vice president of strategic planning and corporate development, was six feet tall, and balding, with a gray beard and oversized glasses. He hated his appearance in Apple's corporate reports. Others, however, found him intellectually attractive and dignified. One read quizzical amusement in the small lines around his eyes. Years of engineering curiosity had put them there.

The secret team had come up with a code name for each project now under evaluation. Robin was alive, but Bluebird had begun to

241

recede. Blackbird, on the other hand, still looked quite viable. As for Turkey, well, it remained one hell of a turkey. A curious interest in birds had arisen inside Apple's executive meetings—that would have been the conclusion of anyone listening at Solomon's door during the months of October, November, and December.

The "SWAT" team was now in the thick of it, and e-mail and memos were flying between the executive committee and team members. Solomon had been set up as team leader, overseeing the secret assessments now under way. Evaluations of the options would continually be presented to the executive committee and later to the board.

Solomon sat on Apple's executive committee. After fourteen years at the company, he had worked in virtually every part of the organization, from product development to market intelligence. He'd worked with Steve Jobs the first time around. These days Solomon reported directly to Amelio, with dotted-line responsibility to Apple's CFO, Fred Anderson, for corporate development activities.

These days Apple was getting at least a call a day from companies proposing their technology. "We've got strange people calling," Solomon would note to his colleagues. "From one-person companies to major corporations with ideas about what we should do." Sometimes Solomon caught himself drumming lightly on the boardroom table. He had been a drummer for years, with a variety of bands. He loved jazz, Ahmad Jamal in particular. And Vladimir Horowitz's rendering of a Chopin polonaise was enough to make him feel that he could survive any corporate fiasco.

The phone rang. Amelio, whose office was a few steps away from Solomon's, was calling from Asia. "Hey, I want you to handle something for me," he said. "I just got a message from Steve Jobs."

Aside from catching the Apple founder on Rollerblades occasionally on the streets of Palo Alto, where both men lived, Solomon hadn't seen Jobs in years.

How had things come to this point? Lead engineers at Apple were in a state of disbelief. They had pursued for more than two years what they thought to be a heroic path: the creation of Apple's answer to Microsoft's Windows 95. The Maxwell Program Office had been started in 1994. Maxwell was yet another code name for Copland.

Apple engineers, gleeful in their capacity to create a little 007-like intrigue, established a policy of dual code names for unannounced projects. One set of names was invented by marketing, to be leaked freely to the outside world and the press. The other set was for internal use only. (This got confusing of course for Apple insiders, who couldn't keep all the names straight, and eventually Apple returned to a single set of code names. After all, whatever names they went by, when it came to company secrets, Apple—like most of its Sili Valley neighbors—had a history of springing more leaks than the *Exxon Valdez*.)

With Copland, a brief tradition began of using inventors' names internally and musical names externally. Inside Apple, Copland had become known as Maxwell. The namers of Copland, however, had already broken ranks. As opposed to referring to the Scottish physicist James Maxwell, Maxwell was an acerbic comment on what had come before, paying homage to the Beatles' song "Maxwell's Silver Hammer," in which a murderous character named Maxwell Edison wields a silver hammer to kill off his foes. Maxwell was to depart from the past as never before, and it would gradually take a silver hammer to the Macintosh operating system legacy.

As a whole, Copland was to be Apple's long overdue "modern operating system," a complete rewrite of the existing Mac OS. It was the largest software project Apple had ever attempted.

Wayne Maretsky had been the technical lead for Copland ever since work on the project had begun. Now Maretsky stared at the page in front of him. "We're fucked." The words, scrawled across the top of a confidential notebook page from reams of notes taken by lead engineers during the last days of Copland, succinctly summed up the situation.

The obvious problem was that the architecture was all wrong and the project had gone out of control. A parade of inept managers had failed to recognize the situation. Apple was now out of time, and on the brink of disaster. Not even Bill Gates could be blamed for the way Apple had botched its future.

Copland engineers found themselves dangling at the end of a broken chain that could be traced back to the introduction of the Mac, in 1984. Since that time the Mac OS had been layered upon year after year like a palimpsest. Ancient shards of code that had once had meaning and purpose lay under the surface, increasingly causing problems for newer software. It was the problem with all "legacy" systems, but, unlike its competitor Microsoft Corp., Apple never knew how to manage software projects and for the most part had conducted business as if it were a hardware company.

It had been in May 1996 that it started to dawn on Apple engineers that Copland was in deep trouble.

Winston Hendrickson had served as senior technical lead for all user experience components of Copland. He'd been at Apple for about a decade. When he returned from his sabbatical in September, he found his colleagues embroiled in an evaluation of technologies from four different companies: Jean-Louis Gassee's Be Inc., with its Be OS; Sun Microsystems' Solaris; NeXT's operating system; and, he was surprised to discover, a version of Microsoft's Windows.

Blackbird, Robin, Bluebird, and Turkey were the code names for each, within Apple.

While he'd meandered through Europe, sunned himself in Hawaii, and puttered around the house building bookshelves and cleaning up the garage, Copland had been killed. Upon his return, Hendrickson was immediately pulled into the evaluation team.

Back in June, ironically, Hendrickson had advised Apple management that Copland would need a new architecture if it was ever to be viable. It was now time to convince the board that he was correct. Hendrickson had written what would turn out to be the libretto for Apple's future. He called it the Alpha Paper, a confidential white paper on how Apple could accomplish its new architecture and easily add features while retaining compatibility with past software.

By August it was clear that Copland would never make it out the door. The former vice president Ike Nassi had commissioned some task forces to look at what needed to happen with the OS strategy and the architecture to get Copland back on track.

In a series of meetings before leaving on his sabbatical, Hendrickson had made a presentation. Apple needed to divide the operating system into two parts. The two parts would sit on top of the core operating system or kernel. Diagrammatically, on the left would be a box that represented the current Mac OS and programming interfaces, which would provide compatibility with what had gone before. On the right would be a box representing the brand-new interfaces for the "modern OS." The box on the left would always be filled by Apple's own technology. The box on the right, however, needed to be filled somehow. The work Apple had done just didn't cut it.

Gil Amelio's eyebrows were almost airborne with arch sentiment. There was a lot he didn't want to hear. "I'm not ready to give up yet," he said.

Now his team was confronting him with a modest proposal from Bill Gates—the essence of what Apple called Project Turkey—that would head off all future and pending litigation between Apple and the software giant. It would also mean an all-Windows world.

Huge evaluation matrices had been put together to measure all options—Sun's Solaris, NeXT, Be, Windows NT, and what remained of Copland. Key on the list were features such as multimedia; international, graphics, and font technology; how robust the system was; stability; the ability to license the software to computer makers; Apple's ability to innovate on the platform; and so on. Of these, the five top executive priorities were stability; the Mac "look and feel"; time to market; Mac OS compatibility; and the ability to differentiate against Microsoft.

It was the day after Thanksgiving, and Turkey, the technological coup now being lobbed at Apple by Microsoft, was getting hot. An analysis of the impact of Microsoft's proposal had been prepared

by several Apple managers and directors for the presentation unfolding for the executive committee. It was powerful. Essentially,
Microsoft wanted Apple to replace the Mac OS with Windows. The
fact that the proposal had gotten this far was nothing short of mind-
boggling, Amelio's top executives muttered to themselves.

Before sitting down to a final face to face with Microsoft, Apple
executives were doing a thorough internal analysis of the proposed
deal. A list of top concerns was put together, including technical
and business questions. Besides being a PR disaster, what would a
partnership with Microsoft mean? Apple's senior executives listened nervously.

Highlighted by slides, the briefing gave a sobering view of the impact of Apple basing its future on a Microsoft Windows NT–based
core. Amelio, Hancock, and Solomon were given a cold-blooded
view of one situation by lead engineers.

"The [Windows] NT operating system is clearly the best in class
implementation of a modern, robust design," the presenting engineer stated. Based on work started by Dave Cutler at Digital
Equipment Corp. in the mid-1980s, Microsoft had redefined enterprise computing around the NT standard. Amelio and his top executives were told that "Microsoft clearly adopted a product
direction that will push the NT kernel down into the desktop market, where it would replace the fragile and troublesome Windows
95 core OS."

Should Apple adopt the NT core as the base of its Macintosh
business, Apple could rest assured it would be using the most pop-
ular and robust OS in the business, the engineer continued. However, at the same time Apple would find itself in a tenuous position
"with a product offering based on narrow and ill-defined advantages."

If we falter, Microsoft will be on par, the engineer said. If we trip,
they will quickly duplicate our capabilities and eliminate our potential differentiation."

Perhaps the most problematic aspect of adopting NT, he said, was
that "we will be forced to compete with Microsoft on their platform." The staff looked horrified.

The entire investigation team felt that if Apple were to announce it was embracing NT, it would have a threefold impact on Apple's business. First, Macintosh sales would be stalled until such time as Apple's new product and market position became clearly established.

"It would also lead to the total abandonment of the Apple's programming interfaces as a platform standard, and complete the transition to Windows as the industry programming interface. That is, all developers would give up development for Macintosh.

"Finally, the deal would eliminate Apple's ability to influence the future of PowerPC, because the PowerPC partners would likely believe Apple would port the Macintosh experience to the ×86 and other platforms regardless of its announcements to the contrary," Amelio was told by Apple engineers.

"This threefold scenario would force Apple to embrace Windows as a cross-platform standard, with only Java as a possible alternative," Amelio was told.

Java was Sun's technology that Gates and his executives had been obsessing over in their e-mail communications. It, like Netscape's Internet browsing software, threatened to destabilize Gates' monopoly.

Amelio's advisers went on. If "Turkey" were adopted, Apple "would effectively cease to create OS software, middleware, and [programming] layers. Its products arena would be defined by its intellectual property and customer value differentiation, along the lines of plug and play, ease of use, industrial design, and so on," one engineer explained.

The assessment was that only by "relentlessly pushing forward in these areas and actively increasing the gap between an Apple label product and the equivalent Wintel product could Apple survive."

In discussion, Apple realized that its advantage in the marketplace would be narrowed so much—"because as an engineer put it Microsoft would be copying us as fast as it could get away with it"—that if the company ever screwed up, any advantage Apple had would disappear.

"The Microsoft machine would just consume us with this dopey grin on its face," the executive committee was told. Throughout the briefing there were references to sleeping with the enemy.

On the sunny side, Apple senior executives scrutinized the possible benefits of such an alliance for the industry as a whole. Unlike any other of the deals Apple was looking at, "a deal with Microsoft may well enable Apple to drive an industry standard component software solution across all platforms, resolving the OLE, OpenDoc, Java, JavaBeans confusion," the engineer informed the committee. The later technologies represented the warring realms of technological standards, the first owned by Microsoft, and the rest by Sun Microsystems and other companies. "This would be an overwhelmingly positive thing for the industry and could be a clear indication of the value of the partnership between Apple and Microsoft." Apple could potentially shine by thinking of the benefits for the industry. The alliance could clean up confusion about component software standards.

The jury was still out. But Apple had not rejected Gates' offer, as sacrilegious as it would sound to its flock of Mac enthusiasts.

On December 10 a gaggle of Microsoft directors and engineers congregated with a group of lead engineers from Apple in a conference room in City Center IV, the corporate development building adjacent to the building that housed Gil Amelio's office and boardroom. Engineers considered the room, which took up about one-quarter of the top floor, "sexy"; it had a gorgeous view.

Wayne Maretsky's counterpart at Microsoft was a "gut specialist," like Maretsky. That is, he knew the inner workings of code like the back of his hand. He had come to Microsoft from DEC along with Dave Cutler, the brain behind Windows NT. He was the technical lead for Microsoft as Apple pried into the intentions of its archfoe. A half dozen other Microsoft engineers accompanied him.

Apple engineers listened closely as their Microsoft counterparts gave technical and strategic presentations. It was not lost on them that, unlike themselves, the Microsoft bunch had been funded for success. The tone of the meeting was surprisingly respectful. All seemed aware that it could easily have disintegrated into name-calling and bitterness.

The Microsoft team made it clear that although they weren't there to discuss the terms of a deal, Microsoft was prepared to wheel and deal with Apple for this business. Apple engineers asked particular technical questions and were given general answers that Microsoft was "willing to consider almost anything, but of course it would be subject to detailed negotiations." This actually was an improvement on what Apple engineers had been used to when dealing with their Redmond rivals. "Usually the answer had just been no," said one lead engineer.

Apple was clear that it did not want to simply run Windows NT, which was all that Microsoft had previously licensed to outside companies. "We want layers of NT," Maretsky told Microsoft. "Stuff you've never made source code or APIs available for before."

Within the NT system, Microsoft engineers would talk about the "executive," the real NT kernel. On top of that were different "personalities" that supported applications—the Windows 3.1 personality, the DOS personality, and so on.

Microsoft suggested that Apple build a "Mac personality" for NT, so Mac applications could be run on it just as DOS applications could. A heated discussion broke out about that notion. The Apple team recognized that, with such an approach, Microsoft was buttonholing Apple's entire Mac business as a compatibility mode for Windows. It still made Windows the dominant software when the customer sat down to use the computer. That didn't make a lot of sense for Apple.

Said one engineer present, "It was obvious. They fessed up pretty quickly. It was almost like they were tongue in cheek. We'll see if we can slip this one by these guys."

"We're not interested in that," Maretsky said.

Microsoft backed off and replied, "Well, of course you might want to do something different as well."

Apple took issue with the fact that with Windows applications the menu bar is inside the window. On Apple's platform, it's at the top of the screen. "Would you be willing to do it our way, and not have Microsoft at the top of the screen?" Maretsky asked.

A Microsoft executive said, "We'll consider it."

As the presentation was winding down, a Microsoft executive dramatically put his hand to his heart. "This would truly be a great alliance," he said. "Apple and Microsoft could make a great business team. It's a shame we couldn't work together before this."

"Imagine that," Maretsky piped up, unable to control himself.

"Well, you did sue us," the Microsoft engineer snapped.

Maretsky had no idea that Apple was still holding another lawsuit over Gates' head. "Well, you did steal our stuff," he shot back. He had the last word.

Silence filled the room, and the Apple team had huge smiles on their faces.

At one point the evaluation team had concluded that the best solution would be a hybrid, using Sun's Solaris as a core operating system with NeXT technology as the programming interface for new applications software. But a bit of past history got in the way of making that a reality.

Years earlier a consortium of Hewlett-Packard, DEC, Sun, and NeXT had been established to create OpenStep, NeXT's technology that would run on a range of computer hardware platforms. As it turned out, none of the companies except Sun actually ported OpenStep to their operating environments. Sun succeeded in bringing OpenStep to its Solaris operating system. Sun therefore had the rights to OpenStep. The Apple evaluation team originally thought it might have hit the jackpot. That is, Apple could get OpenStep through Sun without having to do a separate deal with NeXT.

However, as was soon discovered, Sun's deal with NeXT included giving any changes it made to the NeXT technology back to NeXT. So Sun eventually would have had to give the Apple OS technology back.

Apple was still interested in Solaris, but Sun was making things difficult. It wanted control over the Solaris component of Apple's implementation, and Apple did not feel it would have the freedom to innovate on that platform, a key consideration of the executive committee.

Eventually, it was envisioned that either Solaris or NT could be the core OS. If Solaris was chosen, the Apple team still had no solution for what it would plug in as the "modern programming interface."

By mid-December, in a closed executive meeting, Amelio boiled down the company's choices to Gassee's Be versus NeXT. They offered very similar technology, but NeXT's software had been delivered to thousands of customers. Be was all vaporware, from Apple's point of view. Amelio hadn't liked that. Gassee also offered no international or localization capabilities, which were critical for Apple because it had customers all over the world. NeXT had the international features built into the software.

Be had virtually no playback or authoring capabilities—areas that were strong for Apple. The Be software also did not offer dynamic configuration, or the ability to "plug and play." NeXT didn't have this either, but it would be added.

There was green-gold carpet in Apple's City Center III headquarters building. Steve Jobs followed it to Gil Amelio's eighth-floor conference room. It was the first week in December, and Solomon, Amelio, and Hancock welcomed Jobs. Unlike the dramatic boardroom on the same floor, this was a modest conference room, with a long wooden table that could seat eight comfortably. Large windows looked out toward San Francisco. A door led to a balcony. On a clear day you could see the city.

Jobs had in hand his bottled water from the refrigerator where Amelio had retrieved a Diet Coke. As he usually did, Amelio poured the contents of the can into a glass.

After a polite span with the four seated at the table and Amelio going on about the direction of the company, Jobs migrated toward a large white board on one wall. He was diagramming and presenting like a master, and with surprising humility and compassion, the future of Apple. Gradually, the conversation turned to technologies and products. Amelio and Jobs were doing all the talking.

Of course Jobs had heard the rumors in the press about Apple's potential acquisition of Be. He was not interested in giving a sales pitch, he said, but he talked about the "really great technology" at NeXT.

"Come see for yourself," Jobs said. "If there's anything you want to license, or any other arrangement you'd be interested in, let's talk. I want to see Apple thrive." Jobs was hoping that Apple would adopt the NeXT operating system as a replacement for Copland. He made one point strongly. "Once you look at the OS, I think you're going to want it," he said. "And if you're going to want it, you're going to want the whole company."

The following day, with Amelio's nod, Solomon dispatched Kurt Piersol and Winston Hendrickson to NeXT's Redwood City offices.

A few weeks later, it was show time at the Garden Court Hotel. The Apple executive committee had assembled at the hotel in Palo Alto for a secret off-site meeting that would last two days. The team was moving quickly toward a decision about acquiring a new OS. It was now early evening, and the group awaited the arrival of Jobs and his chief technologist, Avie Tevanian.

It was finally decided that Apple would acquire NeXT outright.

On the evening of Friday, December 20, 1996 Doug Solomon was feverish and barely managing to keep himself upright at the press conference.

Earlier that day the full details of the NeXT acquisition had been presented in the eighth-floor boardroom and approved by the board. Apple executives waited for all the lawyers and investment bankers to congregate. The bunch from San Francisco was taking longer than expected to arrive. A lot of details in the contract still needed to be worked out. Amelio and Jobs were wrangling over Jobs's role at the company. What exactly could be said to the press?

After it was all over, Solomon went home and got in bed; he didn't emerge for three days.

Thank you, George.

Kurt Piersol was raising his eyes to the ceiling as if the great director lurked there somewhere. He held George Lucas responsible for the beating he was now taking with a Nerf sword after a long, hard day at Apple Computer. His three-year-old son had seen him as Darth Vader coming through the door.

Months had passed since the NeXT acquisition and the corporate swords had been out in force that week. Piersol and his colleagues had just begun to regroup and recover. At lunchtime sushi had drifted by in little boats. It was like a surreal version of system software construction. Operating system features floating by all so tempting but rather expensive. Piersol could not succumb to the "feature creep" Apple had been plagued by in the past. While in Japan he had always thought it odd to present food in little boats. At the end of a meal you would count the dishes to see how much money you owed.

Apple's "user experience" tsar had to give the nod now to what he saw as good features. Some, perhaps, had been on the boat a little too long.

Accompanying him was a networking manager from Apple. Networking was a big deal as, once again, the company found itself in the midst of a dual strategy. It had to make two different networking systems work seamlessly on the same machine with the new operating system.

AppleTalk had been used for years, and quite extensively in the publishing business, one of Apple's core markets. Rhapsody, the replacement for Copland, however, needed to take a more Internet-centric approach to networking. "We don't want our current customers to think we're going to blow away the stuff they have now by going and doing something else," Piersol said. "We have to make them work together really well."

Millions of little issues like this lay before him.

Now, Piersol sat, stately in his red suspenders, black shirt, and black trousers; it seemed a victory that he was still upright. After seven and a half years at Apple Computer, Piersol's dark brown hair and dark beard were graying in splotches. By all accounts, his coif should have gone all white this week.

It was about 10:00 A.M., and Gil Amelio's head could be seen talking on video monitors throughout the Apple campus. The Apple chairman was broadcasting his "communications meeting" to console and inspire whoever was left standing at the company. The workforce had been slashed by 30 percent this week. Some 4,000 bodies were in the process of disappearing. Literally overnight, callers trying to reach phone extensions for people who had been fixtures for years were informed, "You have reached a nonworking number at Apple Computer."

Piersol caught snatches of Amelio's talk as he raced around. A first-thing-in-the-morning tour of Macintouch, his favorite Web site, revealed rumor and rancor concerning what was going on at Apple.

Steve Jobs's office, one floor above Piersol's in Building 2, was dark today, as usual. To all appearances, Jobs had little to do with anything going on here, at least for the moment, despite the ruckus the press had made about his return to the company. After all, Pixar, with its Hollywood clientele and cutting-edge technology, was his baby. Apple was stuck in the past. In fact, Apple's newly returned cofounder Stephen Wozniak was playing the more important role. He never seemed to miss an executive committee meeting. Back on December 20, the press conference announcing the acquisition of Jobs' old company NeXT had been delayed for six hours while Amelio pleaded with Jobs to join Apple. To take the money and run would look bad, Amelio had told him. Now more than ever Apple needed a hero of mythic proportions. Jobs was that.

The rounds of layoffs and reorganizations over the past several years had become like musical chairs. In the wake of this week's carnage, Piersol and his managers, Ly Pham and Avie Tevanian—who'd come with Jobs from NeXT—were scrambling to figure out who was going to pick up the pieces. Piersol's colleagues noticed that excess energy seeming to be draining out of his left foot, which vibrated continually as he spoke.

Back alone in his office, Piersol glanced about at the artifacts that had collected over the months. A rather forlorn-looking bottle of brown ale sat on the shelf above his desk. The Copland team, under the belief it was on the road to success, had brewed the stuff. "User Experience Brown Ale," read the label. Piersol considered the little bits floating around in the concoction. It hadn't been very good. A computer nerd's version of brown ale, bits floating randomly to the surface.

Months earlier Piersol had been anointed the tsar of User Experience. The team had only narrowly prevented Amelio from succumbing to the last-minute coup by Bill Gates.

These days the word *scary* seemed to slip into every other sentence uttered by the deep-voiced Piersol. The distinguished engineer, as Apple termed the best of its some 1,000 software engineers, liked to poke fun at himself and brushed off his accomplishments as merely "the geek's-eye view" of the world. Yet he took his challenges personally and had had the sense over the previous six months that he and a handful of others carried the company's future on their shoulders. Some of the stuff he had looked at for Amelio should have run missile warheads instead of personal computers, he liked to joke.

The goal in the coming weeks was to sketch out a new "look and feel"—gluing together shards of Copland and new technology from NeXT. Melding the old world order with the new was the "single biggest thing Apple could do badly," Piersol would remind his colleagues. The past was the past. That had been repeated over and over in the last few days by Amelio, Ellen Hancock, and Avie Tevanian, now Apple's senior vice president of software engineering. The past was the past. But it could not be ignored.

———————————

By March 19, 1997, the tall and lanky chief scientist Avie Tevanian sat inside a circle of computers. In a striped shirt and gray pants, he was informally dressed for work. Tevanian's office remained fairly empty, except for two armchairs and his magic circle of computers—four of them, running NT, OpenStep, Mac OS, and a black slab not yet connected to the Internet.

He was slowly moving objects from his Redwood City office to his office at Apple. Today he'd brought in the baby pictures of his two-year-old son.

Crossing the blue-gray carpet on the second floor of Building 2, the research and development building, Tevanian noted that what worried him most was that "Microsoft is spending $2 billion a week on R&D." Earlier in the week Apple had slashed its own research budget substantially.

The day before he had prepared for his first internal "communications" meeting. It took place in a town hall–type meeting room that could accommodate a few hundred people.

Tevanian was an ally of Jobs. The war within Apple would reach such an intensity that Amelio would be ousted, as would Hancock, but not before Bill Gates settled with Apple and made an investment of some $250 million in the company. Gates made the covers of magazines all over the world for his gesture, which was seen as a huge act of generosity.

Ed Stead attributed the deal Gates had been able to nail to the influence of Steve Jobs and thought it was an enormous mistake, according to his colleagues. Apple could have received royalties from Microsoft in perpetuity if it had pursued the massive patent infringement suit he had in mind.

Jobs also had been agitating for Apple to switch to Microsoft's Internet Explorer, and to Microsoft's version of Sun's Java technology. Hancock had been a steadfast believer in the more open approach offered by Java.

Before any of the deals were made public, Stead left the company to join the entertainment industry. He became chief counsel of Blockbuster Entertainment. It would be only a matter of time before he was butting heads with Bill Gates again, he knew, as Gates was moving fast into entertainment and media.

"Who knows what motivates Jobs," he would muse to his colleagues, finding the full circle that Jobs had taken, from founder of Apple, to Gates reported ally helping Microsoft out of Apple's copyright infringement suit, to his return to lead Apple, this time increasingly relying on Microsoft technology.

The Justice Department was investigating the deal.

17

THE DONUT
WHEEL

The wheel was turning. In October 1997, the U.S. Department of Justice finally made a move to show that its 1995 consent order had teeth. Microsoft, it asserted, was in contempt of that order, which strictly forbade predatory licensing practices and product tying. Meanwhile, evidence continued to be collected not only for a new case that Justice hoped to bring in 1998 but in the private suit that was being expanded to include allegations of Gates' predation since the early days of the DOS market as well as damages related to Windows 95 and its successors, which effectively and permanently tied DOS to Windows, excluding other would-be entrants to the market.

Justice's case hinged on the issue of product integration, Gates contended, accusing the feds of trying to interfere with his ability to design innovative products. But Justice attorneys had evidence of Gates' real reasons for product integration in their files.

While waiting to decide the case, a federal judge issued a temporary injunction demanding that Microsoft immediately unbundle Internet Explorer from Windows 95. Gates' perverse way of complying with the order infuriated both the judge and Justice, inviting yet another contempt suit from federal regulators.

After an embarrassing courtroom demonstration, the judge showed that he was not as stupid as Gates and his top executives imagined. Sun sued Microsoft for infringing on its Java technology. By March 1998, the feds had expanded their probe focusing on allegations about the way Microsoft leveraged power with browser contracts and by attempting to strong-arm Internet content providers, as well as ripping off and manipulating Java for advantages that would continue to lock software developers and consumers into using only Microsoft products.

By the spring of 1998, Gates faced what Rockefeller had faced before him: a case was being developed to address Microsoft's restraint of trade on a state-by-state basis. Justice was also planning a new suit that promised to affect Gates' planned marketing of Windows 98.

Less powerful companies continued to look toward the future, and freedom from Gates' monopoly. Scott McNealy of Sun had a new secret project up his sleeve. In mid-1998, about a decade since the feds began probing Microsoft, the new warriors gathered at the Donut Wheel, a greasy donut shop at the heart of Silicon Valley. They had a vision that had nothing to do with Bill Gates.

In his Justice Department office, Joel Klein stood in a dark jacket, his white pate gleaming, as stately and weary a Dickensian solicitor as ever there was one.

It was October 20, 1997, and high time to prove to the world that this thing he had stood up for—while Anne Bingaman had flailed her arms beside him like an ungovernable sapling—had teeth, and sharp teeth at that. Like some gleeful Cerberus, he was aiming the maw of the Justice Department's 1995 court order straight at Gates' trouser seat.

Back in the winter of 1995, Klein, who had been Bill Clinton's deputy counsel at the White House, had found himself in the unlikely position of being on Microsoft's side. He and Microsoft's chief counsel, Bill Neukom had stood together to defend the Justice Department's settlement which Microsoft negotiated in July 1994.

Judge Stanley Sporkin was wrong, said both men. There were no legal grounds for the consent agreement to be scrapped. At the time, Bingaman had hinted to Sporkin that her antitrust lawyers would probably be back in court soon, if Microsoft continued on the course it had set. To them, the settlement was merely a foot in the door. They would be continually monitoring Microsoft's business practices now, she had assured the outraged judge.

Not long after, Bingaman left the Justice Department for the private sector, and Klein took over. It took him almost two years to find a way to wield that consent order in order to bite Microsoft in a meaningful way. Now Klein and his boss, Janet Reno, having filed a contempt case against the software giant, were about to stand up before a press conference to explain what Gates had done in defiance of the 1995 order.

Interestingly and perhaps predictably, Neukom was singing a new tune. In 1995 he had defended the court order he'd pounded out with the Justice Department. The alternative would have been to have it thrown out and let the Microsoft empire be subjected to perhaps more stringent limitations on the way it did business.

Now, in a midday conference call which he'd dialed into from an airport phone, Neukom told the press that Justice was misreading its own order. "They don't understand how software publishers do business," he said. Reno had stated that she would seek a fine of $1 million a day against the software giant until it complied with the order.

While Reno and Klein's latest action was creating quite a stir, no one was paying attention to Ralph Palumbo's lawsuit, and he was glad of it.

Personal loss versus corporate loss. Both were on Palumbo's mind a lot these days. In his business dealings, he routinely wrestled with the value of things, legal awards, and damages. Profit and loss. Market share. Power and misuse of power. Money changing hands; tides of profits like Himalayan floodwaters.

Now Ray Noorda was after billions of dollars in damages. It had been in the summer of 1996 that the former Novell chief had hired him to sue Microsoft in a case Palumbo suspected would crest like a tidal wave that had been building since the early days of the operating system market.

But more than anything, while mulling the claims of the high-powered clients of his Seattle firm, Ralph Palumbo was haunted by the spirit of his daughter.

Palumbo was a smallish but sturdy figure. His twenty-year-old daughter had been missing for more than a year following a flood in the Himalayas where she had been traveling with her college boyfriend. Her presence lingered with him wherever he was.

Himalayan waters had swept over her in all her beauty, the young one who had set out to see the world. Great walls of floodwaters had rushed over her, pulled her down into the enormity of eternity with her lover.

She was gone.

Market forces could be like forces of nature, and then again, nothing like them at all. Still, his colleague, litigator Steve Susman, had been described as "a force of nature" by those who had dealt with him and had witnessed his ability to win massive awards in corporate disputes.

While the documents subpoenaed from Microsoft came pouring in, and he reviewed the corporate record of Gates' repeated overtaking of the efforts of smaller companies, it occurred to Palumbo that nothing in the corporate world could compare to that single act of nature. The universe seemed to have its own idea of power and value.

He pondered the public versus private; where the two intersected and how one pierced the other.

Bill Gates earlier had refused to shake his hand.

In Seattle on September 21, 1997, Palumbo had stood with Gates, Paul Allen and Warren Buffett, and John Whitacre, the Nordstrom magnate, at the football game at the University of Washington. Gates and he barely made eye contact.

Now it was October, and about a year since Ray Noorda had recruited Palumbo and other attorneys, including Susman, one of the nation's hottest trial lawyers, to serve as litigators for the tiny Caldera Inc., funded and created by Noorda to purchase DR-DOS from Novell. Susman was famous for winning mammoth awards in jury trials from large corporations. Palumbo and Steve Hill, an attorney colleague also hired by Noorda, looked upon Susman as an enlightened being. Caldera was seeking damages from Microsoft that went back to the early days of the DOS market and continued through Windows 95 and beyond.

In July 1996, Susman, Palumbo, and their colleagues had filed the Caldera lawsuit before the federal judge Dee Bensen, in district court in Salt Lake City. It accused Microsoft of monopolization of the DOS market and violation of Section 2 of the Sherman Act; of "illegal tying" resulting in restraint of trade; exclusive dealing; and "tortious" interference with economic relations—including the use of false statements, cover-ups, and encrypted code. The complaint argued that Microsoft's DOS monopoly enabled it to control standards (or APIs) to which all applications for IBM-compatible PCs had to be written and enabled the company to collect enormous amounts of money from licensing DOS at negligible ongoing cost or risk.

The early sessions of butting heads with Neukom's legal team on this case, with Microsoft's Tom Burt doing most of the talking, had been mostly by telephone. On October 16, 1996, Palumbo and his colleagues would have their first face-to-face meeting with their Microsoft counterparts.

Neukom and Burt had been attempting to get the venue changed to Seattle. The last thing Neukom wanted was a jury trial in Noorda country. The Caldera lawyers had made it clear that they intended to be the first on the planet—not employed by Microsoft or the feds—to lay their eyes on most of the documents the Justice Department, and earlier the FTC, had subpoenaed in the course of its investigation of Microsoft. At the time they had informed Noorda that they expected to be granted that privilege by Judge Bensen, who would order Microsoft to release to them all the material.

It would be interesting to see how Microsoft responded. In a little-known earlier copyright infringement suit in Seattle, a judge had ordered Microsoft to turn over the subpoenaed documents. Rather than do that, Microsoft had settled. But now there was no indication that Neukom would consider a settlement.

The previous Sunday, Palumbo had coincidentally taken the same private charter flight as Bill Gates. Gates often hired his friend Sam to fly him to meetings. Palumbo had offered the Microsoft chairman his hand. Gates had turned his back.

It had been a cool morning on October 15, 1996, when Noorda

had sat around a mahogany table in Salt Lake City with his team of lawyers—among them Palumbo, Hill, and Parker Folse—a partner of Susman. The group compared notes. Things had still not settled down abroad. Jeff Kingston, an attorney at Brobeck, Phleger & Harrison, was representing yet another company that had filed a complaint about Microsoft in Europe. Eighteen economists in the EC were now reviewing the case.

Coffee cups were being refilled. Presently, Ray Noorda strolled into the room in a red shirt and black jeans, tall and lanky like an old cowboy. With him was Bryan Sparks, the young president of Caldera.

Months earlier the former DRI and Novell engineer Roger Gross had been on a mission in the UK to find the original source code to CP/M, which Gates had cloned to create the original MS-DOS. Gross had searched for weeks; finally, he'd found it in a safe in London. He was now heading up a European development center for Caldera.

All along Bill Neukom had characterized the Caldera suit as "frivolous." Nonetheless, he and a sizable team of Microsoft's top counsels—the same men he had used to represent the company's interests to the Justice Department—had traveled to the first hearing before Judge Bensen in Salt Lake City in January 1997. There was Neukom and Richard Urowsky, Microsoft's outside counsel who had helped with the settlement negotiations with Justice, the outside counsel Steve Holley, and two of his associates from Sullivan & Cromwell, Microsoft's Tom Burt, and two additional in-house attorneys.

At the hearing, the judge seemed amused by Microsoft's suggestion that a venue transfer might be appropriate. He granted Caldera immediate access to all the information Microsoft had produced for the FTC and the Department of Justice.

Microsoft was fighting to keep certain information secret, while Caldera's attorneys argued that the software giant's secrecy was frivolous. Jim Jardine, a leading Salt Lake City attorney hired by Microsoft, argued that Microsoft's DOS source code was the company's "crown jewel," comparing it to the formula for Coca-Cola.

Palumbo turned to his colleagues and, referring to Gates' and his senior executives' position on DOS since the release of Windows 95, said, "Gee, I thought DOS was dead!"

The press, which had barely taken note when Caldera had announced the filing of its case, thought Noorda was just an obsessed old man. Palumbo and Susman knew, however, that the Justice Department's latest move was simply a very late gesture in a case that had not quite caught up with itself. The government would only take on a case that would result in remedies that had the potential to save a still viable portion of the marketplace. Nothing could remedy the fact that the operating systems market was dead and gone. But they could at least seek damages, and at the same time get some of Microsoft's dirty laundry out in the open. Maybe the feds would finally start to notice a pattern.

Susman, Palumbo, and their colleagues all had taken the case on contingency, with the expectation of receiving a percentage of whatever sum the judge awarded. All were counting on a jury trial. As the feds had known earlier, Microsoft's internal records—albeit incomplete—were overflowing with evidence on which numerous private lawsuits could be based.

By the end of October 1997, Susman was preparing to depose Bill Gates. The team was also, just before trial, planning to subpoena Stefanie Reichel, Theo Lieven, and Bengt Akerlind, among other players from Microsoft's Germany office.

In early November 1997, Palumbo traveled to Germany with his colleague Steve Hill to do a little fishing. Both had talked about the Vobis account with Juergen Huels and with Heinz Willi Dahmen, who still worked for Vobis.

A few weeks earlier Susman had deposed Gates while Palumbo had deposed Brad Chase. Microsoft's counsel Steve Holley had been present. Susman had confronted Gates with an e-mail message to Steve Ballmer in which Gates had railed on about the fact that DR-DOS was cutting into his ability to keep prices for MS-DOS high. Gates responded that he was a product guy and never got involved with profitability. He dismissed the e-mail as poking fun at Ballmer.

Susman and his colleagues were quickly catching on that Gates refused to give a straight answer to any question.

In the course of his deposition, Gates admitted that it would be wrong to threaten Vobis with not getting product if it licensed DR-DOS.

Gates was asked about the numerous e-mail messages to and from Gates and his top executives that mentioned "FUD"ing the competitors. Did that mean creating fear, uncertainty, and doubt?

Gates replied that inside Microsoft FUD meant fair and accurate marketing.

Numerous teams of lawyers—from Stac's to the FTC's to the Justice Department's—knew that a jury was going to hate Gates. They'd never seen a more unlikable witness.

Gates was asked if he had entered into a consent decree with the government and if he could describe it. He said he couldn't remember what he had agreed to, despite the fact that that very decree had been thrust in his face by Justice continually over the past several weeks as part of its contempt suit.

Susman went on to ask if the decree had changed Gates' business practices. He replied that it had not changed the company's practices at all.

Referring to the Justice Department's contempt suit against Gates and Microsoft, Susman asked if Gates was familiar with a more recent issue raised by Justice pertaining to the consent decree.

Gates replied that he had heard about that on TV. Just days before he had responded vehemently to the press about the suit and had mocked Janet Reno's million-dollar-a-day fine.

As Gates and Holley left the room together, Susman followed. Still amused, he called after them cheerfully, "Good-bye, Mr. Gates! See you in court!"

Brad Chase had been through scores of depositions in recent years, most notably by the Federal Trade Commission and the Justice Department. And now here was Ralph Palumbo, on a mission funded by Ray Noorda.

Chase was getting grilled once again. Palumbo provided him with a little history lesson. During the course of Novell's attempts to market DR-DOS 7, Microsoft had announced "vaporware," telling the press that it would have an MS-DOS 7. Instead of being shipped to market, the product became "integrated" into Windows 95.

Palumbo asked Chase if there was ever a product called MS-DOS 7. Chase said there wasn't. Palumbo asked if Chase was sure. Chase said he was very sure.

Couldn't one find DOS 7 inside Windows 95, a fully functioning version of DOS, Palumbo wanted to know.

Indeed, Windows 95 was Windows 4.0 combined with MS-DOS 7.0. Programming experts like Andrew Schulman had looked inside the Windows 95 code and found both products, identified by Microsoft programmers as such.

"Scooter" was hardly behaving like a gentleman. In October 1997, just before the Justice Department filed its contempt suit against Microsoft, Sun Microsystems's CEO, Scott McNealy, had lobbed his own lawsuit at Bill Gates. Sun was suing Microsoft for a litany of naughtiness: trademark infringement, false advertising, breach of contract, unfair competition, and interference with prospective economic advantage.

It all rested on Gates' intentions to rip off Sun's Java technology and leverage it to once again lock the industry into a Microsoft implementation of the product. McNealy considered Gates a most dangerous and powerful industrialist, who was attempting to control "the written and spoken language of the digital age." Microsoft's Neukom lobbed a counterlawsuit right back at McNealy, asserting that Sun was the one acting perversely in the implementation of its contract with Microsoft.

Java was a computer language designed to allow software developers to create software that would run on any computer, on any operating system—basically making Windows irrelevant. Java let programs reside anywhere on the Internet, enabling any computer anywhere to use them. Shortly after its introduction in 1995, thousands of programmers started using it. In 1996, realizing the immense threat that Java posed, Microsoft signed a contract with Sun to license Java.

Joel Klein and his federal attorneys Dan Rubenfeld and Doug Melamed, in a new investigation, had noticed that McNealy's hunches about Gates' intentions seemed to be true. Documents subpoenaed from the software giant showed that Gates' top lieutenants were out to neutralize Java. McNealy's chief counsel, Mike Morris, had walked the feds through the situation, in brief after legal brief, white papers, and court documents.

Microsoft agreed, as part of its contract, to incorporate Java technology in certain products, including Microsoft's Internet Explorer, in a way that adhered to Sun's published specifications, or APIs. It agreed to incorporate future upgrades to Java specifications in order to maintain compatibility with Sun's technology for five years. The software giant agreed to refrain from distributing any products using Java that did not pass Sun's test suites. Separately, Microsoft also agreed to mark each product it distributed that used Java with the "Java compatible" logo provided by Sun, but only after the products met Sun's compatibility requirements.

Instead, Sun claimed, Microsoft was deliberately breaking Java's compatibility by changing the technology in a way calculated to force developers to produce programs that operated only with Windows. Microsoft had secretly changed Java's programming interfaces, according to Sun, and those of Internet Explorer and other products to accomplish this. Further, Microsoft was distributing products marked and advertised as Java compatible, including Internet Explorer 4.0, that failed to conform to Sun's specifications.

"We are not 'write-once, run-anywhere' kind of guys," said Microsoft's Steve Ballmer, responding to Sun's allegations. "Our goal in signing the contract was not to neutralize Java," he said.

"Sun is just a very dumb company," he opined. "Nobody was ever one tiny little bit confused that we and Sun had this sort of wonderful dovetailing of strategic interests! Those sub-fifty-I.Q. people at Sun who believe that are either uninformed, crazy, or sleeping."

He and Gates would soon be defending that position to Joel Klein.

Back at the Department of Justice, the basics of Klein's petition were indisputable. The suit simply stated that Microsoft "through its 'Windows' operating system products . . . possesses a monopoly in the market for operating system software for Intel-compatible personal computers and from this monopoly enjoys a corporate profit rate and market capitalization that are among the highest of any major American company."

Gates still denied that his company held a monopoly of any kind.

Again, the contempt suit asserted, "Microsoft maintained its monopoly by using exclusionary and anticompetitive contracts to market its PC operating system software."

Klein's contempt suit pointed out that the final judgment resulting from the government's 1994 suit prohibited Microsoft from conditioning the terms of a computer maker's license to distribute the Windows operating system on that manufacturer also licensing and distributing other Microsoft products. "The purpose of that and other provisions of the Final Judgment was to prevent Microsoft from protecting or extending its operating system monopoly," the petition stated.

In particular, Justice was now challenging Microsoft's requirement that computer makers license its Internet browser "along with, and as a condition of, licensing Microsoft's commercially essential Windows 95 operating system." All the previous year Microsoft had been promoting Internet Explorer 3.0, and on September 30, 1997, it released its newest version, IE 4.0. In violation of the earlier settlement, Microsoft was forcing computer makers to license Internet Explorer along with Windows 95. It was Microsoft's intention, the suit stated, beginning February 1, 1998, to require the same with IE 4.0. By tying its Internet software to Windows, Microsoft was intentionally thwarting incipient competition.

The growth of the Internet and the World Wide Web since the time of the government's settlement with Microsoft had resulted in enormous consumer demand for Internet browser software, Klein had explained to the court. The first version of Microsoft's Internet Explorer had been released in August 1995. Since that time, Microsoft had released three subsequent versions, in each adding features and functionality. Justice had noted that since at least December 1995 Microsoft had attributed great importance to capturing a major share of browsers and browser users.

Internal Microsoft documents had proved to Klein and his staff that Microsoft feared browsers had the potential to become alternative "platforms" on which various software applications and programs could run. Indeed, competing browsers operated not only on Windows but also on a variety of other operating systems. The contempt suit pointed out that "Microsoft fears that over time growing use and acceptance of competing browsers as alternative platforms and interfaces will reduce the significance of the particular underlying operating system on which they are running, thereby 'commoditizing' the operating system." If this happened, PC makers' and computer users' current "critical need for Windows, and thus Microsoft's monopoly power, would be reduced or eliminated and competition could return to the operating system market."

As Klein knew, Anne Bingaman had wrangled all night long over the wording of what the earlier court order prohibited. The final language stated:

Microsoft shall not enter into any License Agreement [with a computer maker] in which the terms of that agreement are expressly or impliedly conditioned upon:

(i) the licensing of any other Covered Product, Operating System Software product or other product (provided, however, that this provision in and of itself shall not be construed to prohibit Microsoft from developing integrated products).

Bill Gates had forced that parenthetical clause down Bingaman's throat, and, it was now apparent, for good reason. However, Klein, in his petition, pointed out, "As the Competitive Impact Statement filed with the proposed Final Judgment made clear, this provision was designed to prevent Microsoft from attempting to extend or protect its operating system monopoly by conditioning its Windows license agreements on [computer makers'] licensing or use of other

Microsoft products." It defined Internet Explorer as an "other product" and not an "integrated product" within the meaning of the final judgment.

In addition to requiring computer makers to preinstall Internet Explorer at the same time they load Windows 95 onto their computers, their contracts with Microsoft forbade them from modifying or deleting IE 3 as delivered to them without Microsoft's consent. Without such license prohibitions, computer makers "easily could remove Internet Explorer from the Windows 95 package they install on their PCs without compromising the functioning of Windows 95," Justice recognized. Nevertheless, Microsoft had refused requests from at least three major computer manufacturers to remove Internet Explorer from the PCs they sold.

In the fall of 1997, James Von Holle, director of the software and global products group at Gateway 2000, found himself being grilled under oath by an assortment of federal and states attorneys. Justice Department attorneys had been joined by the assistant attorneys general from Minnesota and Texas. Numerous executives from U.S. computer companies were being deposed in preparation for the department's lawsuit against Microsoft. Von Holle went on about how Microsoft had licensed Windows 95 to his company, requiring that all icons on the computer screen be preconfigured by Microsoft.

Under the terms of its Windows 95 contract with Microsoft, did Gateway have the ability to ship a machine without Microsoft's Internet Explorer, or to remove Internet Explorer from the computer screen?

Von Holle answered, "We are not allowed to remove any of those icons that Microsoft preconfigures there." He went on to explain that, given the way Microsoft had required computer makers like Gateway to install Windows 95 along with Internet Explorer, it was not possible to allow consumers to launch an alternative product like Netscape's Communicator directly from the Windows 95 screen.

Consumers would have to specially activate a button to get to anything but Internet Explorer. Von Holle was asked if it would be of value to allow customers to launch Netscape products directly from their Gateway PCs if they so desired, and if Gateway was able to customize its computers in this way.

"Right," he said.

"Would it be of value to the end user?" his interrogators asked.

"We believe it would be. It would be a much simpler environment for the end user to immediately use the PC as they order it," he said.

"You mentioned this sort of new or different interface that can be presented by Communicator. Do you believe that over time a separate interface, an interface that sits on top of the operating system such as the Communicator interface, has any potential to affect the need for a specific underlying operating system?" Von Holle was asked.

"Yes, I think that it would," he said.

"How do you think that might happen?" the interrogator went on.

"If the user is not required to boot or launch an application directly from Windows and there was some sort of an underlying layer that sat between the interface and the PC operating system that abstracted those commands, then there would not be—then there would definitely be a threat to Windows," Von Holle replied.

"Why would there be a threat?" the questioner continued.

Von Holle's reply was simple. "The requirement for Windows would not be there," he said. This was exactly what federal attorneys had seen Microsoft senior executives obsessing about in their internal e-mail communications.

Back in early June 1996, Celeste Dunn, vice president of Compaq Computer's Consumer Software Business Unit, received a letter from Microsoft, threatening to cancel Compaq's Windows 95 contract if the company refused to include the Microsoft Network and Internet Explorer icons on its computer screens as part of the operating system. It had been addressed to Compaq's attorney David Cabello.

Compaq had told Microsoft that it wanted to offer Netscape products to computer buyers who preferred them. Through the rest of the summer and early fall, the companies had wrangled over the issue.

On October 6, 1996, Dunn had called Don Hardwick, group man-
ager of Microsoft's OEM sales division, in response to the "Notice of
Intent to Terminate," and he had responded in a letter the same day.
His letter was copied to Microsoft's top licensing moguls, Joachim
Kempin and Bengt Akerlind.

Hardwick wrote that, to resolve the issue of terminating Compaq's
Windows 95 license,

> Microsoft is requesting that Compaq replace the Microsoft
> Network and Internet Explorer icons on ... Windows
> 95. ... In addition, the Microsoft Network and Internet Ex-
> plorer icons and Internet Setup Wizard icon should also be
> put back into their original locations and functionality under
> the "Start" button on Windows 95.
>
> If you are willing to give Microsoft a clear written assurance
> that the above will be implemented on all Compaq Presario
> machines within sixty days of the date of this letter, Microsoft
> will withdraw its Notice of Intent to Terminate letter.

Almost a year later, Compaq executive Stephen Decker was deposed by Justice Department attorneys, who asked him to explain
why his company was shipping no alternatives to Microsoft's latest
version of its browser software. The product at the time was available only on a separate CD, and computer makers were required to
ship it via a memorandum of understanding with Microsoft.

"Why has Compaq ... not considered Netcaster today as an alternative to Internet Explorer 4.0?" Decker was asked.

"I would say that the major reason that Compaq hasn't is because
the category of browser is fulfilled with the Internet Explorer product which will be a part of the Microsoft operating system," Decker
said.

That is, even though IE 4.0 was not yet built into Windows 95,
Microsoft was requiring computer makers to sell it as though it were
an inseparable part of Windows.

Decker went on, "Therefore, Compaq will get this as part of the
operating system code and that category will be filled."

What had been Compaq's response to Microsoft's threat to terminate its Windows contract when it had not included the Internet Explorer icon on its Windows 95 computers?

"We went back and reworked the code so that we put an icon back on [the screen]," Decker said.

"That was a direct result of the threat to terminate the license agreement?" asked the questioner.

"Yes," Decker replied.

Why did Compaq want to remove Internet Explorer at the time?

"We had a relationship with Netscape, and we had been shipping their product for a while. And therefore Netscape was actually the browser partner, and we wanted to give [it] that position on the Compaq Presario desktop," Decker said.

Justice was readying itself for a brawl with Microsoft on the issue of product integration. Its lawsuit clearly demonstrated that IE held a "significant commercial existence of its own, wholly apart from Microsoft's operating system." It noted that there was a separate demand from computer makers and consumers for Internet browser products and for Windows 95. Based on confidential and public documents it had subpoenaed, Justice also knew that Microsoft itself recognized this demand by separately marketing, licensing, and distributing each version of Internet Explorer "to an extent far greater and in ways materially different than it does for any true, integrated feature or component of its operating system products."

Microsoft offered Internet Explorer through electronic downloading over the Internet and entered into IE distribution agreements with on-line service providers and Internet service providers, companies that connect computer users to the Internet. It also preinstalled and distributed Internet Explorer on other devices, such as printers, and bundled IE with applications software. In addition, it offered the package as a stand-alone retail product.

The company also offered versions of IE 3.0 for earlier versions of Windows and Apple's Macintosh operating system, and would continue to do so for IE 4.

In internal documents, Microsoft could be seen intensely and closely tracking customer usage and overall "share" of Internet Explorer and competing Internet browser products. It was clear that aggressively increasing market share in this area was a strategic goal of Bill Gates.

It was also both physically and commercially possible to separate each version of Internet Explorer from Windows 95. Computer makers had requested that Microsoft permit them to remove Internet Explorer from Windows 95 to avoid customer confusion and to allow customers to choose freely among browser products. Further demonstrating that IE could function separately from Windows, and that Windows operated well without IE, Microsoft had already begun distributing IE 4 to computer makers on a compact disk completely separate from the disk on which Windows 95 was distributed.

That of course would change with the release of Windows 98 in a matter of months, if Bill Gates was allowed to continue with his tying strategy.

Nondisclosure agreements (NDAs) were also again rearing their ugly heads. In its lawsuit Justice again asserted that Microsoft was using these secrecy clauses in its contracts to obstruct federal investigations. A slightly different but related issue was the elimination of Microsoft's use of NDAs to restrain trade, which had been part of the 1995 settlement. Now Justice stated that such NDAs "threaten the ability of the court to enforce and the United States to determine and secure Microsoft's compliance with the final judgment." (The court did not address the issue.)

While the terms of particular agreements varied, many defined "confidential information" broadly, in some cases so broadly as to include any information that Microsoft designated as confidential or that related to the "marketing or promotion" of any Microsoft product or any Microsoft "business policies or practices." Many NDAs stated that those who signed them could not disclose confidential information in accordance with "judicial or other governmental order," unless they gave Microsoft prior notice. Ralph Palumbo was coming up against the same problem in the Caldera suit. And in a matter of weeks the state of Texas would sue Microsoft because of NDAs it asserted were obstructing its ability to investigate the company. The court would throw out that complaint.

Klein and his attorneys had given Microsoft a chance to settle once again, if the company agreed to change the predatory practices now spelled out in the contempt petition. Neukom and Gates had been unwilling to resolve these issues, however, right up to the moment Klein decided to sue. "Through the above-described acts and failures to act, Microsoft has knowingly disobeyed and resisted the lawful orders of this Court, as set out in Section IV(E)(i) of the Final Judgment, and therefore is in civil contempt of this Court's authority," was the suit's conclusion.

To remedy the situation, Klein asked the federal court to demand that Microsoft cease and desist within thirty days from the behavior he had spelled out. In addition, Microsoft was directed to inform each computer maker licensing Windows 95 that the inclusion and preinstallation of Internet Explorer with Windows 95 was in violation of the court order and that they were no longer required to include Internet Explorer on PCs.

The Justice Department demanded also that Microsoft notify each purchaser of any computer with Windows 95 (who had registered) that Microsoft had required the manufacturer to package and preinstall it in violation of the court's final judgment. It had to tell customers that they did not need to use Internet Explorer in order for Windows 95 to function properly, that any Windows 95–compatible Internet browser could be installed or used on their computers without harm to the operation of Windows 95, and that other browsers were readily available. Finally, Microsoft was required to provide each purchaser with easy-to-follow instructions describing how to remove the Internet Explorer icon from the Windows 95 desktop if the purchaser chose to do so.

In a matter of weeks, Judge Thomas Penfield Jackson issued a temporary injunction against Microsoft, demanding that it unbundle

Windows 95 from Internet Explorer until further review by a special master. He declined to fine the software giant, because the language of the consent order had been ambiguous regarding product integration. Any fine would be decided after an in-depth probe by Lawrence Lessig.

But within weeks Gates would spur Justice on to a second contempt suit. The bizarre manner in which Microsoft decided it would comply with the judge's injunction should not have surprised anyone.

After all, Gates' right hand man Steve Ballmer, during the last round in Sporkin's court, had told reporters that the problem was that the judge "needed a brain." And after Reno and Klein had announced to the press the filing of the DOJ's original contempt suit, Ballmer had told reporters "to heck with Janet Reno."

Meanwhile, in a deluxe presidential suite in Phoenix's exclusive Hotel Phoenician, on October 22, just hours after Justice had filed its suit, Gates was scowling and mocking Janet Reno as he sat talking with friends. He had no worries about the Justice Department's latest move, he confided. Reno's proposed fine of $1 million a day, the largest ever imposed by the feds in a civil case, was a joke to him. "Every two and half hours I make a million!" Gates bragged.

An unlikely letter arrived in the mailbox of Harvard Professor Lawrence Lessig in late December 1997. Richard Urowsky, counsel to Microsoft, was urging Lessig to get lost. "In light of the evidence that has now come to light," the letter began. The attorney, who'd used the word twice in the same sentence, seemed to be preoccupied with "light" as much as he perceived the special master to be surrounded by the forces of darkness, Lessig noted. The Microsoft attorney went on. "Demonstrating your actual bias against Microsoft, it is difficult to see how you can in good conscience preside over further proceedings in this matter."

Lessig, who had been appointed by the court to investigate Microsoft business practices, could not have guessed that private e-mail he had penned months earlier to Netscape's global public policy counsel, Peter Harter, would result in accusations of "bias" by Microsoft's legal team. The law scholar had joked that he'd "sold his soul" by installing Microsoft's Internet Explorer on his Macintosh computer.

His e-mail had been prompted by his anger over what had happened to his computer after he installed Microsoft's Internet Explorer. The installation had apparently altered the list of preferred Web sites on his Netscape browser. In fact, Professor Charlie Nesson, one of his Harvard colleagues, had urged him to sue Microsoft over the matter.

Lessig wrote to Harter, "OK, this is making me really angry. . . . I installed Internet Explorer 3.0 on my Mac system only because I wanted to be entered into the contest to win a [Apple PowerBook] 3400, sold my soul, and nothing happened. The next time I went into Netscape, all my bookmarks were screwed up. Did IE do this?"

The Justice Department shot back at Microsoft in a brief to the court, disagreeing that Lessig was unfit to serve on the case. "Having combed Professor Lessig's extensive writings for useful nits, Microsoft has proffered three out-of-context quotes, accompanied by inaccurate and tortured characterizations of his writings, in order to support the notion that Professor Lessig has 'preconceived notions' about 'Microsoft and the government's proper role in the development of software products.' "

Judge Jackson was incredulous, and barely able to contain himself. "It seemed absolutely clear to you that I entered an order that required that you distribute a product that would not work? Is that what you're telling me?"

It was January 14, 1998, and Joel Klein, Bill Neukom, and their respective armies of lawyers were back in front of the federal judge. Jackson was now grilling David Cole, among those brought forward to defend Microsoft's disingenuous compliance with the preliminary injunction issued in December. (Cole was known to Justice insiders as being the same Microsoft vice president who had been involved in designing the "sneaky code" to disparage DR-DOS.)

"In plain English, yes," Cole retorted. "We followed the order," he said. "It wasn't my place to consider the consequences." Indeed, it was not, seeing that the instructions on Microsoft's special way of complying with the court order had come directly from Bill Gates. The court had ordered that Microsoft offer a version of Windows 95 without its Internet Explorer. In response, Microsoft offered two stripped-down versions of Windows 95, one that didn't work and another that lacked key features of the most recent version of the operating system—making it undesirable. Microsoft argued that IE and Windows 95 were inextricably linked, sharing many files indispensable to the proper functioning of both.

Microsoft had appealed both the injunction and the appointment of Lessig. The previous day Judge Jackson had issued another order sharply denying Microsoft's request that Lessig be dismissed, calling its complaints "trivial" and "defamatory." The hearing had gone on for two days now.

The Justice Department argued that what Microsoft had done was perverse. It should have simply used a widely available "uninstall" program that removed twenty-six small files, including the desktop icon for IE, without harming Windows.

Meanwhile, the U.S. Court of Appeals for the District of Columbia had appointed a three-judge panel to hear Microsoft's appeals. Oral arguments were scheduled for April 21. On the panel was Judge Laurence Silberman, who in 1995 had sided with Microsoft in throwing out Judge Stanley Sporkin's decision reinstating the consent decree that, according to Justice, Microsoft had now violated. Along with Silberman would be Judges A. Randolph Raymond and Stephen F. Williams; all had been appointed by Republican presidents.

Later that month, Gates managed to partially derail an EC investigation by giving up certain of his practices in Europe.

The Directorate-General on Competition, headed by Commissioner Karel Van Miert, had wrangled with Microsoft many times before. This time the company agreed that it would revise contracts with at least two dozen Internet service providers in Europe. The contracts had forced the companies to offer Microsoft's Internet Explorer in return for being listed in the Windows 95 operating system. This electronic listing enabled consumers to connect with providers with a few mouse clicks.

Netscape had complained to the Justice Department that Microsoft had the same arrangement in the United States.

In the winter of 1998, Sam Goodhope viewed himself as a knight-errant inside the Texas attorney general's office. As a "special projects" guy, he often found himself on what others would consider fools' errands. Now he could not believe that all the other states were making such a fuss about the browser issue. To him, the much bigger case was Gates' leverage into all kinds of new markets and his end plan with Windows NT—which hadn't even been part of the Justice Department's settlement. The ironic thing was Goodhope and his colleagues started it all.

Goodhope and Texas Attorney General Dan Morales had been buddies at Harvard Law School. Back in early February 1997, Bill Neukom and his staff had received a subpoena from Morales' office. What was this, some kind of a joke?

The eyes of Texas seemed to be on the Internet and on-line commerce. The civil investigative demand indicated that Texas was in the midst of an investigation and ordered that Microsoft turn over documents related to competition in the Internet market. But it failed to state what company was the target of the investigation—Microsoft.

The irony was not lost on Steve Ballmer. Both Morales and Ballmer were on the Harvard Board of Overseers and recently had competed for a committee chair. Morales had won.

Texas prided itself as number one in growth of high-tech business and had been collecting evidence of Microsoft stifling competition in the state. Now Microsoft had to respond to the subpoenas within thirty days.

Netscape had also been subpoenaed a few weeks earlier to provide information on Microsoft's alleged predatory conduct. Goodhope, Morales, and their colleagues were particularly concerned about the impact of Microsoft's business practices on a number of companies that conducted business within the state and nation-wide, including the Fort Worth–based airline reservation system Sabre, owned by American Airlines; Southwestern Bell; and computer manufacturers such as Dell and Compaq.

In the case of Sabre and other airline companies, the Texas attorney general had a number of concerns, including that Microsoft's monopoly in computer operating systems and bundling of Internet services gave it an unfair advantage that would eventually make it impossible for independent Internet-based airline reservation systems to compete.

The Texas investigation also sought to determine whether Microsoft had used predatory pricing and free gifts to deter computer manufacturers and others from using Internet browsers from competing companies. Phone companies like Southwestern Bell, which also sought to compete in the Internet services market, allegedly had been harmed by the software giant's leveraging of market power.

The Texas team was eyeing a coordinated effort with other state attorneys general sharing concerns about Microsoft's business. They were well aware that a concentrated effort by several states had recently resulted in a major settlement with America Online. But they were having a hell of a time getting witnesses to come forward.

In Washington, D.C., Ken Wasch of the Software Publishers Association was preparing a list of "principles" for the Justice Department, and for Orrin Hatch's Senate Judiciary Committee, that would identify potential remedies to solve the Microsoft problem without damaging competition.

Wasch prefaced his principles with a refresher on the basic goals of antitrust law. His guidelines for the digital marketplace aimed at striking a balance between the interests of a successful incumbent and those of smaller rivals and new entrants.

Wasch and the SPA board members, at the risk of permanently alienating Microsoft—which was a member of their organization and not pleased that all the other members seemed to be engaged in a gang war against it—compiled the following:

1. Maximize Innovation

The overriding objective of competition policy as applied to our industry should be to maximize innovation and dynamic competition for the benefit of consumers.

Microsoft had all along contended to federal regulators that, since prices were low, consumers were only benefiting from its success. It had dismissed less immediately obvious, longer-range concerns over long-term competition and product choice.

2. Nondiscriminatory Licensing of Interface Specifications to Third Party Software Developers

If the owner of a commercially available dominant operating system licenses the intellectual property in its interface specifications to any third party for the purposes of developing application software, then it should (i) provide that licensee, and any other licensee, with the licensed information regarding these specifications without delay but within a commercially reasonable time from the time it first provides the information to its own application developers, and (ii) permit that licensee, and any other licensee, to use its certification marks to represent truthfully that the application is interoperable or compatible with the operating system. Compatibility laboratories managed by the operating system vendor should adhere to publicly available procedures to ensure that laboratory certifications are applied on a fair and nondiscriminatory basis.

This would address the unfair advantage, which some attorneys had termed technological tying, Microsoft maintained by keeping technological information secret. It was part of the essential facility concerns, that if one controlled such a facility—in this case the operating system—one had to provide access to that facility to all in a nondiscriminatory way.

3. Leveraging an Operating System into the Sale of Products and Services

The owner of a dominant operating system may have the ability to leverage the operating system into the sale of favored products and services, including those utilizing electronic commerce. Operating systems should not be used to unfairly favor its own products and services (or its favored partners) over those of competing vendors. The operating system vendor should not include its own services or products as part of the operating system or user interface unless it gives the same ability to integrate products and services into the operating system to competing vendors. Competition for the valuable "virtual real estate" of the desktop should instead occur downstream in the distribution system. In addition, artificial barriers should not be established that unreasonably limit the ability of a hardware manufacturer or end-user to reconfigure the desktop to utilize other software, content or services, except where such a reconfiguration would impair the core functions of the operating system.

This item cut to the quick on Microsoft's alleged product integration. Again, it could be founded in part on the legal theory of essential facility.

4. Competitive Licensing of Software Applications to Original Equipment Manufacturers (OEMs).

Each original equipment manufacturer only has limited hard disk space and limited software licensing dollars to devote to bundled applications. Practices such as tying the pricing of the operating system to the price of software applications, and the tying of certain applications to the sale of other applications, have the effect of restraining competition among independent software vendors (ISVs) for the "virtual shelf space" of the OEM. It is critical to the long-term health of the computer software industry that this competition with and among ISVs be encouraged rather than allowing the OEM to be monopolized by a single vendor.

This practice had long been clearly prohibited by the antitrust laws, so no new issues were being raised here. However, the Justice Department had not yet adequately addressed the matter; Microsoft, it was alleged by state attorneys general, still routinely offered operating system price cuts to computer makers who agreed to bundle its other products. Since it held a monopoly position in operating systems, such practices were clearly predatory.

5. Equal Access to Retail Customers

Many software publishers still depend upon retail stores to reach their customers. Competition is undermined by practices that monopolize limited retail space.

6. Disadvantaging Competing Software Products

A software vendor should not intentionally disable, cripple or otherwise interfere with the intended functionality and execution of other products. Similarly, a vendor should not suggest that other products may be incompatible that are in fact known to be compatible.

Representations of compatibility or incompatibility should be truthful and based on reasonable testing and evaluation. In particular, no software vendor should include error messages, warnings or other messages to users that are not completely truthful. Such messages should fully disclose to the user the consequences of following any instructions suggested in the message. The promotion of interoperability and open standards generally enhances competition and innovation in the software industry.

Microsoft continued to deny that it had ever intentionally designed a product to create the appearance that competing products would not run as well despite the fact that Justice had read about such intentions in the company's internal e-mail. Most recently, Microsoft's changes to Sun's Java technology appeared to be motivated by the desire to make Sun's version incompatible with a Windows-specific version, so Sun had alleged.

Brian Behlendorf, one of the organizers of the Apache Project, said the group "wanted to take our future into our own hands." By 1998 the Apache software was being used by Fortune 500 companies—McDonald's, Texas Instruments, and Kimberly-Clark Corp., among others—to run their websites. Estimates were that the software was used in almost half of the 2 million websites on the Internet—more than twice the share for server software held by Netscape or Microsoft. (The total Web server market in 1997 had generated more than $400 million in revenue.)

Across town, in a tiny donut shop, a new generation of software developers and entrepreneurs were stopping in to talk excitedly about everything from complex systems to biodiversity.

Fostered by the Internet, a new aesthetic was apparent here. This was Sili Valley, and the biggest dinosaur of all was far away in Seattle. Why should any of the young developers still feel its shadow looming over them?

Miko Matsumura, a Silicon samurai, had black hair, with wisps of blue and pink, that fell to his shoulders. He wore an oversized black jacket with huge shoulders, and baggy pants that hung too long, breaking into overlapping folds where they hit his shoes. Matsumura was a small and powerful figure. At age thirty he looked like a fierce twelve-year-old but for a faint whisker here and there. He had deep black eyes that peered about him as he spoke, and he tilted his head slightly downward at whomever he was addressing so that his gaze always seemed to be shielded by the fortress of his eyebrows. Of Japanese descent but raised in Minnesota, Matsumura was part philosopher, part neuroscientist, part all-American boy.

He stood amid the ersatz surrounding of the Donut Wheel, the greasy donut shop just across the street from JavaSoft in Cupertino.

Matsumura was part of what one might call the new clergy of Silicon Valley. He was an "evangelist" for Sun Microsystems' star technologies. With Java being damaged by Microsoft, Matsumura and a secret team were already off on a new adventure. Their method for ditching Bill Gates once and for all was Jini.

Jini would be made up of a "federation" of computers and services that could be openly accessed by the public via the Internet
and by dialing into computer services of interest. It would require
no operating system, and would make dependence on Gates a thing
of the past.

Scott McNealy, Matsumura's boss, was planning to unfurl Jini as
"Java Tone" in the fall of 1998. It would be the digital age's version
of the dial tone, and he hoped it would become as pervasive and as
open as the way people used the telephone to get whatever information and products they wished.

McNealy had already secretly signed up major computer and
telecommunications companies to participate—IBM, Oracle, Sony,
and a range of other computer giants. McNealy's chief scientists
had sequestered themselves away for more than a year working on
this thing.

Just before the feds filed a massive lawsuit in May 1998 against
Microsoft, Jini had been quietly integrated into Sun's official product and marketing groups. It was out of the lab and ready for the
real world.

The months leading up to the filing of the biggest antitrust case
since the breakup of AT&T had been fraught with conflict. The evidence in the Microsoft file was as hot as it could be. Justice alleged
that Gates' strategies and intent in market after market, supported
by one predatory act after another, could not have been clearer. It
was all spelled out in Gates' own words and those of his top executives.

Yet the case would be complex and overwhelmingly political. The
situation, however, was not nearly as Machiavellian as Gates and his
chief counsel liked to paint it. No one was denying the huge success
of Microsoft, and its enormous contributions to the American economy and the computer industry worldwide. No one wanted to hobble
Microsoft. The feds simply wanted to make sure that Bill Gates competed fairly and did not continue to snuff out other innovators by
using his monopoly power to squeeze them out of the market.

Since November 1995, when Microsoft had begun giving away Internet Explorer for free as part of its campaign to leverage itself into Netscape's market and force the small company out, the feds had been collecting a detailed account of what Microsoft was up to. Paul Maritz, Microsoft group vice president in charge of the Platforms Group, told a group of industry executives about its intentions vis à vis Netscape: "We are going to cut off their air supply. Everything they're selling, we're going to give away for free."

Gates also warned Netscape in 1996, Justice noted, "Our business model works even if all Internet software is free. We are still selling operating systems. What does Netscape's business model look like? Not very good."

Like it had done with Vobis, to ensure that the German computer giant would no longer ship a competing operating system, Microsoft in early 1996 had even offered to pay off AT&T's $17-million commitment to Netscape in the form of "reverse bounties," credits for the amounts AT&T would have had to pay Microsoft for subscriber referrals, the Department of Justice alleged. AT&T would also have to promise that it would exclusively promote and feature Microsoft's Internet Explorer and drop its previous relationship with Netscape.

Gates himself, in an e-mail written in July 1996, noted his willingness to pay Intuit in order to get the company to cease doing business with Netscape and instead switch to Microsoft's browser.

"I was quite frank with him [Scott Cook, CEO of Intuit] that if he had a favor we could do for him that would cost us something like $1M to do that in return for switching browsers in the next few months I would be open to doing that," Gates wrote.

The feds had noticed just the latest in the software giant's longtime predatory practices: it had bought exclusion of competing products—both indirectly, by leveraging the dominance of Windows and the promise of distribution through Windows, and directly, by paying for it.

By May 1998, Justice had filed a sweeping lawsuit against the software giant, along with twenty states. It had provided glances, in snippets throughout the suit, of internal Microsoft documents and e-mail originating at the top levels of the company, backing up its charges.

Bill Neukom had characterized the filings as insignificant and the material as being mostly from junior staffers at the company. Was Bill Gates a junior staffer? Were numerous members of Microsoft's executive office junior staffers? Were corporate officers junior staffers?

The "junior" staffers, as Neukom called them, were the same band of high level executives—in Gates' inner sanctum—who had masterminded the locking up of the DOS market back in the late 1980s. There was Jim Allchin, David Cole, Brad Silverberg, Brad Chase, Paul Maritz, Joachim Kempin, Gates himself, and of course Neukom.

Microsoft's own legal department had been closely tied to, and well aware of, these efforts. It apparently had drawn up the language that was supposed to warn computer users they were using an "alien" operating system, back when DRI was trying to make a go of it. Gates had taken a note, "purge e-mail," in meetings with his legal counsel, Neukom, and had been grilled about this by Justice and by the FTC. Federal judges had granted "motions to compel" to both Sun and Caldera, who had noticed Microsoft's pattern of blocking production of evidence, and in the case of Sun, Bill Gates' failure to produce evidence and his own e-mail, which had been separately collected from other employees at Microsoft.

Justice noted Microsoft trying to cover its tracks and conceal its true intentions. If product tying was illegal under the antitrust laws, it would have to create the appearance that Internet Explorer was not a separate product but had always been intended to be part of the Windows operating system. Over the past couple of years, Microsoft executives had been told by chief counsel Neukom to be "careful" not to refer to its browser software in such a way that it appeared that the software was a separate product. Internal memos written by Paul Maritz confirmed these instructions from Neukom.

Microsoft executives were "very concerned" that statements in the ordinary course of business made Internet Explorer "appear separate" and concluded it was "critical" that there be "a thorough walk-through looking for places in the UI [user interface] that can be corrected." Aware that the feds were looking at Microsoft's own website for evidence, Microsoft executives suggested there be a "sweep" of the Internet Explorer website to remove references inconsistent with Microsoft's present legal position. Justice attorneys noted that it was agreed that there would be a "review of Win 98" by Microsoft executives and "someone from legal staff" to "ensure IE is properly presented."

Justice, as the FTC had before it, had documented a pattern of predation on the part of Microsoft that had nothing to do with winning in the marketplace based on the merits of great products.

In February 1997, they noted, Microsoft's Christian Wildfeuer had concluded that it would be "very hard to increase browser share on the merits of IE 4 alone. It will be more important to leverage the OS asset to make people use IE instead of Navigator."

In early May, Neukom and Gates had arrived in Washington to engage in settlement talks with Joel Klein and a handful of representatives from state AG offices. After a disastrous day and night session, the feds had given up. Bill Gates was up to the same maneuvering that Anne Bingaman had experienced back during her 1994 settlement, when she had told her colleagues that Gates was trying to "two-time" her.

Microsoft had entered the talks indicating it would stall shipment of Windows 98 if the feds held back on suing, and that it would be willing to make some concessions. Hours into the talks, Gates had informed his lawyers that he refused to make the changes that they had already suggested he was open to.

Days later, the suit was filed. The states' suit would fill out areas that the Justice Department had not been explicit about, but also sought to address while in trial—including illegal tying of the Office applications software to Windows—issues that Lotus, WordPerfect, and numerous other software companies had tried for years to get addressed by the FTC and then Justice. These concerns were finally being recognized as destroying competition in the applications software market—long after scores of companies in that market had succumbed to Microsoft's predation.

Only a few weeks before the filing, at an informal social gathering, Gates had told his confidants that he was particularly nervous about the feds going after a case based on the tying of Office to Windows. They hadn't bothered to open up that can of worms before.

In its suit, the Justice Department also accused Microsoft of entering into illegal contracts with Internet service providers that forced them to stop selling and promoting rival products. It sought a preliminary injunction that held back from asking the software giant to cease shipment of Windows 98, but instead asked that it either disable Internet Explorer inside the product—as it had done under court order with Windows 95—or agree to also ship Netscape's web browser along with Windows 98 so that customers had a choice. Neukom and Gates had been outraged at the suggestion.

Microsoft's share of the Internet browser market had grown steadily from less than 5 percent in early 1996 to more than 60 percent, largely because of leveraging its monopoly power, Joel Klein hoped to prove.

Gates had been so aware that market share was everything when it came to winning in the Internet browser market that he was even willing to cannibalize his own on-line service, the Microsoft Network (MSN), to achieve his goals. Seeking to disadvantage Netscape, Gates agreed to give America Online a preferential placement on the Windows screen at the expense of its own MSN. Gates had told Silverberg in an e-mail that this would mean "putting a bullet through MSN's head."

Internet service providers, like America Online, MCI, and numerous others, now had the power that the computer OEMs had in the early days of the computer industry. They were the most effective way for any company to distribute and market their products. Being the default browser for those providing Internet service to the majority of computer users meant everything.

In June 1996, in an e-mail message, Paul Maritz pointed out that in order to win its browser-share objectives, "In addition to shipping IE 3 on [Windows 95 and NT], we need to get AOL & Compuserve shipping IE3."

Now the government was trying to keep the market open for free trade in the burgeoning digital age. It was attempting to stimulate innovation and ensure that future innovators—like Netscape—did not continue to be stomped out by Microsoft.

In what way did consumers receive innovations or product improvements by being forced to use Internet Explorer versus Netscape? Where in Microsoft's internal documents did it show that the goal of integrating the two products was innovation? That it was not couldn't have been spelled out more clearly.

In a January 5, 1997, internal presentation at the company, Gates' intentions were obvious. "Integrate with Windows" was a way to "Increase IE share," he had said. Only a few days earlier, his senior vice president Jim Allchin had written that if Microsoft was to defeat Netscape, it needed to start "leveraging Windows from a marketing perspective."

He went on, "We have to be competitive with features, but we need something more—Windows integration." Memphis, a code name for the next version of Windows, would play a key role, he added. "We are not investing sufficiently in finding ways to tie IE and Windows together . . . Memphis must be a simple upgrade, but most importantly it must be a killer on OEM shipments so that Netscape never gets a chance on these systems."

The integration of Internet Explorer into Windows had nothing to do with innovation and everything to do with keeping Netscape out of the market.

The State of Texas, which had been the first of the states to investigate Microsoft for alleged predatory conduct, had, ironically, not joined the multistate lawsuit filed along with the Justice Department action. The reason: computer makers based in Texas—Compaq and Dell—did not want to see their PC sales hurt by an injunction against Windows 98. They also did not want to put their relationships with Microsoft in peril.

It was the historic problem: these companies were so dependent on receiving product from Microsoft that any glitch in their operating system supply would have a domino effect on their businesses. There was no other game in town but Microsoft. So while resenting the power the monopolist wielded over them, to continue on with the way things were would be less damaging than an abrupt change in the situation.

Besides, at the Texas state AG office, special projects' Sam Goodhope, assistant AG Mark Tobey, and their colleagues believed that by now the browser integration issue was a moot point. A much larger issue was Microsoft's potential to foreclose competition in on-line businesses such as travel, media, and larger information networks. But if computer makers didn't care, and consumers were in the dark about what Microsoft was up to, who were they to invest scarce resources and taxpayer dollars in a probe that sought to fix a situation that was not yet apparent to most?

The complex and controversial nature of the case against Microsoft could not have been shown in greater relief than through the mid-June appellate court decision throwing out Judge Jackson's earlier injunction against Microsoft in the earlier contempt case. Not only rejecting it on procedural issues, the court's three-judge panel issued an opinion—with Judge Patricia Wald dissenting— that it did not have the expertise to interfere in product design and could see nothing improper with a corporation integrating new features into an existing product, if benefits were brought to the consumer.

A *New York Times* editorial days later called the decision "erroneous," and a heated debate kicked up in editorials and news broadcasts throughout the world. Microsoft hailed the decision as a victory, but it had little to do with the much broader case that Joel Klein and his Justice Department colleagues were pursuing.

The appeals court had backed off, it seemed, making a simplistic decision in the face of the technological complexity of a digital business case that had not ever been tested by the courts. It was the same reason that the Justice Department itself had earlier, during Anne Bingaman's tenure, shied away from pursuing a complex case that would have arguably addressed some of the most egregious predatory practices of Bill Gates and his powerful corporation.

In June 1998, while the headlines blared victory for Microsoft in the face of the appeals court reversal, Joel Klein was preparing to take center stage in federal court on September 8, hoping to unleash a barrage of evidence that had been hidden from the public eye, sealed in carton after carton on the slippery floors of his office.

The appeals court decision was just an inkling of what, as his special assistant Jeff Blatner put it, "we're up against with this case." Whatever the outcome, it would represent a landmark in the history of antitrust law.

Meantime, in online chats taking place all over the Internet, some consumers were fuming about the lack of benefits, let alone "innovation," as Bill Gates insisted on terming it, of Windows 98, which in late June had appeared in retail stores and computer shipments around the world.

"One thing I notice right away: Netscape is toast," wrote one technically savvy early Windows 98 user on a public forum. "Not because Internet Explorer is any better (in my opinion it is not) but because it is there." The consumer went on, "Microsoft has embedded it so much in the old Explorer interface, that I do not see many, if any, people bothering to choose Netscape over IE. Most dealers will default to IE, as it is easier to support one browser than two. Since you cannot remove IE from Win 98 easily, and the code is already loaded when you are running the operating system, the IE load time will always be quicker than Netscape. The winner in the end by default is: IE."

The message continued, "I have only had an hour or two with the install, and I have yet to find a way to turn a few features off. I assume they can be turned off. Also the . . . style of desktop I am told can be turned off. However I have not yet found that ability nor have I been prompted for any choice during install. What this means is that 90% of all users will not even bother to look for the methods to switch this, and will assume that this is the norm. Hence again re-inforcing the IE choice over Netscape."

The user then apologized for his analysis, "Sorry to be so dismal, but this is really the problem . . . The average users of Microsoft products don't know of anything better . . . As far as 90% of them are concerned, the computer industry is moving too quickly and they think that this movement is a result of innovation from Micro-soft. I try to tell some of the users I know that indeed it is the re-verse, but I am bowled over by naive users . . . I fear this is the same all over North America and the rest of the world."

Others in message postings on public forums and online chatrooms all over the Internet railed that the government should leave Micro-soft alone, and indeed could care less what company made their soft-ware, as long as it enabled them to do what they wanted to do.

While debate ran hot in the weeks following the appeals court de-cision, back in Redmond, Washington, the breezes of Puget Sound eased the humidity of summer.

As daylight waned on Microsoft's sprawling campus, a rectangle in Building Eight seemed to burn more brightly.

Quite late, Bill Gates stepped out into the expansive night. Star-light generated billions of years ago filled the heavens, trivializing the business of the day and the minuscule glow of electronic cir-cuits.

If day was technology, night was everything unnamed and un-claimed.

ACKNOWLEDGMENTS

"Everything was perfect in the circus; a spangled fraud with music," wrote novelist Julio Cortazar. I had a similar impression as I embarked on this surprising journey in pursuit of the shining American icon that is Microsoft Corp.

There were many attractions and distractions along the way: The attractions were the many fascinating discoveries and the people who took the time and effort and had the guts to help me uncover information that had been out of the public eye and was almost impossible to get. The distractions included Bill Gates' personal attempts to censor my work by contacting several newspaper and magazine editors and telling them—without giving any reason—that they should not be publishing a word by me. Happily, those editors stood behind me, ignored the words of the richest man in the world, and helped me break numerous news stories on the subject of what was really going on behind the scenes—at Microsoft and in the antitrust probes of the company.

For their support, I thank Owen Youngman at the *Chicago Tribune;* Larry Edelman at the *Boston Globe;* Eric Nee, former editor of *Upside;* Louis Rossetto at *Wired;* John Soat at *InformationWeek;* Andy Lawrence at *Computer Business Review* (London); and Tom Steinert-Threlkeld and Al Perlman at *Interactive Week.*

Thanks to CBS News, National Public Radio, the Canadian Broadcasting Corporation, PBS television, BBC Radio, and BBC Television for featuring my work in their broadcasts in the nascent stages of the book.

I'd also like to thank John Russell at CMP Media, who gave me the opportunity to dig beyond the surface of things very early on, and gave much encouragement and support, and Alice Greene and Bob Evans, for those young but intense days in the news business.

I am greatly indebted to many people at Random House, but especially Ann Godoff, whose brainstorming with me in her office during three days in 1995 provided endless inspiration and wonder at the process I had just begun; Tracy Smith, who was one of the first to notice; and early editor Karl Weber, who never doubted.

Great admiration and appreciation go out to John Mahaney, my editor at Random House, whose expert editing and gentle manner enabled me to forge ahead, heartened by his unflagging confidence and encouragement. I owe much to Luke Mitchell, John's editorial assistant, who kept me buoyant with his humor and irreverent phone messages. Also at Random House I am indebted to production guru Nancy Inglis, who accommodated with much grace up-to-the-minute developments, and to publicity wizards Will Weisser and Mary Beth Roche, who spread the big word.

There are many important confidential sources whose names never appear in this book who I commend for their courage and trust, and especially would like to thank Deep Vision (Woodward and Bernstein have cornered the nickname Deep Throat), who allowed me to see most clearly into the inner sanctum.

For their warmth, encouragement, and companionship during the many times I was on the road in Los Angeles, I thank Steven, Gaye, Nicky, and Zach Lalich; Helene Klosner; and John C. Reilly and Alison Dickey. In New York, I thank Liz Sipes, Liz Norman, and Ian Klapper for humanizing dinners, and my dear pal Robert Auletta, for his endless inspiration and Blakean delight.

For phone messages filled with encouragement, early readings of "snippets," and a respite in Lexington, Kentucky, I send much love to Karen Tice and Dwight Billings, and also to Dan Mason, who sent overnight packages filled with music, flowers, and encouragement.

Closer to home, for those "cauldron" nights under the trees that bubbled with imagination, I thank my dear friends Gail Richman, Bibi Tinsley, S. L. Daniels, and playwright Steve Serpas, who was in his own throes—like me, forever being led around by the nose by a bunch of syllables.

For a gleeful retreat in Malibu, and for creative integrity amid the racket of the world, I thank Gillian Anderson. I send hugs and gratitude out to Jeannie Scheller and her daughter Christina Scheller— a great future writer—for adventures in child-swapping when I was on never-ending deadlines.

To Rachel Slavick, my longtime friend and transcriber, and Ann Slavick, I owe much for emotional support and numerous dinners with friends during hours of darkness; Lew Koch, who kept me fueled with great literature and laughter; Terry Rohm, whose lyrics via e-mail made every day vibrant; John Kilcullen, who propped me up with praise; Dan and Sandy Gookin, for sunlit days and friend- ship via e-mail; and to Bill Gates, for that strange encounter in Vegas. I also thank Perry Myers at Chicago's Myers' Service, Inc., a certified fraud examiner, for his help on details.

I cannot forget my agent Bill Gladstone, and the Dichters, who kept me aloft, and memorable dinners with investment bankers and the Tibetan monk! I would like to thank my parents, Audrey and Sid Goldman, for their unflagging support and encouragement, not to mention my father's brilliant title ideas such as "Schlmozzle Power"; my brother Jeffrey Goldman and Premiere Properties of Boston, who on more than one occasion gave me an idyllic place to get away and write free of distractions; my brother Gary, who trav- eled hundreds of miles to my doorstep, to brighten the gloom with a paintbrush; and my sister Cindy for shedding a few tears on my pages. I am always sending beams of gratitude heavenward to the memory of my life mentors, Joseph Halpern and George F. Butter- ick, who nurtured me in the deepest ways.

I thank Josip Pasic, the iconoclast, for lighting the way when I was navigating dark passageways; he reminded me that words could never be more than "a finger pointing at the moon," and somehow gave me freedom to continue, without judgment or doubt.

Finally, but most important, I thank two people: my wonderful daughter Madeline who fills my life with love and light, and whom I can never repay for understanding when our house turned into one large filing cabinet and Taco Bell dinners became habitual right before deadlines; and Ric Murphy, who always sustains me with his open heart, playful mind, and a few transformational apple tarts.

INDEX